Why the Bible Is Number 1

Why the Bible Is Number 1

The World's Sacred Writings in the Light of Science

Kenny Barfield

BAKER BOOK HOUSE
Grand Rapids, Michigan 49516

ISBN: 0-8010-0950-2

Printed in the United States of America

To the students, friends, and alumni
of Mars Hill Bible School

Contents

Preface 9
Introduction 11

PART ONE **The Body Inside: Sacred Revelations and Medicine**

1. It's a Wonder They Survived 17
2. Out of the Frying Pan, Into the Fire 28
3. A Breath of Fresh Air 37
4. Biblical Sanitation Laws 42
5. Biblical Food Laws 53
6. Biblical Sex Laws 60
7. Biblical Laws and Stress Management 68
8. Biblical Law of Circumcision 73

PART TWO **The Sky Above: Sacred Revelations and Astronomy**

9. Down the Wrong Path 79
10. Climbing the Wrong Mountain 85
11. The Light Shines Through 91
12. Star Light, Star Bright, First Star I See Tonight 95
13. To the Stars and Beyond 102
14. The Blue Planet 107
15. Searching for Flaws 115

16. Trouble at the Center 121
17. Answering the Critics 129

PART THREE **The Earth Beneath: Sacred Revelations and Earth Science**

18. What On Earth Is This? 135
19. The Magic of the Rocks 151
20. Quite a Foundation 160
21. Waste Not, Want Not 164
22. The Pieces of a Puzzle 167
23. Into the Depths 169
24. Rain, Rain, Go Away, Come Again Another Day 176
25. Putting the Pieces Together 182
Appendix: *The World's Scriptures* 186
Notes 187
Abbreviations 216
Bibliography 219

Preface

Surely the being capable of producing the universe would understand the laws by which it was made. And any revelation from that being would also demonstrate a deep and almost prophetic comprehension of those universal laws we come to accept as "truth."

We might well wonder if there could be among all the so-called revelations of the world's religions one document that is untouched by the foibles and fallacies of men, one record that reveals an accurate understanding of man and nature, one collection of writings that holds an immutable relationship to scientific truth? One book—and only one—can meet these qualifications. It is known as the Bible.

Although the Bible is obviously not meant to be a scientific textbook, any honest observer must admit that through the centuries the Bible has held a close, unchanging relationship to now-verifiable scientific principles. In addition, when the laws of science are reflected within its pages, they are presented correctly. Finally, when one understands the times in which the various books of the Bible were written, that tie to truth becomes even more impressive.

We shall isolate various fields of science, note the error-plagued ideas that saturated the cultures of biblical times, observe that these errors found their way into the sacred books of the non-Hebraic/Christian religions, and examine the Bible to determine whether biblical writers absorbed the same errors as their contemporaries.

This study, it should be noted, compares writings and not peoples. There is no evidence that any one group of people is inherently either more or less intelligent than another. It should also be noted that various cultures have made important progress in the sciences. This progress is understandable on the basis of human genius, equally present in all peoples. Interestingly, within this equality of people is an amazing disparity in certain "sacred" writings. The disparity should not be there. But it is.

Introduction

In this study, each section—"The Body Inside," "The Sky Above," "The Earth Below,"—is divided into three units. The initial chapter in each section describes the errors and misconceptions of early "scientific" efforts in a particular discipline. The chapter that follows documents similar errors found in the sacred scriptures of the world's non-biblical religions. The third part of each section, consisting of approximately five or six chapters, demonstrates how errors that permeated antiquity are notably absent from the Bible. Other biblical statements that are remarkably accurate—and from a scientific standpoint far in advance of the time when they would have been understood or described on purely naturalistic terms—are noted and discussed.

Unfortunately, necessary constraints on the length of this manuscript will not allow certain areas of concern to be addressed in detail. Such editorial decisions will, no doubt, prove distracting to some. Two such important issues involve the dates when various teachings occur and the charge that "evidence" has been chosen subjectively.

Dates

Although this work is not primarily concerned with specific dates, they have not been ignored. Surprisingly, however, a specific chronology is basically irrelevant to the reasoning outlined in this study, for only the degree of error is involved and not the exact origin of the error. Every scientific mistake described in these chapters existed to one extent or another throughout ancient history. The fact one decade, one century, or even one millennium gave somewhat less credence to these mistakes than did another is of little importance to this discussion. The issue is simple—every ancient civilization and culture embraced scientific misconceptions in varying degrees, and biblical writers avoided those errors at a time when they were prevalent in secular documents.

Further, during the period when all the major religious writings were composed or compiled, ideas about medical, astronomical, geological, and meteorological concepts were at least partially in error. And, with the exception of the Bible, all religious writings reflect some erroneous concepts regardless of the time frame. That is why this work does not attempt to detail time frames.

In noting these omissions, this work nonetheless accepts the concept that civilization moves in rhythmic patterns of advancement and degeneracy and that not every citizen of an ancient country would accept every error noted in these pages. An idea once accepted as plausible may be rejected later.

Selectivity

Others reading this work will be concerned because not all poetical or declarative statements in the Bible have a scientific underpinning. These critics feel that therefore the apologist is left in a position of choosing those examples that fit his thesis and ignoring or explaining away those that do not. Still others will argue that biblical writers never intended their words to be used in a scientific manner. Rather, they were concerned only with ceremonial, moral, and spiritual lessons. For example, dirt was not the chief reason for washing, nor was preventing disease the reason for Old Testament food laws. Consequently, it is often asserted that it is illegitimate to ascribe any meaning other than the original, author-intended meaning to a biblical passage. Though such arguments are somewhat persuasive, there are several reasons why they do not justify an *a priori* rejection of this apologetic:

First, one of the two unstated warrants that forms the basis of this objection is really an argument-from-silence. The argument runs as follows: "There are biblical commands, poetic statements, and the like for which no scientifically valid foundations are known. They are unknown because they do not exist. Since they do not exist, the apologist is guilty of selectively using the examples that fit, while ignoring those that do not."

Trends in science, however, have consistently diminished the applicability of such an argument in the current context. For example, two centuries ago, the medical validity of circumcision or sanitation or cleanliness was unknown, and a little over a century ago, no one recognized the existence of the great ocean currents. The list is lengthy. In other words, as knowledge has increased in the various sciences, so has the perceived validity of certain biblical statements. Thus, what would have once "fit" the critics' argument-from-silence will not necessarily "fit" the same argument today.

Second, the other unstated warrant on which the objection resides assumes that if one biblical statement has a scientifically intended foundation, then all statements must have such a foundation. That assumption, however, would be hard to prove, even today. Here the argument turns on "intent." As a result, the argument is valid only if the writer's intent is the sole concern when one examines a passage of Scripture. As voluminous studies have already been prepared in this area,[1] they will not be repeated here.

Briefly, however, the thesis here is that no human author, working singularly or in connection with others, had the ability to write, compile, or imagine the information described in the Bible. Given that possibility, the intent of a human writer, though admittedly of great import in examining a passage of Scripture, can never provide an exhaustive meaning.[2]

For instance, if writer intent becomes the *sole* criterion by which all biblical exegesis must occur, how can one possibly determine that intent? Of couse, there are many inferences to be drawn, but they will always remain speculative. It is doubtful that Moses understood the total prophetic meaning of Genesis 3:15. He may have, but there is no way that can ever be known.

Likewise, it is doubtful that the prophet understood the full significance of the beautiful passage in Isaiah 53. He may have possessed a general understanding, but most scholars would question whether the writer saw every detail perfectly. Thus, if *all* biblical statements (remember, one cannot "pick and choose") are to be interpreted solely on the basis of author intent, laymen and scholars alike are in a quandary.

As Payne has noted, "God can reveal more through the words of a writer of Scripture than he [the writer] fully understood."[3]

Third, to discover that a principle of science undergirds a particular passage does not decrease either the validity of the spiritual message or its historical significance. Rather than diluting either aspect, such discoveries enhance a passage.

One example can be drawn from the biblical command regarding washing after coming in contact with something unclean. The passage has historically been treated from a ceremonial perspective, and conservative scholars have noted that it was designed to instruct readers that sin also produces spiritual uncleanness, which likewise must be removed to facilitate fellowship between man and God. Spiritually, the symbolism is the same whether or not there is a scientific undergirding to the command.

Furthermore, modern scholarship is searching constantly for additional historical and linguistic insights into passages of Scripture. The strong aversion by such scholars to allowing scientific insights is inconsistent. They are guilty of an *a priori* exclusion of one line of evidence while allowing others.

Fourth, those who utilize the "pick and choose" objection in this context are almost universally guilty of using the same reasoning. The fact remains that some biblical statements can be more completely understood in light of modern scientific discoveries. Likewise, there are statements that cannot be understood, at least at the present, in light of current science. Yet those who complain that works such as this one are guilty of picking only those examples that "fit" use identical reasoning by accepting only those that have no obvious scientific ties and then trying to explain away those that do. In other words, they, too, "pick and choose."

Part One

The Body Inside
Sacred Revelations and Medicine

1

It's a Wonder They Survived

Most biblical writings that touch upon medical principles were penned hundreds of years before the time of Christ, at a time when medical thought was engulfed by pagan sophistry. Any discussion of these writings, therefore, must be considered within that milieu. What were the beliefs of the day? Who were the leading medical authorities of the time? Answers to such questions provide valuable insight into the cultures that produced the leading philosophies of the day.

Medicine in Ancient Egypt

A survey of ancient thought reveals that more medical advances occurred in Egypt than anywhere else in the known world. Writers of antiquity seem unanimous in praise of Egyptian medicine.[1] Homer's *Odyssey* (1100 B.C.) noted, "In Egypt the men are more skilled in medicine than any [other art]" and Xenophon's *Cyropaedia* added that Cyrus and Darius were served by Egyptian physicians. Obviously the Egyptians made very commendable advances in certain areas of the sciences.[2] Yet, for all the advances, the lion's share of Egypt's medical arts consisted of fruitless rituals that, in many instances, intensified disease rather than cured it. One scholar claimed that "only three out of every ten children born into a family could survive to adulthood"[3] in a land where the average life-span was only thirty.

Sources of Medical Knowledge

Much of what we know about medicine in ancient Egypt comes from two papyri found in Thebes in 1862. They are known as the Ebers and Edwin Smith papyri. Several other medical papyri available to the Egyptologist—such as the Kahun papyrus (2000 B.C.), the Hearst Medical, and Lesser Berlin papyri (all dating from approximately 1600 B.C.), the Berlin papyrus (1350 B.C.), and the London Medical papyrus (1000 B.C.)—merely mimic the brushstrokes painted by the two major papyri.

Combined, the two major papyri measure nearly twenty-five meters in length and comprise over half the manuscript evidence available on the medical sciences of the early Egyptians. The Edwin Smith papyrus, though rich in surgical material, says little about internal diseases, and many of its medical recommendations are simply those of common sense and could be observed by anyone with a penchant for medicine. On the other hand,—while dealing with serious internal diseases and termed "a most imposing and important document"[4]—the Ebers papyrus ventures into a field where mere observations were insufficient to produce accurate knowledge regarding the causes and remedies of disease. As a result, the Ebers papyrus passes along some frightening prescriptions—a stark reminder that its composers were offering their readers nothing more than the speculation of human minds. That errors were numerous should not surprise us.

The papyrus prescribed the following remedy for those with "trembling in the limbs": the fruit of the dom palm, garlic, honey, copper, and verdigris. After the mixture had been consumed, a dog's hide was to be placed on the patient and he was to be delivered to the gods for healing. For the treatment of embedded splinters, Egyptian doctors were advised to prepare a remedy that included "worm's blood" and "asses' dung" and were told to apply the resulting compound to the infected area. When one realizes that dung is filled with tetanus spores, it becomes obvious why short life-spans were prevalent.

These Egyptians were apparently also plagued with numerous diseases of the eye, and the papyrus instructed them to rub gall of tortoise and honey on their eyes when white spots appeared.

Numerous eyewashes were advised by the authors of the old medical text and were prepared with cattle urine and pig bile.[5]

Perhaps the most revolting remedy found in the pharmacopeias of the physicians of the Nile, however, relates to their prescribed treatments of infantile diseases. For some mysterious reason, baby mice were believed to be protectors of children. Therefore, when other prescriptions failed to cure sick children, the physicians skinned baby mice and gave them to infants to be consumed whole.[6]

The pride of this ancient people, so obvious in their temples, monuments, and pyramids, was also evident in their personal grooming habits. Remedies were given in the Ebers papyrus for such things as baldness, gray hair, and personal hygiene. The drugs to be used in these "medical" treatments included all kinds of excreta and urine.[7] Waste products figure so often in the prescriptions that medical historians have labeled the Egyptian practice as "sewage pharmacology."[8]

In retrospect: "Nothing even remotely resembling it is used today"[9] because it was "deeply immersed in myth and magic,"[10] was filled with the "bizarre and disgusting," and derived only from "wild guesses."[11] Even when physicians prescribed less revolting herbs or other mixtures, only occasionally did the remedies fit the disease. And, though we still use some of these old ideas in modern medical practice, "many of the substances [used by the Egyptians] are of no known therapeutic value."[12]

The Ancient Doctrine of Signatures

Egypt, along with the rest of the ancient world, was attracted to a "doctrine of signatures." This theory advised physicians to

Papyrus Prescriptions

1. A dog's hide
2. Worm's blood
3. Gall of tortoise
4. Cattle urine
5. Pig bile
6. Baby mice
7. Heel of a greyhound
8. Burnt quills of hedgehog
9. Backbone of raven

search for drugs that physically resembled the disease or the afflicted organ. Thus, a plant or flower shaped like an ear would be prescribed for an earache, yellow plants would be prescribed for jaundice, and red berries would be given for a rash on the skin.[13]

If an Egyptian incurred a battle wound from a spear, a leaf that resembled a spearhead was used to doctor the injury. Such examples could be multiplied not only among the Egyptians but also throughout the ancient world. All the major world cultures seemed equally impressed with this medically barren idea. The concept, though intriguing, is totally false. Those who followed it were misled.

The Link Between Disease and Witchcraft

Egyptians and their physicians also associated disease with witchcraft. Records in papyri, tombs, and monuments reveal that Egyptians were careful about concealing anything that might have been a part of their person. They feared that even a drop of blood, a hair, or a toenail clipping in the hands of wizards could bring on disease. Once a wizard obtained any part of a person's body, however small it might be, it was their belief that he could simply put that possession in a lump of wax, mold the wax into a person's image, expose that image to fire, and then fever would develop.[14] During the thirteenth century B.C., a superintendent of Ramesses' cattle was found guilty of paralyzing some of the friends of the pharaoh through just such an action.[15]

It was during such times, that Moses began composing the materials that later became the first five books of the Judeo-Christian Bible.[16] It should be remembered, that Egypt was a leader in the medical arts of that day, comparable to the position enjoyed by the United States in today's world. As might be expected when the best medical practices of that era were shrouded in darkness and ignorance, error was even more rampant throughout the rest of the world. It would take another thousand years before the Greeks could even light one candle to dispel some of the darkness.

Medicine in Ancient Babylon

Meanwhile, the errors that plagued Egyptian medical experts were found in Babylon to an even greater degree. In addition to using some rather unattractive drugs and following the doctrine of signatures, the physicians of Mesopotamia were also obsesssed with the idea that all disease was produced by the demons or evil spirits that permeated society. They taught that disease-producing specters lurked in mountains, infested plains, waited beside rivers and roads, and concealed themselves on roofs. Then, the minute that people found disfavor with their gods, these disease-bearing spirits pounced.[17] This belief explains the requirement that the sick be treated with such substances as swine's fat, dog's dung, and other sorts of excrement and urine. It was surmised that these substances would disgust the demon and cause it to seek more palatable surroundings.[18]

Such tactics were of little help of course. Nor, for that matter, were the drugs, which included gall of the black ox, gall of scorpion, gall of pig, head of stork, human bones that had been reduced to ashes,[19] and the forms of human waste already mentioned.

Rituals, Omens, and Astrology Dominate

More important than medicines, however, were the methods by which Mesopotamian physicians and priests arrived at their diagnoses. At least three classes[20] are noted: liver-divination; casual phenomena such as dreams, the movement of animals, or freak births; and astrology. All were used in preventive fashion to discover future misfortunes, that, when known, could be dispatched by using the appropriate ritual or exorcism.

1. *Divination by the Liver.* Through liver-divination, or hepatoscopy, the livers of sacrificial animals, usually sheep, were inspected to make predictions regarding the health of a patient. Throughout Mesopotamia, archaeologists have uncovered hundreds of models of livers that were used in such practices. The ancient site at Mari alone yielded over thirty such models,[21] complete with cuneiform tablets that explained their use. One such tablet read:

> If a flesh tumor is found at the bottom of the na (unidentified part of the liver), the patient will get worse and he will die. . . .
>
> If the gall bladder is long, the king will live long. If the processus pyramidalis is shaped normally, he who makes the sacrifice (of the sheep) will be in good health and live long.[22]

Correct prognosis by such methods, obviously, was mere coincidence. Nevertheless, hepatoscopy was practiced widely in that time; clay, bronze, and occasional golden models of the liver have been found throughout the ancient world. Even the Etruscans, who preceded the Romans in Italy, were counted among its devoted adherents.

2. *Divination by Casual Phenomena.* For those unable to purchase sacrificial sheep, other methods were available. One of the simplest of these involved placing a drop of oil in a bucket of water. The cuneiform tablet recommending this informs: "If the oil sinks and rises to the top again, it means misfortune for a sick man. If the oil forms a ring in the easterly direction, it means that a sick man will recover."[23]

When neither a sacrificial animal nor oil were available, or when an additional prognosis was desired, large numbers of everyday "omens" could be thrust into service. One ancient medical tablet[24] read:

> If a man go to the house of a sick man [and] a falcon goes along at his right, that sick man will get well.
>
> If the falcon goes along on his left side, that man will die.
>
> If, in the morning, in the rear of a sick man's house, a falcon proceeds from an inclosure at the right to an inclosure at the left, that sick man will speedily recover.
>
> If, in the morning, in the rear of a sick man's house, a falcon proceeds from an inclosure at the left to an inclosure at the right, his sickness will be protracted.
>
> If, in the morning, in the rear of a sick man's house, a falcon fly away, that sick man will die.

The extent of such prognosticating may be better understood by the fact that "about 30 percent of the twenty to thirty thousand extant tablets from the library of Ashurbanipal at Nineveh are omen texts."[25]

3. *Divination by Astrology.* Mesopotamia also gave birth to astrology. Early in history, priests of this region earned the title of "star-gazers." They recorded very precisely what they saw in the heavens and meticulously compared these data to simultaneous events occurring on earth. From these records and obser-

vations, the pseudo-science of astrology was born. For medical practitioners of Mesopotamia, the movements of the stars had a direct relationship with illness, recovery, relapse, difficult birth, and one's destiny in love, society, and business.[26]

All the astrologic healer needed was a graph of the zodiac and a knowledge of the planet in conjunction when the patient was born and/or when he became sick. From these "facts," the medical astrologers could then give both cause and cure of the disease without ever having seen the patient. Totally lacking in scientific validity,[27] astrology has been described as "the greatest obstacle to medical progress" in antiquity,[28] a "desperate error on which the intellectual powers of countless generations were spent," and "the most impious and immoral of all religions."[29] Nonetheless, it was a way of life in Mesopotamia.

Other diagnostic errors seeped into the medical texts of the Babylonian people. One centered around the imagined cause of toothaches. A clay tablet unearthed at Nippur and dating from at least the second millennium B.C. noted:

> As the god Anu created the heavens, the heavens created the earth, the earth created the rivers, the rivers created the canals, the canals created the mud, the mud created the worm. The worm came weeping to the Sun, before Ea flowed his tears. 'What givest thou me for my food?' 'I will give thee dried figs and apricots. Set me amidst teeth, let me dwell in the gums. I will suck the blood from the teeth and chew the marrow from the gums.'[30]

From such evidence as outlined here, we can conclude that the civilization that would ultimately build the greatest city of the ancient world was immersed in error and ignorance.[31]

The Role of Exorcism

After diagnosis was determined, Babylon's physician-priests set about to find an appropriate ritual to solve the medical problem or prevent it from happening in the future. Among the methods chosen were (1) the use of amulets, (2) the recital of incantations or conjurations, and (3) the implementation of substitution.[32] Seldom were they used in isolation.

Ancient societies blamed demons for all the diseases and evil present in society. Though their supposed appearance changed from culture to culture, the belief in their evil nature did not. Pictured here are the Moabite demon Belphegor (Num. 25:3), and the lion-headed, eagle-footed Assyrian-Babylonian demon of disease and evil, holding the mace of wounding and the dagger of killing. Courtesy, *Devils, Demons and Witchcraft* by Ernst and Johanna Lehner, Dover Publications, Inc. Right is photograph of a Canaanite demon god. Courtesy, The Louvre.

Clay model of a sheep's liver, inscribed as a guide to Babylonian diviners. This model, found in Southern Babylonia, dates from 1700 B.C. Courtesy, British Museum.

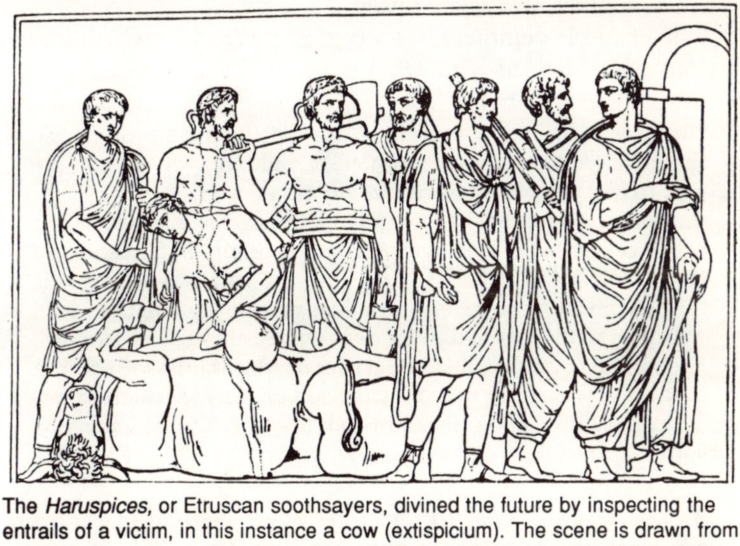

The *Haruspices,* or Etruscan soothsayers, divined the future by inspecting the entrails of a victim, in this instance a cow (extispicium). The scene is drawn from a relief in The Louvre. Courtesy, *Atlas of Classical Antiquities,* Macmillan and Co. 1895.

1. *The Use of Amulets.* Just as people in modern times may still carry a rabbit's foot or wear a good luck charm, the Mesopotamian peoples wore amulets to ward off demons, ghosts, and evil spirits. Their wide use is demonstrated by the sizable num-

ber unearthed by the archaeologist's spade and by their presence in omen-texts and other literature of the period. Even the god Marduk was said to have carried an amulet into his battle with Tiamat for "he held in his lips [some object] of red clay, clasped in his hand the venom-quenching plant."[33] (See chapter 15.)

Among the amulets known to modern scholars, most contain drawings of demons or evil spirits, along with an appropriate incantation that, when used in combination, would render the noxious beings harmless.

2. *The Use of Incantations.* Ritual chants were also common. They were used in association with amulets, fire, and magic for many purposes, including medical and surgical procedures. In ancient Mesopotamia, nearly nothing was done without an incantation! These ritualistic sayings were supposed to drive out evil influences, foil the "machinations of human wizards and witches," and "exorcise particular types of evil spirits."[34] There were, of course, many other uses.

One example demonstrates a typical method by which incantations were blended with other magical elements in exorcism:

> Unleavened bread was prepared from specific ingredients to the threefold recitation of incantation: "Dead folk, why do you appear to me, you whose towns are the ruins, whose houses (?) are the bones? As for me, I do not go to Cuthah, the assembly-place of the ghosts: why, then, do you come after me? Be Ye exorcised by . . . [names of deities follow]." As the sun was setting, the magical bread so prepared was taken to a newly-dug hole, into which it, with flour and water, was poured through an ox-horn, a torch then being applied to a censer nearby. Whilst the column of incense was rising to the setting sun another incantation was recited, calling upon the Sun-god to exorcise the offending spirit. . . ."[35]

3. *The Use of Substitution.* One other method of exorcism was substitution. Such an option was usually the last resort and followed a number of milder forms. Clay tablets discovered at the great library of Ashurbanipal are filled with rituals such as:

> A suckling pig (take and lay against) the head of the patient. Tear out its heart and (place against the [heart] of the patient) with the pig's blood (smear) the sides of the (sick) bed. Cut up

> the pig and spread the parts over the patient. . . . Give the pig as his (the patient's) substitute. Flesh (of the pig) for his (the patient's) flesh. . . . Let them (the demons) take it.[36]

Medicine in Ancient China

Chinese medical science fell prey to many of the same errors seen elsewhere, as well as to several additional mistakes unique to the oriental culture. Because many of these were directly traceable to the Taoist religion, they will be considered in the next chapter. It should be noted, however, that the early Chinese medical practices included demonology, divination, alchemy, and various forms of magic.

One example will suffice to demonstrate the occurrence of magic in pre-Taoist China:

> [At birth,] the placenta should be stored away in a felicitous spot under the salutary influences of the sky or the moon, deep in the ground, and with earth piled up over it carefully, in order that the child may be ensured a long life. If it is devoured by a swine or dog, the child loses its intellect; if insects or ants eat it, the child becomes scrofulous, if crows or magpies swallow it, the child will have an abrupt or violent death; if it is cast into the fire, the child incurs running sores."[37]

Examples such as this one could be multiplied by the thousands.

Summary

Throughout the ancient world primitive medical science included many misconceptions about the cause and treatment of disease processes. Some errors were held almost universally; others were unique to certain geographical areas and cultures. Modern-day readers should be slow to ridicule those who were deceived by what is known today as "superstition" and "foolishness." After all, knowledge in many areas of science was then in its infancy. In fact, it is admirable that our ancestors made as much progress as they did. They were, like all of us, imperfect mortals searching for answers.

2

Out of the Frying Pan, Into the Fire

In what the ancients wrote about the medical arts, numerous errors are to be expected. However, if there is a God behind this universe, and if that deity has in some way revealed truth to mankind, then one test of a supernatural revelation—as opposed to literary inspiration or human genius—would be the absence of errors in the revelation. There would also be an unexplainable presence of advanced ideas then unknowable in the ancient world because of a lack of technology. With these criteria in mind, can divine inspiration be claimed for any non-biblical scriptures?

Medicine in the Hindu Writings

The Hindu system of medicine, known as Ayur-Veda (the science of life) is included in sacred writings known as the *Atharva-Veda,*[1] the *Charaka Samhita,* and the *Susruta Samhita.* Of the three, the *Atharva-Veda* is the chief source of Vedic medical knowledge.[2] Its one hundred hymns, intended as cures for diseases, are the oldest Hindu writings that deal with medicine, dating from around 700 B.C.

Demons as the "Cause" of Disease

In line with the erroneous teachings of their day, authors of the *Atharva-Veda* ascribe all disease to supernatural demonic powers that enter the body. One commentator observes: "Some of these demons took the form of worms and were the cause of headaches as well as diseases of the ear and eye. Still others singled out the victims on the basis of sin in their previous life. Thus, a mortal sinner automatically became a leper, an alcoholic automatically had black teeth, and one who killed a cow would be struck blind."[3] The *Atharva-Veda* also conceived of lightning as a demon that caused fever and cough[4] and prescribed either a covering of grass for the patient's head[5] or heating an axe in water, then pouring the water over the head of the diseased person.[6]

Prescriptions that Failed

Other Hindu medical practices are equally ineffective. The *Kausika* recommends earth from an ant hill as a cure for diarrhea (xxv.–7) and earth from a mole hill to relieve constipation (xxv–11). The latter is obviously selected because moles travel through dark passages! Dropsy was to be cured by sprinkling water over a patient's head by means of twenty-one tufts of sacred grass.[7] And, like secular writers of the time, the Hindu scriptures recommend such substances as dog saliva, slime from the teeth, spittle, and rotten fish, in the belief that any medicine that tasted or looked bad enough would disgust a demon sufficiently to cause it to leave the body of an infected individual, who would then be able to recover from the illness.[8]

Even later works did not dispel superstition, but instead recommended the use of "drugs" such as the ground bones of goat, bile, animal blood, and urine. Other remedies were prescribed on the basis of the doctrine of signatures (already noted in chapter 1 as obvious error). One can read, for instance, that the leaves of a *parasu* (axe) tree were to be applied to an abscess because the axe-shaped leaf would "open the sore." Wood from the *karunka* tree (a bow) was applied to wounds caused by poisoned arrows. Growth of hair was to occur when the root of the *nitani* plant was utilized. Since the *nitani* was noted for its root system, its use was supposed to cause the hair to take root.

Color signature is also recommended—yellow plants are invoked as cures for jaundice; red plants are proposed as remedies for rashes and fevers which cause a person to look "red" or flushed. Similar prescriptions occur throughout Hindu literature. The medical consensus today is that these remedies were useless.[9]

Even remedies that might be considered partially effective were submerged in meaningless magical rites. According to the writings, some drugs, to be effective, had to be mixed in a cow's horn or stirred with a poisoned arrow. In other references, one is informed that drugs must be prepared at a crossroads or some other special place before they can take effect. The recovery of a patient was often deemed dependent on where or when a drug was administered or even the type of clothing the patient was wearing when receiving the treatment.

Since such errors are numerous, one can safely conclude that the Hindu religious writings, while beautiful, thoughtful, and creative, give no evidence of being of divine origin. They are written as ordinary humans would write and include the same type of errors common to secular writers. They teach "largely magic."[10]

Medicine in the Buddhist Writings

References to the medical sciences in the *Tripitaka,* the sacred writings of Buddha, are almost nonexistent. One would expect to find in them little of note regarding the healing arts, in light of the Buddhist view that the human body and human life are of no real value, that man's real goal is to reach a state of *nirvana*—nothingness—and the belief that any good at all comes from suffering.[11] The verdict of medical scholars? They conclude unanimously that "the Buddhists cannot claim any credit for medical advancement."[12] Their low view of human life prohibited any real progress in the prevention and treatment of disease.

Medicine in the Taoist Writings

The sacred writings of the Taoist religion—the *Tao-te-Ching* and the *Chuaung Tzu*—contain numerous medical teachings. As is the case with other non-biblical writings, however, they offer little of lasting value in light of modern medical research.[13]

Alchemy and a Long Life

By far the greatest medical difficulty in the *Tao* is the doctrine of alchemy. Briefly, alchemy is the belief in the transmutation of elements. For example, it teaches that lead can be changed into silver or silver into gold. Insofar as the medical sciences are concerned, the doctrine teaches the existence of an "elixir of life" that supposedly can cure all diseases, heal all wounds, bring wisdom and virility, restore permanent youth, and resurrect the dead.

This miracle liquid prompted a search among the disciples of the *Tao* that would make Ponce de Leon's search for the fountain of youth look like child's play. Alchemists began by listing certain substances that they felt should comprise this life-giving liquid. These substances included some materials from the animal and vegetable kingdoms but were predominantly taken from the mineral world.

Specifically, the minerals selected were mostly metallic substances, such as mercury, silver, and gold. These were then mixed in various compounds and consumed in the hope of attaining immortality. Reliance on these elixirs proved especially unfortunate because the prescribed elements, when taken into the human system in sufficient quantity, are themselves lethal. Yet the death of countless multitudes by metallic poisoning seems to have been ignored. So firm was the belief in alchemy that noted British historian Joseph Needham was able to compile a lengthy list of Chinese emperors who probably died as a result of its use.[14]

The Use of Charms and Talismans

In addition to championing the errors of alchemy, the sacred Taoist writings also recommended the use of charms and talismans for healing. Magical diagrams were written on paper, then burned and swallowed to cure diseases.[15] These magical devices were believed to ward off the evil demons that, according to Taoist doctrine, abounded in the countryside.[16] It is conclusive that the writings of the Taoist religion contain numerous serious errors in medical knowledge. In short, Taoist writings "hindered the progress of medicine in ancient China for many centuries."[17]

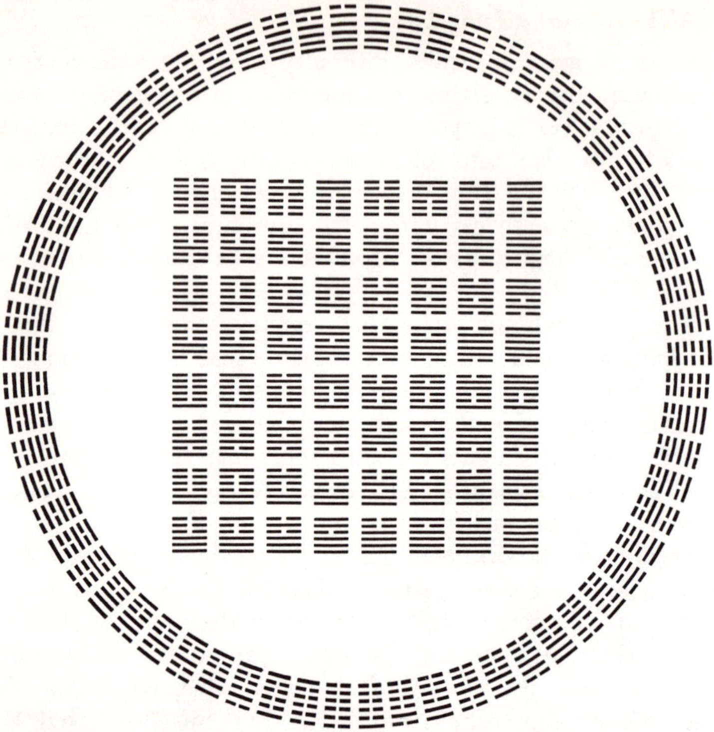

The famous 64 hexagrams of the I Ching are arranged both in a square and a circle. Using these hexagrams, Chinese "seers" were supposedly capable of determining the causes and cures of illnesses. Often these hexagrams would be copied on paper, burned, and the ashes would be swallowed to promote proper healing.

Medicine in the Zoroastrian Writings

The Zoroastrian religion looks to the *Avesta* for its sacred revelations. The section known as the *Vendidad* (law vs. demons) is the primary source of teachings relating to medical ideas. As was believed in most of the ancient world, the Zoroastrian document attributed all disease to demons who wandered through the land searching for victims. Consequently, cures were aimed at destroying or driving out demons rather than at the natural causes of disease. Zoroastrian scriptures taught such rituals as the sprinkling of cow urine over a patient to disgust any demons

A Taoist nostrum said to cure all diseases. Courtesy, C. A. S. Williams, *Outlines of Chinese Symbolism and Art Motives* (New York: Dover, 1976) p. 64

hidden in the body.[18] Even the simple process of sneezing was ascribed to demons. The remedy was simple: "Whenever a person sneezes, he should offer the prescribed prayers."[19] The *Vendidad* is filled with magical prayers and incantations designed to assist in expelling demons.

At least one other medically related item, perhaps the most significant, should be noted from Zoroastrian writings. Embedded in these scriptures is a prohibition against burying the dead. The text reads, "A sin for which there is no atonement—the burying of the dead."[20] And the reason for this law? It was taught that a corpse placed in the earth would render the earth unclean and thereby produce disease through crops that receive their nourishment from the soil. Such practices actually multiplied the disease-producing bacteria among these societies.

Medicine in the Shinto Writings

Shintoism, as expressed in writings such as the *Ko-ji-ki,* [the *Nihon-gi,*] the *Yengi-shiki,* and the *Manyo-shui,* reflects the same basic errors that plagued other Eastern religions. It is deeply entrenched in the teachings of alchemy and blindly accepts much of the attitude of futility that pervaded Buddhism.

According to Shinto writings, all disease was ultimately to be traced either to divine influence or evil and dead spirits. As a result, medical advice primarily emphasized magic. Diseases were to be treated on the basis of such totally unrelated omens as the number of lotus leaves on one stem, the condition of water in a pond, or the burning of bones. Remedies included prayers, incantations, exorcisms, sacrifices, and elements such as the liver of a wild pig. Even the method of purification performed in the *chazu-bauche* (holy water placed before shrines in which all the faithful are commanded to wash their hands and rinse their mouths) has been labeled as that which actually spreads disease and infection.[21] Once again, supposedly divine scriptures are found to have feet of clay.

Medicine in the Islamic Writings

Discussing scientific teachings in the Islamic *Koran* and *Traditions* proves more difficult than an analysis of the other sacred writings, for two important reasons.

First, Muslim scriptures were composed several centuries after the completion of the Bible, the *Tripitaka,* the *Vedas,* and most other sacred writings from the world's major religions. The writers obviously had the opportunity to draw on not only the scientifically acceptable teachings of earlier religious texts, but also on centuries of progress and advancement in the various sciences. For example, in the medical field, the idea that demons were the cause of all disease had been fairly well eradicated from much of society, and the tenets of Greek and Roman medicine had already permeated the Arabian world when Mohammed began to teach. We would thus expect to find less of the grotesque and the absurd in Muslim scriptures, even if we considered them to be written by an author not supernaturally inspired.

Second, the *Koran* almost never speaks of medical concepts or practices. Any comprehensive interpretation of the original Islamic medical beliefs is thereby made difficult, if not impossible.

Medicine in the Non-Inspired Jewish and Christian Writings

Finally, mention should be made of writings by non-inspired Jewish and early Christian authors. If these writers *were* able to write without error, then our argument for the divine guidance of biblical authors would lose its force. On the other hand, if there existed in their works errors similar to those in other non-biblical texts, this would become an additional argument in favor of the Bible's supernatural origin.

Such an inquiry produces immediate results. The writings of non-inspired Jews and Christians are littered with misconceptions and inaccuracy. Many believed and taught the errors of astrology. Others had false ideas concerning the function of certain drugs. Rabbi Jochanan, for example, advises the use of amulets, the digging of pits, the burning of vines, and the recitation of formulas to eradicate disease.[22] Josephus believed demons could be expelled through a patient's nose, then forced to overturn cups of water to demonstrate that they had left.[23] Examples could be multiplied, all indicating that non-biblical Jewish and Christian authors shared equally with other ancient writers in their erroneous medical beliefs.

Summary

At this point, three conclusions can be drawn.

First, although it is true that medical sciences in antiquity were advanced in certain areas, they were also permeated with errors, inaccuracies, and absurdities. Any literature written during this period by human authors would therefore be filled with mistakes. On the other hand, any writings of this time that dealt with the medical arts without error would admittedly be something very special.

Second, the "inspired" writings of the world's non-Christian religions are likewise filled with inaccuracies. They are in that respect not distinguishable from books written by ordinary men who claim no special divine help. Similarly, books by non-biblical Jewish and Christian authors are also filled with inaccurate teachings.

Third, if one believes in a truly divine being, it is difficult to conceive of that being transmitting a string of errors. At best, therefore, the evidence that has accumulated thus far argues against divine authorship of the sacred writings of the world's non-biblical religions.

3

A Breath of Fresh Air

As the same tests applied to other writings are administered to the Judeo-Christian Bible, two important questions must be asked. First, do Bible authors, many of whom were writing prior to or at the same time as the writers of other sacred scriptures, avoid the errors in the medical sciences that ensnared all the others? Second, is there additional evidence that some biblical statements are so advanced that human authors would have been unable to comprehend their significance, given the lack of technological and scientific abilities of the times? If the Bible is what it claims—supernaturally inspired—the answer to both questions is affirmative.

With regard to the first question—do Bible writers avoid the medical errors of the day?—the answer is an overwhelming "Yes!" Of all the sacred and religious writings available, only those in the Bible sidestep the errors and ignorance that pervaded the medical sciences of its time. A thorough study of the Bible, for instance, will yield not one "abominable" prescription. That in itself is amazing, for the Bible (especially earlier parts of the Old Testament) was compiled and written during the same time period when medical science was suffering through some of its darkest years.

Many erroneous concepts actually originated during the time of Moses, when the Ebers papyrus was in vogue. That is even more impressive when one realizes that Moses, in all probability, was well aware of the papyrus. Luke says in Acts 7:22 that "Moses was educated in all the wisdom of the Egyptians. . . ." Many biblical scholars place Moses in the Middle Kingdom, at a time when the Ebers papyrus (or at least its doctrine) was widely accepted. With that dating, we can draw several conclusions about the "wisdom" available to Moses:

First, practices and prescriptions outlined in the papyrus pervaded Egyptian culture throughout the period. Following a detailed study, Eby and Arrowood declared in absolutist terms that "incantations and charms invariably preceded or accompanied the taking of medicine. . . . Remedies revolting to our sensibilities and wholly without reason were commonly prescribed."[1] The authors also noted: "Every physician was obliged to study these writings and to follow the prescribed remedies without alteration."[2] This alone would make Moses' familiarity with the papyrus even more likely.

Second, as a member of the royal court, Moses would have studied Egyptian medicine, for the royalty studied "medicine, astrology . . . and perhaps the more secret aspects of other crafts" as part of their educational curriculum.[3] Eby and Arrowood also comment that "medical science was taught at the great temples" where Moses would have studied.[4]

Third, schoolboys during the time of the Middle Kingdom were taught to "write the symbols of each science"[5] as part of their daily schooling, in addition to writing "essays on magical beliefs and superstitions."[6] Thousands of their copybooks have survived into the modern era. As R. C. H. Lenski concluded, "The priestly caste of the Egyptians was famed for its knowledge of science, mathematics, astronomy, and medicine, and constituted the nobility around Pharaoh. In all their wisdom was Moses educated."[7]

Fourth, the Ebers papyrus, by "general agreement" of Egyptian scholars, was "designed to be a text for study and training."[8]

Yet, when the Pentateuch was written, it did not recommend even one of the repulsive treatments so widely used by the medical establishment of the day. Coincidence? Perhaps. Logic suggests that if these writings had been composed only on the basis of human knowledge, they would have followed others down at least one blind alley. But, from one end of the Pentateuch to the other, not one medical reference pertaining to such cures as human or animal excrement or "gall of tortoise" or "heel of an Abyssinian greyhound" or "burnt quills of hedgehog" can be found.

In addition, one can scour the Bible from cover to cover and fail to find any reference that attributes all disease to demons or that teaches alchemy or astrology. One writer observed that the Hebrew nation was "probably the first people to disbelieve that diseases were caused by evil spirits and demons."[9] Throughout the Old and New Testaments, saints and sinners alike fall prey to disease and/or death without the slightest hint that devils were to blame.

Bible writers do occasionally mention demons. There are major differences, though, between the biblical account and all others:

1. Bible authors never imply or suggest that the demons were the only cause of sickness. When they are mentioned, the demons are described as afflicting the mind, which in turn caused physical problems.
2. Bible authors severely restrict the power of demons.
3. Bible authors imply that demon involvement in human affairs was for a limited time.[10]

Those who reject the biblical account simply because it involves elements of a spiritual dimension usually dismiss any form of the supernatural. That bias will be discussed elsewhere.

Bible writers also rule out the value of divination (Ezek. 12:24; Deut. 18:10) and the use of omens (Jer. 10:2). Whereas healing is on occasion attributed to the miraculous, Bible authors never claim that miraculous measures are required for healing (see Luke 10:30–35; Matt. 9:12). Again, the Bible's writers suggest that even the miraculous healings through human agents were not to occur perpetually, but were unique in human history, as suggested by Paul's famous treatise on spiritual gifts, including "miraculous powers" (1 Cor. 13:7–11).

In short, it is singularly strange that of all the ancient writings, the Bible alone is free from the grotesque, unscientific perversions that were once passed off as medicine. The Bible is, as a medical historian notes, "surprisingly rational."[11]

Identical terminology was used in a 1983 article on Hebrew medicine, which mused, "The Hebrew approach to therapy was

Avoiding Medical Errors

Pitfalls biblical writers managed to avoid

1. Bizarre prescriptions
2. Attributing all disease to demons
3. Magical control of disease
4. Doctrine of signatures
5. Alchemy
6. Astrology
7. Divination and omens

rational. Hebrew medicines, ointments, salves, and baths were basic to treatment, and there was an extensive *materia medica.* The excremental pharmacopeia popular among neighboring peoples was not acceptable."[12]

Sir M. Monier Williams spent nearly half a century in the study of Sanskrit and the Eastern religions. He admitted that he was impressed at first and would have once given the writings equal footing with the Bible. Those thoughts were wiped clean by intense study and, once gone, they never threatened again. Near the end of his study, he wrote:

> "These non-Christian Bibles are all developments in the wrong direction. They all begin with some flashes of true light, and end in utter darkness. Pile them, if you will, on the left side of your table; but place your own Holy Bible on the right side—all by itself, all alone and with a wide gap between them. For there is a gulf between it and the so-called sacred books of the East which severs the one from the other utterly, hopelessly, and for ever; not a mere rift across which the Christian may shake hands and interchange similar ideas in regard to essential truths—but a veritable gulf, which cannot be bridged over by any science of religious thought . . . a bridgeless chasm, which no theory . . . can ever span.[13]

No final conclusion concerning the uniqueness of the Bible can be drawn merely on the basis of what it does *not* say, as important as that happens to be. A second step is necessary, as is our second question—What do Bible authors actually say regarding medical materials and concepts? The Bible should be examined for positive clues that suggest divine inspiration. Five general categories will be studied in the remaining chapters of this section: sanitation laws, food laws, moral laws, laws relating to factors that cause stress, and laws concerning the practice of circumcision.

4

Biblical Sanitation Laws

Scholars are nearly unanimous in attributing the world's first system of sanitary laws to precepts laid down in the first five books of the Bible. One medical historian labels them "remarkable chapters" of ancient medicine.[1] Another concedes that they are "scientifically sound," even in light of modern discoveries, and admits that no other medical code of antiquity was anywhere near as thorough.[2] Another writes that the practices were "remarkably prescient in light of current understanding" and adds that "the ancient Hebrews have been termed the founders of preventive medicine."[3]

Still another scholar adds that the sanitation laws were "superior to any which then existed in the world" and that "to this day they have been little improved upon."[4] Likewise, R. K. Harrison notes that the regulations were "of immeasurable importance for individual and communal health in preventing the outbreak of devastating epidemics" and that "an advanced degree of protection from infectious disease was afforded if the prescribed rules for sanitation, isolation, and hygiene were followed." Finally, he observes that "the principles enshrined in the Pentateuch are in harmony with the basic precepts of contemporary preventive medicine."[5]

The renowned Italian expert in tropical diseases, A. Castiglione, concurs adding that "no one can fail to be impressed by the careful hygienic precautions of the Mosaic period.

The extremely stringent quarantine rules very likely did a great deal of good."[6] Finally, the words of Harry Wain, a current historian of medicine, should be heard. His verdict is that the laws are "advanced," were "superior to any which then existed," and are "as worth following now as when they were first promulgated."[7]

Accolades such as these are especially impressive when you realize that (1) ignorance was prevalent in the ancient world; (2) the very author of the code of laws in the Pentateuch had been taught similar errors since childhood (Acts 7:22); and (3) these laws were passed along to a nomadic people crushed by years of slavery.

Specifically, the laws to which these medical historians refer include the commands for washing and general sanitation, the process of quarantine, and the commands for the disposal of wastes prescribed in the books of Leviticus, Numbers, and Deuteronomy. Before considering each, it should be understood that the primary intent in any of these areas was not to develop some type of scientific principle. As far as can be determined, the real issues were more likely to be ceremonial or religious. The science is tangential, but it is there.

Washing and Sanitation

In the enlightened twentieth century, it is easy to forget that sanitary precautions were once largely unknown. Those familiar with the history of medicine, however, readily draw to mind the traumatic attempts of Ignaz Semmelweis in the mid-1800s to persuade his fellow physicians in Vienna regarding the simple importance of washing hands as a preventive to the spread of disease.[8]

Semmelweis was troubled by massive mortality rates in maternity wards at Allegemeine Krankenhaus, Vienna's large and celebrated instructional hospital where he was an assistant in obstetrics. Though the hospital was supposed to be among the best in the world, one of every six women entering its maternity clinic died of "childbed fever." To Semmelweis that was a catastrophe, and he was determined to isolate the cause of the slaughter.

Obstetricians among his peers claimed the calamity was

Although ridiculed for his suggestions regarding washing and sanitation, Ignaz P. Semmelweis (1818-1865) is now hailed as one of the forerunners of modern sanitation theory. Courtesy, The National Library of Medicine.

brought on by such things as fear or poisoned air. Admittedly, such suggestions were weak, but they were the only ones available. Semmelweis set out to find the real answer. After being placed in charge of one of the wards, he kept careful records and observations. Some time later a tentative conclusion was drawn, but the conclusion seemed so simple that he hesitated suggesting its adoption.

After a few more observations, however, Semmelweis was convinced. He had casually noticed that there was a much higher mortality rate in the section where student doctors, rather than midwives, did examinations. Though the general correlation had been confirmed rather easily, the specific cause had been harder to determine. Yet, the daily schedules of the interns had offered the first glimpse of a solution. Semmelweis had carefully observed that the first order of daily business for doctors and their students was the performing of autopsies on patients who had died during the past twenty-four hours. Then, with no attempt at sanitation, teachers and students proceeded from the dissecting room to the maternity wards to examine their living patients.

Semmelweis issued a strange new rule—no doctor or medical student could examine a patient in his ward without first washing his hands thoroughly. The mortality rate plummeted. One month later, only one patient in forty-two died in the ward. Two months later, the death rate was only one in eighty-four. Semmelweis had found the answer. Even then, it took years to convince the medical profession of the validity of his position that sanitary measures could control the spread of infection. This discovery was both simple and profound. It altered the course of medical history. Perhaps it would be impractical to label it as a discovery. "Rediscovery" is a more appropriate word, for over three millennia prior to Semmelweis's observation, Moses had transcribed detailed ordinances (Num. 19; Lev. 13–15) that certainly suggested the same idea. If carried to its logical conclusion, this code would have prevented centuries of needless death and suffering.

The Mosaic laws were simple. Anyone who came in contact with the dead or diseased was declared to be unclean. Such persons were then to wash themselves and their clothing repeatedly in running water before resuming their place in society. The injunction is especially noteworthy when one considers the scarcity of water in the areas where the Israelites lived. Fresh water is (and has been throughout history) a precious resource in Middle Eastern lands. Even today, those who travel in this region will pay almost the same for a bottle of water as for other beverages. But, despite the scarcity of water, the laws required the people to wash themselves in running water after having contacted anything unclean.

The laws were the first of their kind,[9] and they were effective. More impressively, they are still in wide use today. One scholar described them as being of "profound significance in the control of disease."[10] Another commented, "Washing with soap and water has been shown to be effective in removing patient-acquired micro-organisms and is recommended not only for personal hygiene but also as the most important procedure for preventing nosocomial infections spread by hospital personnel."[11] Another added, "There is no good substitute for routine handwashing with soap and running water."[12] Sadly, it took medicine many centuries to rediscover the importance of washing.

Some may question this last statement on the basis of the massive study by Sir James George Frazer asserting that washing for purification was common among primitive cultures. Frazer's study is irrelevant to the argument here, however. Several observations are in order:

1. With the exception of the Roman and Egyptian examples, Frazer's source material is at least three millennia after the biblical period and, consequently, his work in no way speaks to the time period around 1500–500 B.C.

2. All of Frazer's examples come from areas where the water supply was sufficient. Egyptian irrigation systems of earlier days made that nation's supply much more plentiful and accessible. Biblical commands were given in different environments.

3. In the Egyptian sample, which is the only one cited within one thousand years of the biblical time frame, only the nobility were enjoined to wash, and that command was associated with several other rituals of no known scientific validity. In contrast, the Mosaic laws were universally applied.

4. Non-biblical precepts never specify washing in running water, as does Moses. Modern discoveries are more in tune with Moses' commands than with those of the Romans of late times.

Use of Cleansing Materials

If the biblical story stopped here, it would be amazing enough. But there is more. Not only were the Israelites instructed to wash in running water, but they were also instructed to use a primitive soap in their cleansing (Num. 19:18). McMillen describes this in his latest text:

> "According to the scriptural method, wet branches of hyssop were used to shower soapy water on the unclean person. Most authorities feel that hyssop refers to a type of marjoram plant. . . . The sweet-smelling oil of marjoram . . . contains about 50 percent carvacrol. Carvacrol is almost identical to thymol, an antifungal and antibacterial agent that is still used in the practice of medicine."[13]

It is obvious that the biblical command to wash after coming in contact with someone or something that was unclean was extremely advanced for its time.

Correct Disposal of Wastes

When other biblical sanitation requirements were ignored, there were the same unfortunate results. The Mosaic laws, for example, stressed the importance of the correct disposal of human excrement and blood (Deut. 23:12–13 and Lev. 17:13). Both were to be *buried* outside the camp. Medical scientists tell us that, as a result of these laws, the spread of germs was minimized and decomposition of harmful substances was hastened by micro-organisms in the ground. In addition, the burial of blood also eliminated a known attracter of disease-bearing insects and a culture medium for bacteria. Again, the significance of these injunctions is somewhat muted because sanitary disposal is now taken for granted in industrialized societies.

Yet, even today, hundreds of thousands of people die annually from sanitation-related problems. One must remember that the laws under discussion were composed at a time when most cities and villages were little more than settled dung-heaps where excrement filled the streets. Over the centuries, as a result of the failure of medical science to realize the importance of these concepts, millions of graves have been dug prematurely.

Intestinal diseases such as dysentery, cholera, and typhoid fever have had a free rein in the world.[14] The real tragedy, of course, was that these premature deaths could have been avoided even in the simplest societies if the Mosaic commands had been followed. One medical historian, while noting that the biblical ideas were "simple" and "primitive," was forced to admit that they were "effective."[15]

The Link Between Contagion and Disease

Another concept involved in sanitation is contagion. Again, the ancient world appears to have been totally ignorant of this very basic tenet of modern medicine.[16] At best, isolation of diseased persons was practiced because the sick were taboo to the gods. Most medical historians trace the concept of contagion to the Pentateuch. As one author concluded, the Hebrews were "the first to recognize . . . communicability of diseases."[17] Whether or not they actually "recognized" it is open to debate. Nonetheless, even though "the idea of contagion was foreign to the classic medical tradition . . . the Old Testament is a rich source for contagionist sentiment."[18]

Even the Greeks, whose medical concepts were the most advanced among early peoples, "never had a concept of conta-

Erroneous beliefs about the cause of the great plagues of the Middle Ages led physicians to attempt the absurd to ward off sickness. This woodcut from 1721 shows a physician in a special "plague costume" in hopes of avoiding and curing the disease. Courtesy, The National Library of Medicine.

gion,"[19] and most medical historians suggest that the first theory of contagion from a scientific standpoint was not given until Fracastorius' writings in the middle 1500s. That was two thousand years after the biblical command!

Specifically, laws in Leviticus 13 and 14 that relate to medical concepts of illness include: (1) the recognition and diagnosis of disease; (2) the separation or isolation of the diseased person; (3) the placing of a covering over the nose and mouth; (4) the designation of anything that had been touched by a diseased person as unclean; (5) the process by which the unclean became purified; and (6) the destruction of those items that could not be cleansed. All are followed to some degree by modern medical practitioners. And although advances in technology have made strict isolation no longer essential, "ideally the infected person is nursed in a separate room."[20]

Results of Ignoring Biblical Laws

As was true with other biblical concepts, mankind over the centuries managed to avoid or ignore the ideas, and numerous

The demon of plague. Even as late as the Middle Ages demons were still believed to be responsible for most of the world's desease. H. von Gerodorf's representation of the demonic-caused plagues was drawn for the 1540 publication *Feldbuch der Wundarzney.* Courtesy, *Devils, Demons and Witchcraft* by Ernst and Johanna Lehner, Dover Publications, Inc.

critics of the Christian Scriptures have enjoyed poking fun at the "quaint religious practices." From a scientific viewpoint, the validity of the practices is now obvious. But in the centuries between modern scientific verifications and the original discussion of the ideas in the Bible, the death toll was dreadful. Ancient and medieval human history is filled with millions of human corpses, fallen prey to the plagues of leprosy, the black death, and syphilis. One medical scholar estimates that as many as sixty million Europeans were victims of plague in one century.[21] Millions more lost their lives to leprosy.[22] And all of these deaths were occurring at a time when a biblical command offered a way to avoid much of this needless carnage. The solution had been in the Bible rather than in a test tube, and the idea was imposed by those who studied the Bible rather than those who worked in a laboratory.

Precepts in the Book of Leviticus brought the plagues under control and "accomplished the first great feat . . . in methodical eradication of disease."[23] Once its concept of quarantine was incorporated into medical methodology, the great plagues no longer controlled the destiny of man. Though modern quarantines are not as numerous because of advanced treatment measures, this in no way diminishes the scientific value of the law. During biblical times, no microbial, bacteriological or other microscopic tests existed to distinguish between specific diseases. Therefore, it was safer to assume that all diseases with similar outward symptoms were equally serious. If society should ever lose the ability to conduct modern tests, the Mosaic laws would become once more the preferred alternative. Quarantine is still a useful tool in the battle against disease, even in our advanced culture. It is not uncommon for schools to close when absenteeism due to influenza or other contagious outbreaks rises dangerously. Temporary closures help healthy students stay away from infected ones until the crucial periods are over.

Finally, the use of designated wards in hospitals, and to some degree specialized hospitals, illustrates a modern form of quarantine.

Summary

Biblical sanitation laws were definitely unique in ancient literature. They were given without scientific error well over three

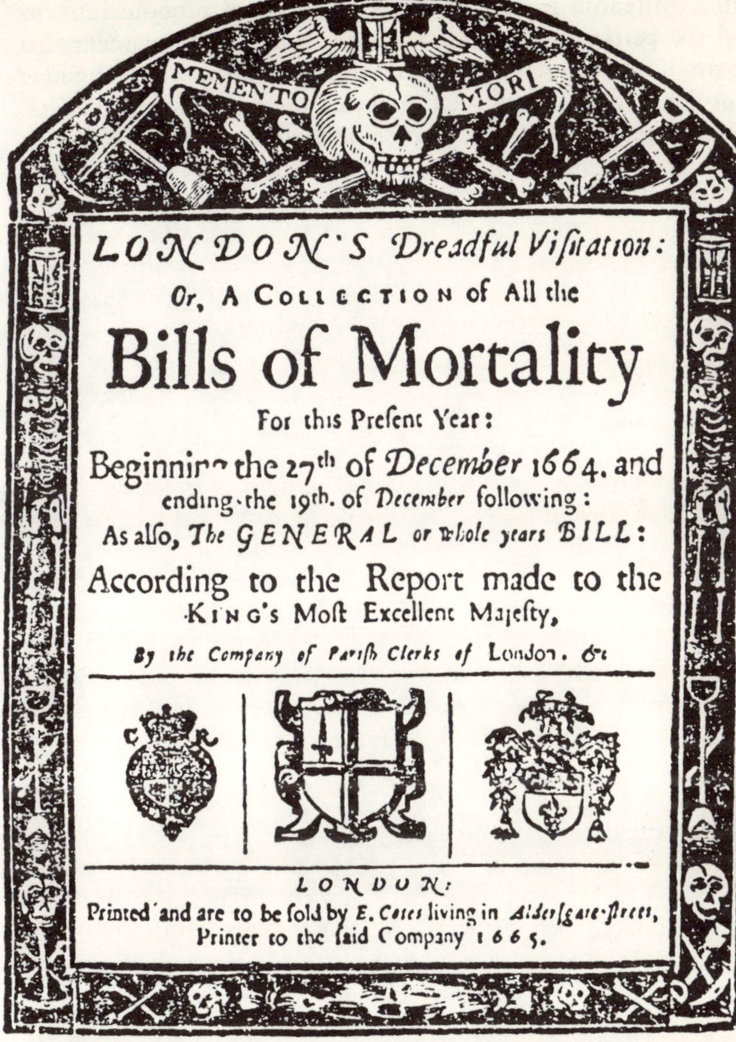
MEMENTO MORI

LONDON'S Dreadful Viſitation:

Or, A COLLECTION of All the

Bills of Mortality

For this Preſent Year:

Beginning the 27th of *December* 1664. and

ending the 19th. of *December* following:

As alſo, *The GENERAL or whole years BILL:*

According to the Report made to the

KING's Moſt Excellent Majeſty,

By the Company of Pariſh Clerks of London. &c.

LONDON:

Printed and are to be ſold by E. *Cotes* living in *Alderſgate-ſtreet,*

Printer to the ſaid Company 1665.

The plagues that devastated the Middle Ages were finally brought under control by following biblical suggestions. The title page from "Bills of Mortality," a printed report to the king regarding those who died in 1665, was ominously printed in the form of a tombstone. Courtesy, *Devils, Demons and Witchcraft* by Ernst and Johanna Lehner, Dover Publications, Inc.

thousand years ago, a time when the technology of the day was incapable of making such discoveries. In most instances, over three millennia passed between the original pronouncements and the pertinent scientific discoveries. It is little wonder that Moses has been characterized as "the greatest sanitary engineer that the world has ever seen" and that the Book of Leviticus has been tabbed as "that fine treatise on hygiene."[24]

5

Biblical Food Laws

Advanced disease prevention also surfaces in the biblical division of food into the general classifications of "clean" (acceptable) and "unclean" (unacceptable). No restrictions were placed on fruits and vegetables, but Bible writers did record severe limitations on eating meat. Among land animals, for example, only those that have a "split hoof" and "chew the cud" were permitted for human consumption (Lev. 11:3).

As far as water life, only organisms with "fins and scales" were approved as food (Lev. 11:9). Birds of prey were prohibited, as were most insects. The most well-known prohibition was the exclusion of pork, although such other modern delicacies as catfish and rabbit were also prohibited.

In addition to outright bans, the consumption of food labeled as "clean" was regulated. For example, "clean" animals were not to be eaten until the blood had been removed (Lev. 3:17; 7:26; 17:10–14; Deut. 12:23–35), and animals that were diseased, that had died, or that had been killed by carnivorous animals were prohibited (Deut. 14:21), as was eating the fat of animals (Lev. 7:22–26).

The ultimate effect of these laws was that they "would go far toward preventing the incidence of food-borne polioencephalitis, the enteric fevers, food poisoning, and the parasitic worms."[1] They were remarkable for the time in which they were composed. In fact, "civilized man, after centuries of experience, has come to approximately the same conclusion."[2]

The Ban on Pork and Rabbit

The ban on the eating of pork and rabbit is said to have "direct public health implications even today."[3] One writer concluded that these types of flesh are safe "only if they are cleanly fed and the flesh well cooked."[4] A survey of ancient customs indicates that neither condition was met with any degree of regularity. Specifically, the exclusion of pork in the Israelite climate was of immense importance:

> The flesh of the pig is particularly dangerous . . . being the intermediate host for several parasitic organisms. . . . *Trichinella spirilis* occurs in partially or improperly cooked pork, and if ingested . . . propagates . . . trichinosis (which causes) malaise, fever, edema of the face and legs. . . . Tapeworm infestation as a result of eating pork is more common than trichinosis. The pig is the intermediate host for a parasitic worm known as *Taenia solium,* which, in a developed form is often much as ten feet in length. In man . . . the worm develops from the *Cysticercus cellulosae* parasite present in . . . pork. Occasionally, this infestation leads to . . . nodules in the brain or the skeletal muscles. . . . (The) pig is also . . . host for the parasitic *Echinococcus granulosus* which . . . is the cause of hydatid tumors in the liver, lungs, and other parts of the body. A further disease, conveyed in particular by pigs and rodents is toxoplasmosis.[5]

Obviously, the ban on pork was "an extremely valuable regulation," as were other exclusions from the diet, such as "dogs, cats, fishes without scales (all poisonous fish have no scales) and oysters, which on many occasions in modern times have caused epidemics of typhoid fever and other infectious diseases."[6]

The respected W. F. Albright adds, "We find no classification as logical as this in any of the cuneiform lists of fauna or ritual taboos." Yet, at the same time, Albright found himself fascinated that such a classification system appeared so early in the history of mankind, noting that such laws "can scarcely have been drawn up on the basis of any knowledge of the aetiology underlying the prohibition. . . ."[7]

Other scholars agree that the Mosaic dietary laws "are unique in the ancient Near East"[8] and note further that "this distinction seems to rest in health considerations"[9] rather than in the "sympathetic magic—sometimes professional magic—about the taboos in the cuneiform texts."[10]

The Ban on Eating Animal Fat

Science has also documented the medically valid reasoning behind the exclusion of animal fat from the diet. The first known scientific study related to the concept was conducted by the Russian pathologist Nikolai Anitschkov in 1913. He reported that rabbits fed a diet high in cholesterol and animal fats quickly developed hardening of the arteries. Since that report a number of highly regarded studies have confirmed the concept.[11]

One of the most widely known studies is the Diet and Heart Disease Study Project begun by Dr. Norman Jolliffe in 1957. Over one thousand men participated, and the results suggest that lowering the amount of animal fat in the diet reduces the incidence of heart attacks. Simply put, the Mosaic law, given three thousand years before its scientific validity was confirmed, was "of great epidemiological significance."[12]

An interesting parallel to the medically valid ban on animal fat involves the food categories themselves.

Experiments have determined the levels of toxicity in the meats of the animals, birds, and fish described in the clean-unclean listing of Deuteronomy 14.[13] Those studies found that the prohibited meats contained more toxic substances and a higher percentage of toxicity per meat than those that were allowed.

Other Food-Related Prohibitions

Another prohibiton in the Bible forbade the eating of any animal that died of natural causes or was killed by wild animals. That regulation happens to be a valuable method of preventing diseases. As one scientist notes, "We know that carcasses may harbor fleas, ticks, lice—all of which are carriers of deadly diseases such as bubonic plague, spotted fever, or typhus fever."[14]

Finally, limiting the consumption of blood is an equally viable concept with easily tested scientific reasoning behind the injunction.[15] Yet, when the Old Testament books were written, it was common for blood to be an important part of the diet. Several religions contemporary with the Old Testament period encouraged the drinking of blood because it was believed to aid in prophecy.[16]

Even religions that forbade blood consumption added numerous qualifications. Egyptian religions, for example, would not allow eating blood because it was held to be sacred to the gods. The *Grihya Sutras* prohibited the eating of blood but nullified any rationality associated with the injunction by explaining that it was equally disastrous to even look at raw flesh or blood, and similar consequences would occur even if the materials were not consumed.[17] Since no scientific study has found anything wrong with looking at blood, we can conclude that the Bible writer states the warning correctly, while the *Sutras* do not.

Considering the Objections

At this point, we must consider several objections to the thesis that the biblical food laws are both medically valid and unique: (1) the laws are based on superstition, magic, and cultic rituals; (2) similar laws are found in other cultures that were contemporaneous with biblical writers; and (3) the regulations were only ceremonial and were never intended to teach hygienic precautions. They were designed solely for religious or spiritual purposes.

Are the Biblical Food Laws Mere Superstition?

Since numerous ancient societies practice food taboos, it is often asserted that biblical prohibitions are merely what one would expect. Those who hold this position refer to the massive study of magic and religion by James George Frazer.[18] Frazer's work concluded that many obviously false pagan religions in modern times have developed food taboos somewhat similar to biblical laws. In addition, many "biblical" ideas are found in cultist societies contemporaneous with biblical authors.

This argument sounds convincing at first, and the massive amount of material presented by Frazer seems intimidating. Truth is not determined, however, by popular vote or by numbers of examples. Examples without logical reasoning are invalid, and such is the case here.

First, the majority of Frazer's examples come from modern times, rather than from the times of the biblical writers and are therefore over three thousand years removed from the time in question. In this instance many scholars are guilty of the fallacy of *post hoc, ergo propter hoc* which mistakes cause for result. To document that a profusion of food-related superstitions exists in either ancient or modern times does not demonstrate that the original intent of a food prohibition was rooted in superstition. Those who refuse to admit the possibility that the original intent was based on valid medical principles (supernaturally revealed) can offer no real proof to the contrary. Since they are *a priori* opposed to anything supernatural, they assume the alternative of the evolution of all food-prohibitions from superstition.

Second, the thesis of this section relating to Old Testament food laws is that even when relationships surface between biblical references and other ancient or modern sources, these relationships are only superficial. Biblical references differ in qualitative ways that are demonstrably reasonable as far as medical knowledge is concerned. Mere superstitions are not scientifically reasonable.

Are the Biblical Food Laws Non-original?

The real question to be considered is "Did similar laws exist in other lands at the same time the biblical laws were being prepared?" If so, we might well conclude that these regulations were hardly original. But research demands an answer in the negative. Even when similarities are observed, non-biblical laws—both in the Old Testament period and later—are associated with a host of invalid concepts. Outside the Bible no scientifically valid food prohibitions are extant from the Mosaic period, and even if critics were correct that much of the Old Testament was written at a later time, the results are the same. If biblical authors borrowed from other sources, they borrowed only those items that were medically valid. For example, the Romans had food taboos,[19] but they were practiced to keep wizards and sorcerers from bringing evil magic among them.

In addition, others in later times banned pork, but they argued that those who ate pork would produce offspring that would look like pigs and have ugly, long noses.[20] The Babylonians also banned consumption of pork but followed the ban only on certain days. Eating pork was allowed at other times.[21] Merely forbidding a food on certain days did little to prevent disease!

Hindu teachings from a much later time period are likewise based on pagan superstitions rather than scientific fact, and their laws are hardly in the same class with biblical injunctions. As an example, the *Code of Manu* allows the Hindu to partake of such disease-prone organisms as iguana, hare, porcupine, and tortoise, but forbids the eating of vegetables like turnips because they grow in the shape of a head. Equally taboo is food cooked by someone wearing shoes, food prepared by a person of an inferior caste, food cooked on board a ship, food that had been cooked with the use of spoons, or food that had been touched with the left hand.[22] Another Hindu scripture prevents the eating of garlic because it is said to come from drops of ambrosia that trickled from the head of a demon (Rahu).[23]

Are the Biblical Food Laws Merely "Ceremonial"?

Of all the objections, the strongest is that the biblical food laws were not intended as hygiene. This view appears in several variations. Wenham, in his excellent short treatise on the subject,[24] has classed these arguments in three categories.

First are those arguments proposed by scholars who believe the laws are simply arbitrary—designed only to teach the Hebrews to obey, with no obvious reason for their existence.[25] Wenham's reaction is typical of many scholars here: "It is basically a negative approach and should be adopted only as a last resort."[26]

Second, some argue that the forbidden or unclean animals were banned because of their association with pagan worship.[27] Though fairly common among commentators, this view also has strong difficulties. As Wenham realized, "This hypothesis explains too little of the evidence to be of real use" because "the Canaanites sacrificed the same general range of animals as Israel" and the bull was "an important cultic animal in both Egyptian and Canaanite ritual."[28]

That this concept is supported by a reference in Origen[29] is certainly questionable, for Origen states that unclean animals were so determined because the Egyptians thought them to "possess the power of divination" and that it was well-known among Moses and the prophets that unclean animals were "possessed by demons." Origen fails to cite any biblical reference that indicated demon-possession by animals. Further, the bull was one of the key elements of Egyptian worship, magic, and divination, yet was still classed as "clean" in the Bible.

Finally, even the fact that numerous references suggest that the old laws were designed to separate Israel from surrounding nations (Exod. 19:5–6; Lev. 11:44–45) in no way eliminates the possibility that hygienic reasons were also involved. God promised Moses that if the Israelites would be faithful in following his laws, he would "put none of the diseases upon [them], which I have brought upon the Egyptians . . ." (Exod. 15:26, KJV).

Third, several critics believe that the primary purpose of the laws was to demonstrate symbolically an understanding of holiness and of God's separation of Israel from those around them.[30] For example: "Their diet was limited to certain meats in imitation of their God, who had restricted his choice among the nations to Israel. . . . As they distinguished between clean and unclean foods, they were reminded that holiness was more than a matter of meat and drink but a way of life. . . ."[31] Yet even this alternative has difficulties. Why certain animals were listed as "clean" and others as "unclean" on the basis of this interpretation alone cannot be explained in light of the best knowledge.

On the basis of all the evidence, the approach taken by Craigie seems to be the most realistic. After reviewing the various positions, he concludes: "The text does not make absolutely clear which position is correct, and it is possible that both positions [hygienic and symbolic] have some merit. . . ."[32] In other words, to claim there is scientific validity behind an instruction does not invalidate an important ceremonial or symbolic interpretation being the primary meaning.

As DeWelt reasons:

> There is a two-fold purpose in the distinctions. . . . (1) It is right because God said it was—[it was wrong because God said it was. . .]. Essentially this establishes in the mind of the sons of Israel the sovereignty of God. (2) These . . . were unclean from a dietary point of view. . . . There is . . . a practical side to God's prohibitions if we look deeply enough."[33]

6

Biblical Sex Laws

In the modern, scientific world of the 1980s, the health burdens placed on human shoulders are often avoidable and unnecessary. The causes of many diseases are known, and the ways these diseases can be prevented are easily accessible to much of the world's population. But all too often these health-care dictums are either neglected or ignored completely. The results are predictable—disability and disaster. Nowhere is this more evident than in the area of the sexually transmitted diseases.

The Curse of Venereal Disease

Venereal, or sexually transmitted, diseases serve as examples of the modern albatrosses that human beings seem to delight in hanging around their own necks. The results are devastating, if not suicidal. In most instances solutions exist, yet the problems continue to grow.

One government publication reported in 1986:

> Syphilis and gonorrhea have not disappeared; they are, in fact, still flourishing. In 1984, gonorrhea had the dubious distinction of being No. 1 among diseases reported to the U. S. Public Health Service's Centers for Disease Control. . . . CDC estimates that there are another million unreported cases. . . . The World Health Organization estimates that each year there are 250 million new

cases of gonorrhea and 50 million new cases of syphilis worldwide."[1]

In 1983, the Center for Disease Control noted 900,435 reported cases of gonorrhea in this country[2] and 32,698 reported cases of syphilis.[3] There were also "260,000 medical consultations for genital herpes simplex infection" in the last available reporting period.[4] And these, too, are the *reported* cases, not the total caseload. Most authorities believe the actual occurrences are much greater, with annual increases in the disease approximating half a million.[5] Finally, studies now indicate that an average of 267,200 women annually are being hospitalized for Pelvic Inflammatory Disease.[6]

Syphilis and Gonorrhea

The problems from syphilis and gonorrhea have been around for centuries. Although the first recorded epidemic of syphilis occurred in the fifteenth century, there are possible cases dating back to biblical days. Gonorrhea can be traced into antiquity.[7]

Again, biblical authors give a number of commandments that could effectively limit the spread of all such diseases, assuming that the laws are obeyed. Specifically, laws found in the Bible prohibit sexual contact with prostitutes (Prov. 7:4–27; Lev. 19:29), impose strict regulations on sexual contacts (Prov. 5; Mark 10:4–12; 1 Cor. 6:18; 10:8; 1 Thess. 4:3–8), and order the isolation of those with possible symptoms from the rest of the people (Lev. 15:1–13). Adultery was prohibited in the Ten Commandments (Exod. 20:14, 17).

In addition to the code of laws, numerous biblical statements and warnings predict unhealthy physical consequences that accrue from failure to abide by the laws. In the Pentateuch, for instance, violation of the Mosaic laws is said to produce fever, wasting disease, blindness, madness, stunting, and bone malformations dating from birth as well as boils, tumors, festering sores, and itches that would be incurable (Deut. 28:22, 27–28; cf. Lev. 21:18–20). Paul declared that fornication was a sin that harmed the physical body (Cor. 6:13–18). In fact, we know today that syphilis often leads to paresis (a type of insanity) and locomotor ataxia (destruction of nerves and inability to control bodily actions) in addition to numerous other disabilities. The biblical statements are medically accurate in that regard.

As in other areas of medical knowledge, the inspired Bible writers proved to be accurate far ahead of the actual scientific discoveries. The price humanity has paid for ignoring the biblical commands is high, and the interest in their accuracy is still mounting. In that light, a medical historian wrote that the Mosaic law "contains an impressive system of pre-Hippocratic medical thought" and concluded that Moses was "one of the most far-sighted proponents of preventive medicine."[8]

Humanly speaking, the causes of these sexually related diseases had not been determined even as late as the fifteenth century. Theodoricus Ulsenius of Nuremburg blamed venereal disease on a malign "conjunction of Jupiter and Saturn."[9] Still others proclaimed "guaiacum" as a possible cure, but it was worthless.[10]

A quick glance at some proposed remedies of antiquity demonstrates the almost total ignorance that pervaded the globe. Some proclaimed the cure for gonorrhea was to be found in refusing to eat peas, because worms with wings inhabited the peas. Others believed the disease could be prevented by being anointed with mercury salve, though a large number who followed that thinking died of mercury poisoning. Still others proposed placing patients in large stoves heated with glowing coals, where they lived on starvation diets. The only thing cured was the chills, and many of those so treated died from suffocation, starvation, and heart failure.[11]

Solutions proposed in Mesopotamia were no better. Prescriptions included black saltpeter, shell of ostrich-egg, and pine-turpentine,[12] all of which "cures" are easily dismissed by modern physicians.[13]

The Medical Value of Biblical Teachings About Sex

In spite of the near-total ignorance that surrounded these diseases, biblical writers were able to (1) isolate the cause; (2) establish effective preventive measures; and (3) correctly predict the results if certain precautions were not followed. As a result, modern scientists can write of the Bible what they cannot write regarding any other ancient source—that the laws "are excellent hygienic measures to hinder the spread of gonorrhea, and precautions exercised for venereal disease might well have been applied to a purulent discharge from any part of the body."[14]

Earlier ways of treating syphilis. The title page from Steven Blankaart's 1689 book, *Die belagertund entsetzte Venus*, depicts an interior scene showing people involved in various methods of syphilis treatment, including mercury fumigation. The victim in the foreground is in the last stages of treatment. Courtesy, The National Library of Medicine.

Thus, biblical emphasis was on the "ounce of prevention" rather than the "pound of cure," and that emphasis has become the crucial element in modern-day dealings with venereal disease.

The real issue in medical practice must be the results. Here, biblical laws are in line with scientific truth. Observance of these laws will produce a more healthy society, while refusing to follow them will bring physical, emotional, and spiritual disaster.

The debilitation from gonorrhea includes such unexpected but related harms as arthritis, meningitis, and septic shock.[15] Of course, premature death is the ultimate of miseries! All these problems will intensify in coming years because of the increasing incidence of a resistant bacterium that actually dismantles penicillin.[16]

Several problems affect citizens in some countries to a much greater degree today than they do citizens of the United States and other developed nations. For example, many of those placed in American institutions for the blind during previous decades (some estimates range as high as 90 percent) were blind because of gonorrheal infections passed from mother to child. Today, while the use of silver nitrate has lessened the incidence of this disaster in the more industrialized nations, blindness from this source continues to be a scourge in underdeveloped countries. It is unfortunate that "the chronic ill health, disability, suffering, sterility, unhappiness, and premature deaths caused by gonorrhea in backward areas of the world are still numbered in the countless millions."[17] Obedience to biblical laws would virtually eliminate gonorrhea.

Herpes, PID, and AIDS

Though gonorrhea-induced blindness is no longer a serious problem in this country, numerous other problems affect children born to parents who have contracted one of the "social diseases." Various venereal diseases remain one of the leading causes of infants being born macerated or stillborn. In modern times, very often the culprit is genital herpes. A baby passing through the birth canal of a mother with active herpes can be infected, blinded, or killed by the virus.[18] This is exacerbated by the fact that "70% of neonates with herpes infections are born to women with no (outward) signs or symptoms."[19] Of course, these are only the beginning of woes that come as a result of this disease. Studies also indicate that women with herpes increase their risk of cervical cancer by five to eight times.[20] And even worse, there is no known cure for the disease at the present time. As one popular college saying goes, "Love may only last for one night, but herpes is forever." What a tragedy, especially when one realizes that venereal disease could be eliminated by adhering to biblical laws.

Mention should be made of at least two other sexually transmitted diseases. The first, pelvic inflammatory disease (adnexitis), or PID, affects an increasing population every year,[21] and studies indicate that the increase can be tied to "more liberal sexual behavior."[22]

Consideration must also be given to the spread of AIDS (Acquired Immune Deficiency Syndrome). Since the issue is dealt with in copious detail elsewhere,[23] a brief overview will suffice here. It must be remembered that the origin and spread of this dangerous disease is related to promiscuous sexual activity. At least in the United States, the problem surfaced in the homosexual community, where those homosexuals who first contracted the disease averaged an astonishing twelve hundred partners each.[24]

Although AIDS' fury has yet to be fully unleashed, it is already obvious that the toll will be monstrous. Conservative estimates by the American Social Health Organization and the World Health Organization indicate there will be close to two hundred thousand AIDS-related deaths in this country by 1991 and an alarming one hundred million cases worldwide.[25] The picture is bleak. One health official predicted that the epidemic would render "earlier medical disasters such as the Black Plague, smallpox, and typhoid pale by comparison. We face the dreadful prospect of a worldwide death toll in the tens of millions a decade from now."[26]

Strict observance of moral principles laid down in the Bible would have short-circuited humanity's latest attempt at self-destruction. Bible writers specifically prohibit both homosexual and promiscuous heterosexual relationships (Lev. 18:22; 1 Cor. 6:9–10). We must remember, of course, that the Bible is not against sex. In fact, its writers teach that sex is beautiful and

Results of the Sexual Revolution

1. 921,895 reported cases of gonorrhea per year in the U.S. (Over one million other cases estimated that are unreported)
2. 31,237 reported cases of syphilis per year in the U.S.
3. An estimated four million cases of chlamydia per year in the U.S.
4. 270,000 projected deaths from AIDS by 1991 in the U.S.
5. 260,000 reported cases of genital herpes in the U.S.
6. One in every four Americans will be infected with some type of sexually-transmitted disease.

natural between husband and wife, as is obvious in the erotic stanzas in Song of Solomon.

The Uniqueness of Biblical Sex Laws

If other religious systems exact similar codes of conduct from their followers, then biblical laws offer no proof of divine revelation. But such assertions are unfounded. The Bible's code of sexual behavior *is* unique.

The Uniqueness of Restraint

Many world religions place no restraints on their adherents as far as sexual practices are concerned. Shintoism is one such example, for "there is scarcely anything in Shinto by way of a moral code."[27] Hinduism provides nothing better, and "infidelity on the part of the husband was neither rare nor considered worthy of moral censure . . . (and the) *Bharadvaja Grhyasutra* (ii, 28) advises a husband how to proceed in the case of going on a journey if he desires his wife to have lovers in his absence."[28]

Muslim teachings are only slightly different, as the prophet himself "showed by his example that women may be regarded merely as man's playthings."[29] In fact, "outside the married state, the husband is allowed to cohabit with an unlimited number of slaves."[30] Not only are most non-biblical religions far more permissive about sex, but the same holds true for the cultures in which authors of the Bible lived. Every major culture of ancient times from the Egyptians to the Romans was lax in its imposition of rules relating to sexual conduct.

As far as the Egyptians were concerned, "pre-nuptial immorality was very lightly regarded; we find no prohibition concerning it."[31] Since the Greek historian Strabo (xvii, 1.46) noted that religious prostitution was a way of life in the land of the Nile, we can assume that biblical sources certainly did not draw their materials from an Egyptian background. Likewise, in Babylon: "The place of sexual intercourse was the public street,"[32] and there really is no need to document the lack of morals in old Rome. In short, even if there were some limitations on sexual conduct in these ancient cultures, they were not nearly as effective in preventing the spread of disease as were their biblical counterparts. Most accounts of antiquity seem to imply that there was very little restraint at all.

The Uniqueness of Reasonability

Those religions that did limit sexual behavior often carried their prohibitions to extremes far beyond what was actually necessary from a scientific and sanitary viewpoint. Buddhism provides the best example of this point of view. Simply put, "the Buddha recommended the life of an ascetic (*samana*)"[33] or, in other words, claimed that the only true happiness was to be found in total abstinence. Total obedience to this principle would, of course, eliminate humanity in one generation, unless Buddhism could supply a new means of propagating the race!

Summary

Slight similarities occasionally surface between biblical laws and laws from other religions that attempt to regulate sexual activity. These similarities are the exception rather than the rule, however, and obedience to the non-biblical teachings would either wipe out humanity altogether through celibacy or have little or no effect on the spread of venereal disease. Only the Bible remains consistent with scientific principles now known to be valid.

7

Biblical Laws and Stress Management

That biblical writers do not name a single cause of all disease is amazing, since other ancient writers made such an attempt. *The* cause of disease was variously labeled, depending on which source one happens to consult, as "worms," "demons," "that which hovers in the air," "bile," and so forth.

Seemingly everyone except the biblical writers took a turn at trying to isolate the one cause of all sickness. This biblical omission has scientific validity, for scientists and physicians are increasingly aware that there is no single causative factor for all disease. Some diseases are spread through the air; some are carried by food; others travel in the water. Some are hereditary; some are not. For some diseases, a specific organism has been identified as villain; for others, science has not yet found the source.

Hans Selye and the Role of Stress Agents in Disease

More amazing than the modern discovery of the multiple causes of disease is the fact that the germs of a particular disease may enter an individual without that person actually contracting that disease, or at least its outward symptoms. Such discoveries have prompted substantial efforts to determine why people from similar backgrounds and circumstances respond differently to the same disease.

The most promising answer revolves around an accidental discovery in the mid-1930s. Young medical researcher Hans Selye was attempting to isolate a new sex hormone by injecting extracts of cow ovaries into mice. Though no new hormone was forthcoming, Selye did note that the experiment produced a number of reactions in the physical state of the mice.

These reactions involved what Selye called "a general syndrome of sickness" that seemed to be superimposed on all diseases. He was sure there were some factors at work in the production of these reactions that had not been noted before. From the simple observations that followed came the theory that stress is in some way related to the outbreak of many, if not all, diseases.[1]

Selye called his theory the "general adaption syndrome." Years of research have refined his concepts, and, while there is some confusion about the way stress lowers resistance to disease, there is substantial agreement that the two are causally related.[2]

Stress-Related Health Problems

Study after study over the past fifty years has demonstrated the effects of various stress agents upon the human system. Many have indicated that disease-producing bacteria do not become overtly active in humans without the help of stress factors.

Estimates "suggest that 80 percent of the complaints people take to their doctors—colds, back pains, upset stomachs, tiredness, loss of appetite—are . . . psychosomatic reactions to the daily stresses of living."[3] An even more recent study regarding the link between stress and disease concluded that the "evidence is enormous at every level."[4] The long list of diseases now known to be either caused or aggravated by emotional stress includes diseases of the digestive system (ulcers, mucous colitis, constipation, diarrhea),[5] diseases of the circulatory system (high blood pressure, strokes, heart attacks, abnormal heart rhythms, migraine headaches, angina pectoris, arteriosclerosis),[6] diseases in the skeletal-muscular system (backache, headache, rheumatoid arthritis, muscle spasms),[7] and diseases due to the failure of the immunological system (allergies, asthma, hay fever, infectious mononucleosis, perhaps all infections, dermatitis, psoriasis).[8] Some research even shows a link between cancer and extreme stress.[9]

Many authorities now believe stress to be the key culprit in over half of man's diseases, and researchers have found a direct relationship between stress and the disease of hypertension, which annually afflicts twenty-three million Americans and underlies hundreds of thousands of deaths in this country alone.[10] One study found that "in 75 percent of heart patients, heart failure followed not long after bitter arguments with family members, illness or death in the family, business failures or other stressful incidents. In the first year after divorce, divorced people have twelve times more illnesses than people who are married."[11]

Stress is obviously related to medical problems, and everyone faces the so-called agents of stress at some point in life. But stress *per se* does not seem to be the problem. Medical difficulties seem to be determined by an individual's reactions to the stress rather than to the stress itself. It is around this observation that a fascinating correlation develops. Biblical instructions regarding emotions are increasingly consistent with medical research as to what constitutes appropriate stress management.

Of course, it is necessary to be cautious in dealing with these materials because it is clear that the main emphases of the biblical injunctions are moral and spiritual, not medical. There is no indication that the writers presenting the information knew or expected to transmit anything other than the obvious ethical recommendations. Still, if one responds to stress agents in a manner consistent with the biblical commands noted below, the likelihood of developing certain medical difficulties is significantly diminished.

Biblical Injunctions Regarding Harmful Emotions

Hatred, one of the prime stress factors, is prohibited in the Mosaic laws (Lev. 19:17), and several New Testament passages warn against harboring anger, resentment, or bitterness (Luke 9:51–56; Heb. 12:14–15; Col. 3:8, 13–14). God's people were instructed not to covet what belonged to others (Exod. 20:17) or to be greedy (Col. 3:5). Not surprisingly, envy is widely recognized in modern journals as a key agent of stress. The Bible writers told the people to be fair in their dealings with others (Lev. 19:13–15, 35), and not to lie (Col. 3:9). They were instructed not to hold grudges (Lev. 19:18) and to control their temper (Prov. 14:17; 16:32; 20:3). David recorded some positive advice: circumstances were not to be feared, but trust was to be placed in God (Ps. 91:3–7). Later, the apostle Paul added that men should learn to be content (Phil. 4:11; 1 Tim. 6:6).

Worry was to be set aside and was unbecoming to a child of God (Ps. 23:1–4; 27:1–3; Phil. 4:5–7). Selfishness and ambition for the benefit of self were to be controlled (Rom. 12:3, 9–16; Phil. 2:1–5; James 3:13). Man was not to walk according to the flesh, "but according to the Spirit. . . . The mind of sinful man is death, but the mind controlled by the Spirit is life and peace" (Rom. 8:4–6).

A later passage cautioned, "But I say, walk by the Spirit, and you will not carry out the desire of the flesh. . . . Now the deeds of the flesh are evident, which are: immorality, impurity, sensuality, idolatry, sorcery, enmities, strife, jealousy, outbursts of anger, disputes, dissensions, factions, envying, drunkenness, carousing, and things like these . . ." (Gal. 5:16, 19–21, NASB).

Amazingly, the attitude and characteristics so vehemently opposed by biblical authors are the very stress agents that modern scientists and physicians find to be the causal or aggravating factor in much of our illness. It should come as no surprise, therefore, that at least one recent study acknowledges that "religion in a devout believer has little equal as an allayer of stress. . . . The Judeo-Christian tradition, for instance, takes on all the primal stresses, and though it does not dispense of them completely it makes them surprisingly bearable."[12]

Statements such as these can be multiplied by the thousands, though only a representative few will be noted here. Among the accolades by doctors, psychiatrists, psychologists, and medical researchers are the following: "The Bible is full of truths that psychologists and psychiatrists are now acclaiming to be among the sound ways of achieving happiness."[13] "The Sermon on the Mount is pure scientific knowledge . . . a blueprint for optimum mental health and contentment."[14] "An amazingly large percentage of . . . disease and suffering can be linked to the various stress agents caused by unwholesome thinking and unclean living. The sincere following of the Bible's teachings would at once wipe out more than half the difficulties, diseases, and sorrows of the human race."[15]

Perhaps the best recommendation of the biblical teachings on handling stress comes from Dr. Carl Jung, a contemporary of Freud and one of the world's leading psychologists. He wrote that, of the many hundreds of patients with whom he had been associated, "there has not been one whose problem, in the last resort, was not that of finding a religious outlook on life."[16]

Surveys of individual stress factors continue to confirm the Bible's wisdom about the role of stress in disease. For example, the biblical authors command that uncontrolled anger is not to continue to be a part of a Christian's life but instead must be quickly resolved. Scientific texts on the subject agree. Anger is known to cause "great harm" and affect individuals "adversely both physically and mentally," causing "headaches, ulcers, ulcerative colitis, respiratory disorders, skin disorders, arthritis, disabilities of the nervous system, circulatory disorders, and emotional disturbances."[17] Many heart attacks are triggered by uncontrolled outbursts of anger.

Summary

It is obvious that these biblical warnings have valid medical reasoning behind them, and there are three principles to be weighed in support of this thesis. First, in ancient times only the biblical authors made no attempt to specify the single cause of all disease. Scientific research supports that view. Second, teachings found in the Bible imply that one who follows the precepts laid down in Scripture will avoid a number of physical problems. Once again, scientific evidence is in agreement. Finally, writers from Moses to Paul warn against certain uncontrolled emotions. These emotions coincide perfectly with current lists of stress factors that are known to cause physical and psychological problems.

8

The Biblical Law of Circumcision

People tend to ridicule what they do not understand. And, for centuries, many people have not understood circumcision. The practice has been viewed in some circles as a religious rite with no medical significance whatsoever, while others have argued that it was a mythical preparation for sexual activity. Still others have claimed that circumcision was a primitive custom showing belief in reincarnation.[1] Though the practice does involve symbolism, it is not without medical validity.

Studies strongly suggest that circumcision reduces the incidence of cancer of the penis and diminishes both the occurrence and severity of balanitis (inflammation of the penis).[2] There is also evidence that circumcision may help control the spread of such venereal diseases as *Trichomonas vaginalis.*[3]

In recent years, a small but vocal group of opponents of the operation have charged that circumcision is unnecessary from a medical standpoint.[4] The evidence does not support that contention.

A Circumcision-Cancer Link

Though cancer of the penis is not as common as other forms of cancer, it does exist and has increased in recent years, especially in Brazil, Jamaica, and Puerto Rico. It has never been denied that cancer of the penis is almost nonexistent in circumcised males. Uncircumcised males have rates many times higher. For example, the rate is nine times higher in the United States than in Israel, though many American non-Jewish males have been circumcised.[5] In India, this cancer occurs far less frequently among Moslems (who are circumcised) than among Hindus (who are not).[6]

Three studies covering five hundred cases over several years found no cases of penile cancer among circumcised males.[7] A review of literature from 1936 to 1975 revealed "only nine reports of cancer of the penis in neonatally circumcised males" during the entire period.[8] By contrast, China, a land where circumcision is not practiced, reports a significant number of such cancers.[9]

In regard to a risk-benefit analysis of the practice, the most extensive study found only one death among 500,000 circumcisions, and that was recorded in a circumcision that took place at home. Even that death could have been prevented had a transfusion been given in time. The same study reported that the failure to circumcise that many children would have eventually allowed the occurrence of 830 cases of penile cancer and, ultimately 275 premature deaths.[10]

Circumcision as Evidence for Inspiration

Can circumcision (the first biblical command for which is found in Genesis 17) be submitted as evidence for the divine inspiration of the Bible? Is it not true that the practice was found in many ancient cultures and that it was around for centuries prior to the time of Abraham? In both cases the answer is yes. Circumcision was used in many cultures and it did predate Abraham. Still, there are critical differences between the biblical practice and the use of circumcision in other cultures.

First, in most other civilizations, male circumcision was paralleled by a type of "circumcision" (excision) for the female.[11] There are known medical values for the former but not for the latter. Since the Bible writers require the former but not the latter, they are isolating only that which is known to be scientifically valid.

Second, circumcision in other cultures was not universal for all males. In Egypt and Mesopotamia it was limited to priests and soldiers. In addition, males with physical blemishes of any type were refused the rite.[12] The earliest universal requirement is in the Bible.

Third, if circumcision is medically beneficial, the time when the rite is performed is critical—as will be shown below. In ancient times most cultures observed the ritual at puberty. Others prescribed its observation at various times from the age of a few months to the age of fourteen years, with the generally accepted time falling between the ages of two and fourteen. On the other hand, the biblical act was to be performed on the eighth day after birth (Gen. 17:10–12). And though three other civilizations decided on the same time table, those decisions were made centuries after the biblical instruction.

The Eighth Day Is Special

Interestingly, some who copied the Hebrew law—the Moslems, for example—set different times for the observation of the act (Moslems are circumcised between ages two and ten). Yet modern science notes legitimate medical reasons for having the operation performed on the eighth day of life.

Two key elements that are necessary for normal clotting of blood—vitamin K and prothrombin—are not present in sufficient amounts in a male child until the eighth day of life. Without these, any bleeding can produce hemorrhages that might lead to serious health problems or death.[13]

Vitamin K is not formed naturally in the intestinal tract until the fifth to seventh day of life. Operations could only be considered completely safe *after* the seventh day of life. Likewise, prothrombin is known to be virtually depleted in infants a few hours after birth and not completely replenished until the eighth day. On that one day, there is more prothrombin present (an extra 10 percent) than is usually necessary.[14] The eighth day of life is the safest day to perform the operation. Only in the Bible is the eighth day specified.[15]

Additionally, a significant amount of medical evidence shows the pain suffered by such small infants to be minimal. Merely delaying the operation by a few days proliferates the amount of pain and discomfort that is suffered.[16] Not only is the operation more painful after the early days of life, but there is a concomitant increase in physical and psychological risk factors.[17] Essentially, all this suggests the impeccability of the biblical account, and we might well wonder where the Bible's writers got their amazingly accurate information!

It might also be mentioned that the biblical account avoids the false ideas proposed by its contemporaries. For example, circumcision is not associated with an act of endurance—as it later was in such other cultures as Arabia and Australia—nor is it performed as a sacrifice to fertility cults.[18]

Summary

Biblical teachings regarding circumcision are unique in ancient literature. Circumcision may have been widely known long before God's covenant with Abraham and the later biblical teachings on the practice, but only in the Bible are superstitions and errors of the times avoided.

In fact, only in the Bible are many other scientifically correct principles utilized centuries before their discovery in laboratories. Modern science continues to appear in this ancient book of truth.

Part Two

The Sky Above

Sacred Revelations and Astronomy

9

Down the Wrong Path

Ancient man gazed at the starry heavens and pondered its mysteries. At times in fear, he imagined awesome omens and signs and became confused by the sky's curiosities. As he attempted to explain what he saw, occasionally his explanations have been correct. More often, however, he was wrong. Hindered in earlier times by the lack of telescopic equipment, the ancients relied on fallible judgments to interpret what they saw with the naked eye. Before any optical or radio telescopes, man was severely limited in his conception of the universe. Forced to speculate, his imagination ran wild. In astronomy especially, it is easy to understand why man "almost universally took a wrong path."[1]

Astronomy in Ancient Mesopotamia

Chaldean star-gazers were among the first astronomers. They looked at the still-unpolluted skies from the warm desert plains of Mesopotamia and tried to understand what they saw. They had few facts to work with, but where facts were lacking, imagination took over.

A Limited Universe

Since everything known to man at that time had definite limits, it was only natural to see the universe in the same manner. To the Chaldeans, therefore, the universe was completely enclosed. A wall supposedly surrounded both the earth and sea, and a dome of hard metal was thought to cover the sky. The metal of the dome reflected the light of the sun during the day and formed a backdrop for performances of the gods (planets, stars, and moon) at night.[2] These ancient star-gazers sized the universe no larger than the observable skies, and the number of stars was seen as extremely limited.[3] They envisioned stellar configuration as everything from gods and their chariots to firebrands and torches suspended by ropes.

Misconceptions of the Earth's Place

With such ideas about the universe, the earth was thought to have a far-larger role in the universe than is actually true. Ancient societies universally held the earth to comprise the plurality, if not the majority, of all existence. The earth—believed to be larger than the sun, moon, and stars combined—was seen as a large, flat plain at the bottom of the universe. Isaac Asimov observes, "All men before the time of the Greeks made the assumption that the earth was flat. . . . If any pre-Greek ancient thought otherwise, his name has not come down to us and the record of his thinking has not survived."[4]

Whereas Chaldean astronomers accurately recorded numerous observations of heavenly events, it could still be said that "astronomy . . . owed little to the early Babylonians."[5]

Mixing Astrology and Astronomy

Another Babylonian idea actually retarded the growth of astronomical knowledge. Chaldean records duly noted the movements of the heavenly bodies as well as the unexpected appearances of such phenomena as comets, meteorites, and eclipses. Inadequate understanding of these events sent their thinkers scurrying for answers that came, once again, from their imaginations. The movements of the heavenly bodies were viewed as demons, omens, or other activity by the gods.[6] This superficial "understanding" gave birth to the pseudo-science of astrology.[7] The result was devastating to the search for knowledge, and almost three thousand years passed before astrology lost its stranglehold on astronomers. Astrology followed the stream of civilization to Egypt, India, China, Greece, Rome, and Arabia. It was considered *the* study of the stars.

Xenophon noted in his *Memorabilia* that even Socrates believed in omens and divination from natural phenomena.[8] Over three centuries later, the Roman writer Cicero gave the doctrine an even stronger stamp of approval in his *De divinatione.*[9] To the list of believers in the astrological teachings can be added Plato, Aristotle, Ptolemy, Hipparchus, and Varro. With such impressive followers, it is easy to understand why astrology reigned so long as the "queen of sciences." Even today, the doctrine survives in a multitude of beliefs in horoscopes and psychic pronouncements.

Astronomy in Ancient Egypt

Not far from the Tigris-Euphrates Valley, another ancient civilization stumbled along the same path, searching for answers to the heaven's enigmas. The Egyptians' mathematical achievements were astounding and their architecture spectacular, but the civilization that rose to glory along the banks of the Nile became entangled in the same snares that wrecked their Chaldean counterparts.

In additon to following astrology, Egyptian astronomers strayed even further from reality. They believed stars were the souls of dead Egyptians who had attained the status of deity.[10] The sun was to be worshiped as a god and was said to be alive.[11] Egyptian teachers accepted the universe as being a large rectangular box, with the earth lying at the bottom. The only noticeable change in the theory was that Egypt, rather than Mesopotamia, was considered to be the center of the earth.

The ancient Egyptians also viewed the skies as a vaulted ceiling held in place by four giant mountain peaks. Stars not thought of as deities were envisioned as lamps hung from the ceiling by cables. The ocean was viewed as a giant river encircling the earth. The sun was pictured as riding in a boat on that river as it made its daily passage.

When the sun became invisible at night, it was said to pass behind a giant mountain.[12] Interesting reading that might be. Science it was not.

It comes as no surprise that the astronomy of Egypt is de-

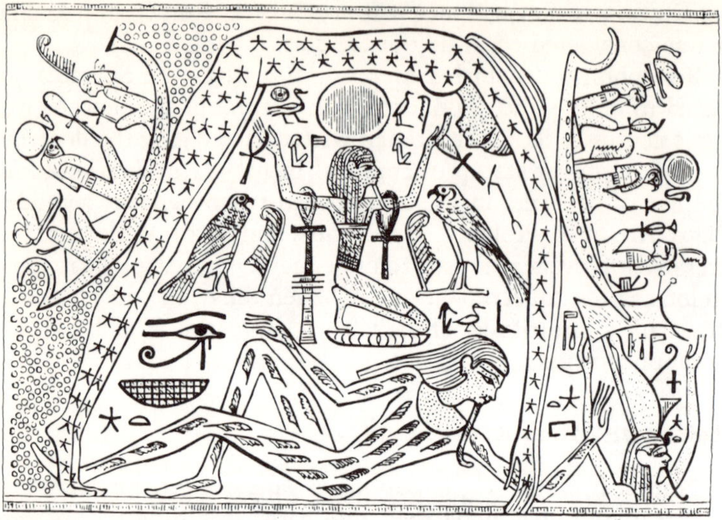

One of the more imaginative Egyptian cosmologies depicted a goddess as the limits of the universe. Courtesy, Hart Pictorial Archives.

scribed as "blended with much absurdity and fable."[13] In fact, its astronomy failed to reach the same stage of development as the Chaldean.[14]

Astronomy in Ancient Greece

Not until the time of ancient Greece was any advancement of worth achieved in the space sciences, and even many of those advances were later shoved aside and forgotten. The Greeks recognized the earth to be a sphere, postulated the earth's rotation, and became more precise in estimating the distances between objects in space. Yet even the Greeks were mostly incorrect in their view of the heavens. A brief view of their works will easily demonstrate their errors.

Among the earlier Greek astronomers, Thales of Miletos (*circa* 640 B.C.) made a few theoretical advances, but his astronomy was "mixed with much error and absurdity."[15] Anaximander thought the earth was the center of the universe and believed the sun to be the same magnitude as the earth. Anaxagoras believed that the sun was a mass of red-hot iron and stone only somewhat larger than the Peloponnesus and that heaven was a vault of stones.[16] He also said that all the planets were flat, that the moon was inhabited, and that meteorites came from the sun.[17] Anaximenes proposed that stars were attached to their positions by nails and that when they passed from view, they went behind mountains at the edge of the world.[18]

Pythagoras fell prey to the error that the sun was only three times farther from the earth than the moon. Philolaus thought the sun was a disk of glass that reflected the light of the universe. Eudoxus was another who believed that the sun and earth were nearly the same size.[19] Hicetas believed that the earth was the only body in the universe that moved, while all others remained stationary.[20] Democritus speculated that the moon was a star.[21]

The best mind of the day fared no better in his ideas about the cosmos. Plato proposed in *Timaeus* that the earth was immovable at the center of the universe. He also surmised that the entire universe was small enough to make a complete turn or rotation every twenty-four hours.[22] A modern astronomer labeled his teaching "a monument of unwisdom and recklessness."[23]

Aristotle made the same type of errors as his teacher. He speculated that all celestial bodies were made of different substances than the earth, believed the earth to be the center of the universe, and thought that comets and the Milky Way were closer to the earth than the moon. As Sarton points out, "Genius even at its best is never continuous."[24]

Astronomy in Ancient China

Misconceptions about the universe were repeated throughout the ancient world. The Chinese, though often revered for their astronomical advances, actually followed a similar error-filled path. Current research concludes that Chinese astronomy "consisted only in the practice of observations which led to nothing more than the knowledge of a few isolated facts." The more that is known about the ancient Chinese science, the more "their astronomy shrinks into . . . insignificant dimensions."[25]

Even Sagan, who was impressed with Chinese records of astronomical data, was frustrated by the fact that these ancients did not understand the basics of astronomy. In his discussion of comets, he writes: "A survey of the early history of cometary observation gives the impression that for almost a thousand years everybody except the Chinese went to bed early." Still, Sagan comments, for all their observations, "They never had an inkling of what comets really were."[26]

Discovery of an ancient textbook in 1970 at the "Number Three Tomb" at Mawangdui has shed a great deal of light on the way the Chinese viewed the comets in antiquity. Compiled around 300 B.C., twenty-nine comets were displayed on a painted silk and "classified by their appearance and by the particular brand of mayhem each foretold."[27] A "three-tailed comet" signified "calamity in the state," for instance; and a "two-tailed comet" whose tails "curved to the right" indicated only a "small war" and a "plentiful corn crop."

Summary

Throughout the world, ancient astronomers were more often wrong than right, and "until about 1500 A.D., astronomy remained an inextricable mass of confusion."[28]

10

Climbing the Wrong Mountain

Ideas about the skies in non-biblical religious writings fared no better and were in some instances considerably less based on truth than their secular counterparts. Various sacred texts were almost universally in error in their understanding and teaching regarding the heavenly spheres. Had there actually been supernatural direction behind these writings, the very opposite should have been true. It is difficult to conceive of any god or supreme intelligence who would have thought the earth was the center of the universe or that stars were nailed to the vault of heaven. Surely, the knowledge available to any supernatural being would pre-empt such mistakes.

Astronomical Errors in the *Koran*

Since the *Koran* had access to centuries of additional information denied to writings conceived earlier, one would expect it to contain fewer errors than the texts that predated it. And, with the exception of the Bible, this is true. Nevertheless, the *Koran* is far from unblemished, and the few references made to the heavens are usually false. For example, repeating the erroneous Aristotelian and Ptolemaic doctrine of the spheres, the *Koran* speaks of seven literal heavens in which all things are said to move[1] and claims these heavens are "seven solid heavens"[2] that contain "lamps" (i.e., stars) whose main purpose is to be "darted at the devils"[3] to keep them from entering the heavens and tempting their inhabitants.[4] Since the heavens were said to be solid, it was natural that they be given a roof.[5] Further discussion of the stars reveals such statements as all stars "move in retrograde motion,"[6] and stars serve (as in astrology) as "guardians for those on the earth."[7] Of the sun, Mohammed wrote that "the sun sets in a sea of black mud."[8]

The *Koran* also claims that the distance from the earth to the edge of the seven heavens was fifty thousand years.[9] All these statements are known to be in error. And yet the *Koran* claims, "Nor is God disposed to lead people into error."[10] If a supreme deity did stand behind the *Koran,* he violated his own standards.

Astronomical Errors in the Hindu Writings

Hindu scriptures are far less scientific than the *Koran.* Even their apologists admit, in explaining why there are so many mistakes: "Vedic astronomical facts are not strictly accurate as it was not the intention of the Vedic writers to deal with astronomy."[11] Given that the *Vedas* and other Hindu writings are "regarded as being of divine origin and as having been communicated to certain priviledged human seers,"[12] it is difficult to understand why they did not speak accurately.

In the *Rigveda,* Surya (the sun) is recognized as a deity suitable for human worship,[13] as are the planets, moon, and the stars.[14] Hindu scriptures also teach that the moon is fifty thousand leagues farther from the earth than is the sun, produces its own light, and moonlight produces the vital energies that give life to the earth. In addition, night is said to come when the sun passes behind a mountain (Someyra) that is located in the center of the earth and allegedly stands many thousand miles (84,000 leagues) high. The earth is said to be flat and triangular, with seven stages or stories, each of which is inhabited and has its own ocean. One is filled with honey, one with milk, and so forth.[15]

Scriptures of the Hindus also envision the earth as resting on the back of four giant elephants that repose on the back of an even larger turtle that is leisurely swimming about in a sea of

These drawings, taken from the 1851 edition of The Iconographic Encyclopaedia of Science, Literature, and Art, illustrate the ancient Hindu conception of the earth and the seven celestial spheres. In the former, the hemispherical earth is shown resting on the back of four elephants which, in turn, ride on the back of a giant tortoise.

milk.[16] If there was a god behind these writings, their astronomies produce no evidence of the deity's accuracy.

Astronomical Errors in Buddhist Doctrine

Buddhism's sacred writings closely parallel Hindu ideas and commit many of the same mistakes.[17] As in the Hindu *Vedas,* the heavenly bodies are conceived of either as gods or vehicles of the gods[18] and are called "world-protectors" or "guardians."

Buddhism also accepts the flat earth of the *Vedas* and places Mount Meru in the earth's center. The mountain was said to reach a height of 84,000 leagues. Yet the moon was said to be only forty leagues in diameter, with the sun only fifty.[19] The sun was also said to be crystal outside with a golden interior, while the moon's composition was silver and jewels. Eclipses were caused by an evil being (Rahu) that occasionally swallowed the sun and moon and then gave them up on the order of the Buddha.

Astronomical Errors in Chinese Religions

Chinese religious books reflect similar errors. One authority on the sacred literature of the Orient noted, "Not being advanced enough in science and culture to distinguish between the pos-

Many ancient societies attributed eclipses of the sun to voracious demons who tried to eat it. This engraving by Samuel David in *The Century Magazine* (Vol. 36, 1899, p.4) is based on Hindu descriptions.

sible and impossible, almost everything which the books have to tell . . . are always reflections of prevailing opinion and of the train of thought of the time in which they were written."[20]

Chinese religions were also deeply involved in all forms of nature worship. Until the Christian Era their devotées offered sacrifices to the earth-spirit[21] and to the various heavenly bodies.[22]

Astronomical Errors in Judeo-Christian Writings

Jewish and early Christian extra-biblical writings are also generally permeated with astrology. Whereas some of these writings oppose astrology (invariably on the basis of biblical teachings), many openly accept its tenets. The Talmudic rabbis, for instance, "found no difficulty in reconciling a belief in astrology with the principles of Judaism. . . . Rabba Ben Joseph made the statement that a man's fate, including the number of years he would live, the children he would have, and his fortune was determined . . . by his horoscope" (*Ber. 64a*).[23]

Other rabbis argued that a person's character was determined by the day of the week on which he was born: "If it were Sunday, he would be a leader; Monday, a wrathful man; Tuesday, rich and sensual; Wednesday, intelligent; Thursday, benevolent; Friday, pious; if he were born on the Sabbath, he would die on the Sabbath"(*Sab. 156a*).[24] It was also held that "even every blade of grass had a planet in the sky which commanded it to grow" (*Midrash Gen.* 10:7).[25]

In addition, both the Talmud and the Midrash fall into numerous other errors. One can read that there are "seven heavens," that the sun at night was "believed to be beneath the earth . . . or ascended into heaven" (*Pes. 94b*), "appearing and disappearing through portals," and that "the size of the smallest star is estimated as the area taken up by a kor of mustard seed" (*B.B. 73a*).[26]

Conclusions

Several conclusions are possible regarding these writings:

1. There were gods behind these writings but they were limited beings who did not understand the skies.

2. There were gods behind these writings, but they were unable to transmit their knowledge to their human secretaries.

3. There were gods behind these writings, but these gods chose to pass along numerous scientific errors for some unknown reason.

4. There were gods behind these writings, but the human agents altered the messages of the gods.

5. These writings are solely the production of men.

If either the first or second alternative is true, the god is so limited in knowledge that he is worthless. More importantly, this deity could not be the creator or the cause behind the universe because whatever brought the universe into being would certainly understand it. Anyone who claimed to invent an airplane but knew nothing about that plane would be recognized as a fraud. Such also holds true here.

The third suggestion is no better. It implies a supernatural intelligence that is limited in vision and concerned only with people in prior generations who lived as if the error were fact. If a book's "science" was written entirely for the past, so were its religious doctrines. The fourth alternative suggests a god who did not know enough about human nature to choose the right people to receive his revelation.

One can conclude that the presence of large numbers of astronomical errors in these sacred writings invalidate their claim to have come from a supernatural intelligence. On the other hand, if they are the work of men, numerous errors would be expected. Since that is what is found in abundance, the fifth alternative is the more logical explanation. They were the products of purely human intelligence.

11

The Light Shines Through

Since there is much evidence that other early astronomers were mistaken, biblical writers must be judged by the same criteria. Again we find obvious differences between the Scriptures and the non-biblical texts. Errors that found their way by the hundreds into other early writings are conspicuously absent from the Bible. In the Bible, for example, the universe was not considered to be limited by artificial walls that surrounded the heavens, nor was the size of the earth in relation to the rest of space overstated. Stars were not designated as gods or torches hung by cables from the domed top of the universe, and astrology was not given credence, much less encouragement.

Many errors of primitive astronomy are simply not found in the Bible. As in the medical sciences, however, this lack of error does not occur simply because biblical authors never speak of things in space. They do. And when they do, the ideas set forth are far ahead of the scientific knowledge and technology of the times.

Uniqueness of Biblical Observations

At the outset of any study of biblical references to space and the astronomical sciences, one must realize that celestial happenings were generally interpreted in magical, superstitious ways in the earliest days of recorded history. Scholars like E. M. Fallaize have called attention to this "universal belief among primitive races that both sun and moon should be regarded as alive and quasi-human in nature."[1] Yet, when reading the description of the sun in the Bible, "its moderation remains striking in comparison with the famous hymns dedicated to the sun by other religions," and "the Old Testament speaks soberly of the moon."[2]

C. F. Whitley admired the way biblical writers drew their distinctions between nature and the supernatural sphere:

> The heavens were personified by the Mesopotamians as the god, Anu, and they were regarded by the Egyptians as the divine Mother; but to the Hebrews they were but one aspect of Yahweh's power and glory. The Mesopotamians, again, conceived of the sun as Shamash, the god of justice; the Egyptians invested it with the properties of a divine creator; but the Hebrews merely accounted for it as one of the luminaries created by Yahweh. The moon was similarly worshipped by the Babylonians as the god Sin, and the stars were thought to determine the destiny of man; but to the Hebrews they were created by God.[3]

The Bible stands in stark contrast to its contemporaries, for it alone includes facts without fanciful interpretations. The uniqueness of biblical observations has been noted by numerous scholars. For example, E. W. Maunder concluded:

> The celestial bodies could not be referred to in a more simple manner. And this simplicity is marred by no myth; there is not the faintest trace of the deification of sun or moon or stars, no suggestion that they formed the vehicles for spirits. . . . It is the expression of man's earliest observation of the heavenly bodies, but it is real observation, free from any taint of savage phantasies.[4]

The Babylonians, Egyptians, and Persians all fell victim to extreme subjective and anthropomorphic ideas. Only biblical writers did not.

Ancient Descriptions of the Heavenly Bodies

Not only did the ancients misinterpret the movements of the sun and moon by granting them life, but other things seen in the skies were regarded in a simliar vein. Stars were pictured as the moon's children[5] and were said to cause earthquakes.[6] Comets were believed by some to be balls of lightning[7] while others claimed they were either rockets thrown from the earth or signs sent from the gods to threaten rulers with death.[8] When Aristotle presented the first "natural" interpretation of comets, his basic ideas were totally in error. Though he claimed that comets were caused by a juxtaposition of the stars, he admitted they could be omens or signs.

Correct Interpretation of Eclipses

Eclipses of celestial bodies were never seen as natural phenomena by the ancients. "The Chaldeans explained eclipses (of the moon) on the supposition that one half of the moon was bright, the other half dark. When she [the moon] suddenly turned the bright side away from men," it was "evidence of displeasure."[9]

The Chinese and Hindus described the eclipse of the sun as an event wherein the sun was being eaten by some animal or demon,[10] and the Confucian religious writing *Tsun Tsiu* claims that the beating of drums during an eclipse would drive the animal/demon away. And who could question the drums' effectiveness? After all, apparently every animal or demon who ever tried to devour the sun or moon had been driven away!

Yet Jeremiah was advising, "This is what the LORD says: 'Do

Comets were viewed in antiquity as balls of lightning, glowing rocks, or supernatural signs from the gods. Even as late as the early twentieth century, Halley's Comet (above) was thought to be the harbinger of evil. Courtesy, National Aeronautics and Space Administration.

A solar eclipse. Jeremiah cautioned his people not to be wary or dismayed at the signs of the heavens, for such customs are "worthless." The Bible writers consistently viewed nature in an unpersonal, undeified manner. Courtesy, Lick Observatory.

not learn the ways of the nations or be terrified by signs in the sky, though the nations are terrified by them. For the customs of the peoples are worthless . . .' " (Jer. 10:2–3). Jeremiah was definitely right—and far ahead of his time. But we can wonder who told Jeremiah. There were no Israelite observatories on Mount Zion in those days. Yet he and other biblical authors not only avoided the errors of those around them but also pointed out those errors and cautioned God's people to avoid them.

12

Star Light, Star Bright, First Star I See Tonight

Evidence of the Bible's superior grasp of astronomy is also found in a number of highly advanced statements regarding the sun, moon, and stars. During the days when the statements were first penned, each of these ideas was previously unknown or "unknowable" to the observer-scientist and was often the exact opposite of popular belief.

Numbering the Stars

Biblical writers implied the impossibility of numbering the stars. Moses, referring obliquely to the inability of man to count Abraham's descendants (Gen. 15:5), compared the number of stars to the grains of sand on the beach (Gen. 22:17). Jeremiah simply stated that the stars were "countless" (Jer. 33:22). Such a disclosure is hardly a revelation to those who live in the twentieth century.[1]

Admittedly, science is not the chief concern of these verses. Rather, in the first reference, an aging patriarch—who was well beyond the time when he could expect to father an offspring—is being told by the Lord that he will have innumerable descendants. Still, the figure of speech that was used is scientifically accurate, though there was no way the human writer could have known such information at the time.

On the other hand, it is surprising to learn that attempts to number the stars were being carried out as late as 1932. Prior to the invention of the telescope, and especially during the times of the biblical writers, it was commonly believed that there were a prescribed number of stars in the sky.

One of the earliest star catalogs was compiled by the Greek astronomer Hipparchus. Some two centuries before Christ, he set out to make a written record of all the stars in the heavens. Although the number of stars he supposedly counted varies,[2] there is no question that he believed the number could be determined. He probably would have laughed at anyone who believed otherwise.

The same general impression regarding the limited number of stars was held universally throughout the ancient world. Ptolemy followed the lead of Hipparchus and published his own star catalog some time later. Although a number of scholars feel this was probably plagiarized from another source, the origin of the catalog is not really the issue. The fact remains that its existence is evidence of a belief that the stars could be counted by the naked eye.

Farther to the east, Chinese astronomers reached the same conclusion. There existed a large number of ancient catalogs that placed the number of stars in the universe at near fifteen hundred.[3] The largest non-biblical estimate in ancient times seems to have been suggested by Chang Hing, who claimed in regard to the stars, "There are in all 2500, not including those which the sailors observe. Of the very small stars there are 11,520. All have their influences on fate."[4]

In light of such commonly held ideas, it is unusual that biblical writers described the stars as numberless, at least so far as man was concerned. Interestingly enough, those same authors did not go to the extreme of that position and claim an infinite number of stars. References to God calling the stars by name (Ps. 147:4; Isa. 40:26) imply that the stars are not infinite in number, though they *are* too numerous for man to count. This distinction is important and one that would have been impossible for the ancients to determine without sophisticated instruments. Modern evidence indicates that while there are more stars than man can count, there is not an infinite number of them.

Describing the Sun and Moon

Bible writers correctly assign the role of "light producer" to the sun, while avoiding such a designation in regard to the moon. Among the terms used in reference to the sun is *hammah* or "the hot one" (Isa. 30:26), which literally means "that which produces warmth."[5] That word accurately describes the sun, as any elementary school student could attest. On the other hand, writers of the Bible did not use such language to refer to the moon but instead speak of it as *lebhenah* or "the snow white,"[6] the cool one. This distinction in terminology is critical because it embodies the Bible's correct depiction of the two heavenly bodies at a time when not everyone was able to make the correct differentiation.

Early Hindu writers believed the reason the moon did not yield as much warmth as the sun was that the moon was much farther from the earth than the sun. Both sun and moon were said to shine by their own light. Centuries later, the more enlightened Greeks still thought the moon was reflecting fire from the center of the universe,[7] while some of the Pythagoreans claimed the moon produced its own light.[8] Once again, the biblical writers were correct, while many others held erroneous concepts.

The Stars and Sound Waves

Biblical writers were also correct in stating that stars emit sound in addition to light and heat. The writer of the Book of Job says that the stars "sang together" (Job 38:7). Poetic, yes—but the statement is definitely true. The Hebrew word translated "sang" is *ranan,* which means the emitting of a loud, shrill, or credulous sound. Of course, no one—not even Job—could have been technologically aware of the truthfulness of the statement at the time. Not until the twentieth century was this phenomenon verified. Though there are scattered references in non-biblical texts to stars giving off human sound, those writers believed the stars to be alive. In such instances they were said to be humans who had been placed in the sky after their deaths.

The only other suggestion in ancient times that stars gave off sound is found in the works of the Greek Philolaus, who argued that the stars produced "whizzing" noises as they rushed through space. He labeled this noise as "the harmony of the sphere."[9] Even centuries later the idea that stars produce sound seems almost totally absent from scientific thought. It was not until the 1930s that the possibility surfaced at all, and then most scholars in the field were slow to recognize what had actually been discovered.

Radio engineer Karl Jansky first noted sounds produced by the stars when he wrestled with "static" in 1932, but he believed them to be nothing more than an ionic reaction in space. Some ten years later, Grote Raber made an attempt to determine the origin of radio static but gave up because his results were "inconclusive."

In that year, U. S. Army scientists were convinced that the radio interruptions were the result of jamming devices operated by Nazi saboteurs. When the origin of the sound was eventually traced to the sun, the age of radio astronomy was begun. But how did Job, thousands of years before anything even resembling radio astronomy, know that stars emit sounds? A coincidence? Perhaps. But somewhere along the line, it becomes dubious to explain the Bible's accuracy as coincidence after coincidence after coincidence.

Describing Distances in Space

In the Bible, stars are correctly noted as appearing small because of their great distances from the earth. The writer of Job remarks, ". . . see how lofty are the highest stars!" (Job 22:12). Other biblical writers express similar ideas. While such conclusions are obvious today, they were the exception rather than the rule in Old Testament times. Anaximander claimed that the stars were actually closer to the earth than was the sun and moon.[10] Xenophanes hinted at the same error when he explained that the sun was only a foot wide, while the stars were merely sparks in the heavens.[11] An identical conclusion was reached by at least one Jewish scholar, who reasoned that the stars seemed small because they were the size of mustard seeds.[12]

These writers obviously thought that stars only the size of sparks or seeds would be invisible if far from the earth. Other ancient thinkers surmised that there were really no stars at all

Karl G. Jansky. Courtesy, Bell Labs.

In this historic photo Karl G. Jansky of Bell Telephone Laboratories is shown with the rotating antenna he used at Holmdel, New Jersey, to discover and authenticate radio waves coming from space. Jansky's investigations during the 1930s into the cause of strange noise in the telephone equipment resulted in the awareness that stars and galaxies produce sound waves and gave the world a new science—radio astronomy. Courtesy, Bell Labs.

in the skies. What appeared to be stars, they argued, was sunlight seeping through holes in the roof, or dome, of heaven. Those holes, they explained, had been caused by giants throwing rocks.[13]

Other Information Regarding the Stars

Biblical writers were even accurate when drawing moral lessons or doctrinal principles from the stars. For example, in speaking of God's power, the author of Job implies that the Pleiades are "bound together" in some fashion (Job 38:31). While some have questioned the identification of the Hebrew *"Kima"* with the Pleiades, the bulk of scholarship rejects this challenge.[14] The significance of the terminology was not completely understood until modern astronomy had come of age.

With the development of large telescopes and the aid of improved photography, twentieth-century astronomers have been able to study the stars in great detail. Because of these devices it is now known that a constellation is made up of thousands of stars and that the major ones are literally held together by strong gravitational and galactic forces. So permanent is the arrangement that they "can probably maintain their identity almost indefinitely."[15]

All great star groups, or constellations, lend the appearance of permanency to the sky. Through the years men have observed them in the same familiar patterns. Modern-day astronomers are aware, however, that this "permanence" is often illusionary, since stars in many constellations are actually moving away from one another. Precise measurements by astronomers show that the two stars at opposite ends of the Big Dipper are moving in one direction, while other stars in the constellation are moving in another. Assuming that the universe will endure, in a relatively short time the Big Dipper will no longer exist since its stars are not "bound together." It is not a true star group.

On the other hand, the Pleiades constellation does constitute what scientists label as a true star group. All stars in the group are moving through space in the same direction at the same velocity. Cecilia Payne-Gaposchkin's excellent discussion of star clusters concludes by observing the difference between the Pleiades and other groups. She writes that many open clusters that "leap to the eye" are not what they might first appear.

The Pleiades, referred to by Job as being "bound together," are now known to constitute a true star group, that is, all stars in the group are moving through space in a uniform manner. Courtesy, Lick Observatory.

Rather, "apparent clusterings, especially in regions rich in stars, turn out on closer examination not to be true groups."[16] On the other hand, the Pleiades are a true star group. They are bound together just as Job says.

13

To the Stars and Beyond

Naturally, one key area in the discussion of astronomy must be the nature of the universe itself. In this area, the inspired biblical writers again demonstrate an advanced knowledge absent in the writings of their contemporaries.

An Expandable Universe

Right from the start, Bible writers correctly observed that the universe is not fixed or solid but capable of expansion. The creation account speaks of "the heavens" or "sky" where the sun and stars are located as the "expanse" (Gen. 1:8, 14–19), a phrase translated from the Hebrew *raqia,* whose root meaning is the "spreading out" of the material under discussion.[1] The word suggests that the material has the capability to spread by expansion. However, authors who stretch the meaning to imply that the universe is still expanding take the evidence too far.[2]

Job mentions that God "spreads out the northern skies" (Job 26:7; cf. Job 9:8 and 37:18). Here the description refers to the stretching of space. It does not teach, as some have alleged, that Bible writers speak of a solid universe. Other biblical writers make similar statements. Isaiah pictures the heavens as stretched like a canopy (Isa. 40:22), a concept also recorded by the psalmist (Ps. 104:2) and Zechariah (Zech. 12:1). Jeremiah implies that the universe is such that man cannot measure it (Jer. 31:37). We can conclude from such passages that Bible writers describe the universe as immense and expandable.

The significance of these statements is better understood in light of other theories about the universe that were popular during biblical times. Lacking the technology needed for scientific study of the cosmos, ancient thinkers believed the universe was fixed in size, extremely small, and encased in some type of box or dome. Even such great thinkers as Plato and Aristotle, who wrote centuries after the Old Testament was composed, fell victim to the same error. Plato revealed his misunderstanding of the size of the universe by saying the entire universe would make a complete turn or revolution in twenty-four hours.[3] Aristotle supposed that the Milky Way was closer to the earth than was the moon,[4] and he and other Greeks closely followed the "doctrine of the spheres," which assumed the fixed nature of the universe.

A Non-Eternal Universe

Another area of scientific foreknowledge appears in the Bible's references to the non-eternal nature of the universe. In ancient times (especially during the Greek period) it was believed that the universe was eternal and unchanging. This concept was intact until the dawn of the modern era, as even the famed Greek philosophers felt compelled to differentiate between the changing earth and what they believed was an eternal sky.

Ancient Belief in an Eternal Universe

Even "shooting stars" and comets could not sway the ancients from their position that the universe was unchanging. Such phenomena were quickly explained away. After all, no stars were noted to be missing from the skies after one of these events! It was therefore assumed that they must be something occurring in the atmosphere, similar to the shifting of clouds or the falling of rain. Even the terms *meteor* and *meteorology,* derived from a Greek word meaning "things of the air," are used in reference to the earth's atmosphere rather than to the heavens or to "meteorites."

Observation of actual changes in the skies did not produce any significant shift in the belief that the universe was eternally the same. Tycho Brahe reported in 1573 in *De Nova Stella* that he had observed a new star that had not been previously seen. Yet the general feeling was that the star had been present all along, but for some reason had been masked from human sight. The dogma thus survived its first serious challenge. Later, in the 1700s, experts still believed there was some type of solid vault that surrounded the universe, which was believed to be unchangeable by natural law.[5]

Formulation of the Laws of Thermodynamics

It was well into the nineteenth century (1865) before Rudolf Clausius first advanced scientific proof that the universe was not eternal, but degenerating. The evidence he gathered helped to form the basis for what is now known as the first and second laws of thermodynamics,[6] both of which are widely accepted and well documented. In speaking of the concept, Einstein wrote that it "is the only physical theory of universal content concerning which I am convinced that it will never be overthrown.[7] Others have observed that the laws are "the most secure generalization from experience that we have."[8]

Lincoln Barnett summarized the concept of a degenerating universe:

All the phenomena of nature, visible and invisible, within the

Albert Einstein. Photo by Johan Hagemeyer, Bancroft Library, Courtesy, American Institute of Physics.

atom and in outer space, indicate that the substance and energy of the universe are inexorably diffusing like vapor. . . . The sun is slowly but surely burning out, the stars are dying embers, and everywhere in the cosmos heat is turning to cold, matter is dissolving into radiation, and energy is being dissipated into empty space. The universe is thus progressing to an ultimate 'heat death.' And there is no way of avoiding this destiny. For the fateful principle known as the second law of thermodyamics, which stands today as the principal pillar of classical physics

The Brookhaven solar neutrino experiment, located 4900 feet underground in the Homestake Gold Mine in Lead, South Dakota, was used to detect solar neutrinos emanating from the sun. The tank, twenty feet in diameter and forty-eight feet long, contains 100,000 gallons of perchloroethylene used in capturing and counting neutrinos. The experiment by Ray David suggested the possibility of measuring the decay of a proton. Several projects now underway have provided evidence of such decay. Thus it seems that matter, even in its most elementary and stable state, is not eternal. Courtesy, Brookhaven National Laboratory.

> left intact by the march of science, proclaims that the fundamental processes of nature are irreversible.[9]

Chemist Henry Bent calculated that the odds that the second law of thermodyamics could be completely negated even at the most elementary level is comparable to the odds for a group of monkeys randomly punching typewriters to "produce Shakespeare's works 15 quadrillion times in succession without error."[10] In any way of thinking that means impossibility!

Examples of Thermodynamics

There are numerous ways this law can be observed. The stars (our sun included) are constantly consuming hydrogen fuel or losing matter from their coronas at an estimated rate of 5.5 million tons of material per second.[11] Presumably the same holds true for other stars. In addition, galaxies are losing tremendous amounts of energy through similar processes.[12] Examples such as these can be multiplied. Truly, "everything deteriorates, collapses, breaks down, wears out, all by itself."[13]—"The universe is decaying to a homogenized nothingness."[14]

Modern knowledge has completely reversed the ancient notion regarding the eternity of the universe. Again, the biblical texts were far ahead of their time. How truly accurate are the words of the psalmist, who wrote concerning this universe: "They shall perish . . . yea, all of them shall wax old like a garment; as a vesture shalt thou change them, and they shall be changed" (Ps. 102:25–27, KJV). Centuries later, the apostle Paul, though deeply imbued with the Greek culture, also rejected the commonly held belief of his day to say that "the whole creation has been groaning" under "its bondage to decay" to which the creation was subjected (Rom. 8:10–22). Jesus had made it even clearer; the heavens would "disappear" (Matt. 5:18) or "pass away" (Matt. 24:35; cf. Mark 13:31; Luke 21:33).

14

The Blue Planet

Not only were biblical writers correct in their statements about the universe as a whole; they were equally accurate in references to the earth and its relationship to that universe.

Suspension of the Earth

Ancient authors conceived of the earth as resting on a strange foundation. Some pictured it as riding upon the back of four giant elephants, which perched atop a giant turtle that spent its days meandering about in a sea of milk. Others surmised that the earth was astride a large catfish that swam in some sort of primal ocean. Those who were repulsed by such ideas placed the world on the shoulders of Atlas.[1] On the other hand, the writer of Job correctly observed that "the earth hangs on nothing" (Job 26:7).[2] Literally, the phrase implies that the earth is suspended in space without observable means of support. Scholars of Job's day certainly had no such conception.

Sphericity of the Earth

The Scripture's writers also speak of the sphericity of the earth. Solomon, for example, mentions "a circle on the face of the deep" (Prov. 8:27, NASB). "The deep" refers to the oceans, and these earthly focal points are said to have a rounded surface. Some three centuries later, Isaiah used the same term, "circle" (Hebrew: *hug*), to refer to the earth (Isa. 40:22). There are some critics who have charged that Isaiah was speaking of the horizon and not the earth. It makes no real difference, for the argument is the same in either case.[3] If the horizon that surrounds the earth is circular, the same is certainly true for that which it encircles. Another Old Testament source speaks of the vaulted (circular) nature of the atmosphere that envelops the earth (Job 22:14) and thereby implies the sphericity of the earth.

A New Testament passage is also pertinent here. In the context of discussing his ultimate return to earth, Jesus implies that when he returns many of the people will be at rest while others will be at work (Luke 17:31–36). The meaning is obvious—it will be both day and night when Christ returns. That necessitates a spherical earth, for those who believed the earth to be flat could find no place in their theories for a time when the sun shone on only half the populace. There were no civilizations underneath this supposedly flat earth!

An objection is often raised that at least some writers of Scripture must have believed the earth to be flat, for they spoke of the "four corners" of the earth. It is easy to see that such an objection is without merit.

First, anyone familiar with the ancients' general understanding of the earth realizes they seldom thought of their flat earth as a square or a rectangle but rather viewed it as a disc.[4] Those who spoke of the "four corners" of the earth would have used the term metaphorically, even if they believed in a flat earth. Even today, though the sphericity of the earth is accepted, we speak of the "corners" of the world.

Second, Bible writers used the phrase "four corners" interchangeably with "four winds," which is considered by most scholars to be a simple metaphor. It is so recognized even by the same critics who so vehemently argue that biblical writers describe a flat earth. When dealing with parallel metaphors, it seems there should be a more consistent interpretation. Either both should be considered metaphors or both should be considered non-metaphors. For example, (see Ezek. 37:9; Dan. 7:2 and 11:4; Matt. 24:31; Mark 13:27; and Rev. 7:1.)

Third, recent discoveries indicate that the earth may indeed

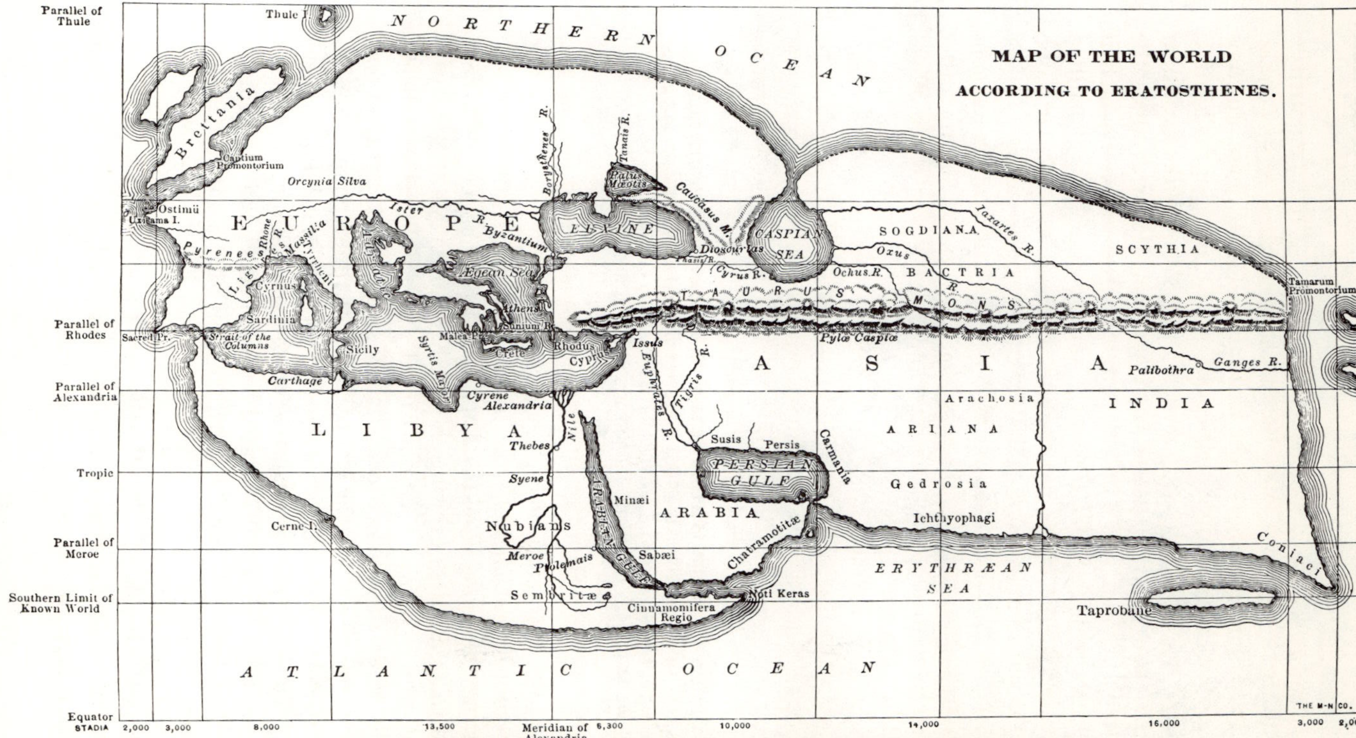

A typical map of the world as it was conceived of in antiquity. This drawing was attributed to Eratosthenes. The rendering appeared in *The Century Magazine* (Vol. 36, 1899, p. 767).

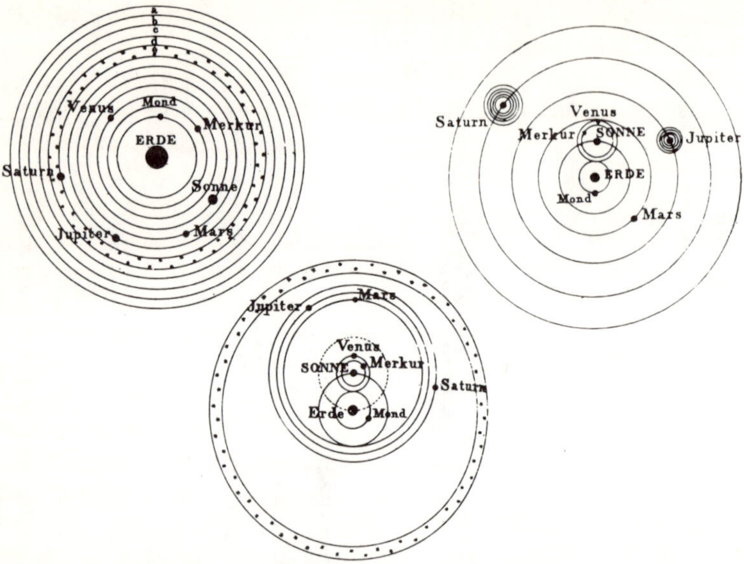

Geocentrism was central to all pre-Copernican theories of the solar system. These drawings, based on the 1851 edition of *The Iconographic Encyclopaedia of Science, Literature, and Art, depict* the earth as the center of the solar system in the works of early Egyptian astronomers, Ptolemy, and Tycho de Brahe.

have four "corners," or high points, though it is certainly not flat. In 1965, scientists working under a grant from the U. S. Navy at the Johns Hopkins Applied Physics Laboratory discovered that satellites orbiting the earth were unable to achieve a true orbit. The study demonstrated that satellites were being pulled from their orbits by a slightly stronger gravitational pull at four points around the globe. One of the high points is in the northern hemisphere from Ireland toward the North Pole. A second extends across the equator from New Guinea northward toward Japan. A third is located between Africa and Antarctica, while a fourth is just to the west of the South American continent.[5]

The Earth's Daily Revolutions

A final biblical reference (Job 38:12–14) suggests that the earth makes daily rotations on its axis. In describing a concept that was very advanced for Old Testament days, the author carefully delineates how the sunlight races across the earth's surface at dawn. Job, claiming the words are those of God, draws an analogy between the dawn of a new day and the use of a seal to produce an image on clay. The physical appearance of the earth is moving from a darkened to an illuminated condition, he notes, occurs as "clay under the seal" (Job 38:14, KJV).

To better understand the imagery, consider the meaning of the word *seal.* In biblical days, several types of seals were used to make impressions in clay. Those impressions were then used the same way as a signature is used today. They were marks of authority and identification. Many seals were in the form of rings either hung about the neck or worn on the finger. Others were cylinders through which holes were bored and solid objects (often well-formed pieces of wood) or cords were inserted into the opening. The Hebrew word for the latter type (*hotam*) is the term used by Job. This type of seal was dominant among both Egyptian and Babylonian cultures.[6]

Since the writer of Job was familiar with various types of seals, it is not surprising that he spoke about the *hotam.* What is surprising is the way the term is used. In speaking of the dawn, the writer says that morning is brought to the earth in the same manner in which clay is turned and given an impression by the seal (*hotam*). Thus, the clay (earth) which receives the impression (dawn, daybreak) of the seal (sun) does so in the same way that daybreak is produced on earth by the sun. The earth turns and, in so doing, produces the dawn.

The Hebrew word *hapak* that carries the action in Job 38:14 expresses the meaning of to "turn, turn about."[7] It occurs in several other passages where the concept of revolving is obvious. For example, in Genesis 3:24, the writer spoke of an angel guarding the entrance to the Garden of Eden, holding a sword that "turned" in every direction (KJV). The New American Bible renders the term *revolving,* and both the New English Bible and *The Interlinear Bible* use the term *whirling* to describe the scene.[8]

The similarities between this ancient description and modern scientific knowledge are remarkable. One, both the clay and the cylinder are described by the writer as being in a fixed position relative to one another. Analogously, the sun and the earth are in a fixed position relative to one another. Two, the seal remains in place while the clay rotates on a potter's wheel. As the clay rotates, the seal makes an impression on its soft surface. Likewise, the sun remains in place while the earth turns. Rays of light from the sun make an impression on the land as they illuminate the ground. A rotating earth makes day and night possible. Again, in a remarkably accurate fashion, biblical authors illustrate scientific knowledge.

Furthermore, these revelations in the biblical record occur long before surfacing in any other literature. The first veiled suggestion of a rotation of the earth came in the works of two early Greeks—Heraclides and Philolaus—and even these references are suspect.

If the Greeks held some nebulous concept about day and night being made possible by a daily rotation of the earth, it certainly was not obvious. That they probably did not hold such views is accentuated by the doctrines of Claudius Ptolemy and his "primum mobile." Ptolemy believed that the earth was the center of the universe and that other objects in the solar system revolved around it. His beliefs held scientific opinion firmly in its grasp for some fifteen hundred years.

It was not until Copernicus and Galileo that the verdicts of scientists were to swing toward a true understanding of the relationship between the earth and the sun. Yet, long before there was a Copernicus, writers of the Bible spoke of that same relationship.

15

Searching for Flaws

The accuracy of biblical astronomy is not without challenge. In fact, there are those who suggest that the Bible is filled with astronomical myths and errors. Such charges may be categorized under three major headings; (1) Bible writers adopt the primitive concept of a universe surrounded by a vault or dome, with the earth resting upon a primeval sea and/or held in place by massive columns; (2) Bible writers teach that the earth is the center of the universe; and (3) Bible writers inaccurately describe physical phenomena.[1] A brief overview of the evidence will quickly reveal that each charge is unfounded.

It is often implied that biblical writers followed mythical, pagan concepts of the universe prevalent at the time. Even many scholars in the religious establishment hold such views. In general, these authorities charge that the Bible writers believed in "a flat earth with mountains round its rim, on which the dome of the firmament rested as on pillars; in the firmament, windows through which the waters above could come down in rain; and in the earth, the hidden channels through which the windows of the underlying deep could flood to make the seas."[2]

But do the biblical writers really suggest these absurdities? If such charges are valid, there is little difference between their material and that found in other ancient books, as far as scientific truth is concerned. The evidence will be examined carefully and honestly for several specific charges.

Babylonian Borrowing?

Examining the proof offered in support of the position that the Bible presents a primitive concept of the universe, we find that critics assume that the Bible's writers borrowed freely from a Babylonian account of creation known as the *Enuma Elish.*[3] This material was rediscovered in the mid-1800s by archaeologists Layard, Rassam, and Smith. The account, written on seven clay tablets totaling slightly over one thousand lines of material, was unearthed among ruins of King Ashurbanipal's library in Nineveh.

The *Enuma Elish* begins at a point when nothing was in existence except Apsu (the primeval sweet-water ocean), Tiamat (the salt-water ocean), and their son Mummu (the clouds). From these sources were produced numerous gods and goddesses who eventually began to argue. A war ensued, during which both Apsu and Tiamat were slain. The body of Tiamat was cut into parts and used to create the universe. Half of the corpse was the sky; the other half was the earth. Mankind was made from the blood that flowed from the severed arteries of another god, Kingu.

To support the assumption that biblical authors borrowed from this story, critics observed that the *Enuma Elish* dominated beliefs about origins for three thousand years.[4] They then assumed—since the belief was almost universal during biblical times, and since the Bible was penned in the same general locality by people who could trace their ancestry to Babylon—that Bible writers must have believed and taught the same world view. But where is the evidence to support this conclusion? It is minimal and open to widely divergent interpretations. Briefly, a few reasons for rejecting the criticism are as follows:

1. The purpose of the two stories is radically different. Genesis presents an account of the origins of nature, while *Enuma* "was not composed to tell the story of creation, but to glorify the god Marduk and the city of Babylon."[5] Another scholar argues persuasively that *Enuma Elish* is based on a more ancient account and that *Enuma* is, in fact, not a creation epic at all.[6]

2. Major differences exist in the ethical and religious concepts of the two accounts.[7]

3. No extant process is available for the transmission and reworking of the material. As Millard observes:

> All who suspect or suggest borrowing by the Hebrews are compelled to admit large-scale revision, alteration, and reinterpretation in a fashion which cannot be substantiated for any other composition from the Ancient Near East or in any other Hebrew writing. If there was borrowing then it can have extended only as far as the 'historical' framework, and not included intention or interpretation.[8]

4. Evidence suggests that the Babylonian account is a degenerative account of the Hebrew version rather than the opposite.[9] Whitley points out that the Genesis material offers "greater detail" and a "more coherent pattern," whereas the Babylonian was "a confused combination of various traditions." He concludes that the "recognition of similarities does not necessarily imply dependence on the part of the Hebrew writer."[10]

5. Throughout the biblical account, the elements are described in a "depersonalized"[11] and "non-mythical"[12] sense. As Westerman notes, these differences suggest that the biblical writer "does not reflect in this act of creation the contemporary world-view, rather he overcomes it."[13]

An Inaccurate "Firmament"?

It is usually asserted by critics that the usage of the term *firmament* (occurring some seventeen times in the Old Testament) proves that biblical pensmen are referring to a solid sky. But studies demonstrate that the English word is not translated from the original Hebrew term (*raqia*) actually used by the writers, but it is derived instead from a Latin term (*firmamentum*), used by Jerome in his Vulgate translation.

Jerome followed the lead of the Greek Septuagint rather than the original Hebrew. The Greek word does mean "that which makes or is made firm,"[14] but to understand what the Old Testament authors meant, the original meaning must reflect the Hebrew, not the Greek. Why the Septuagint transcribers chose to render the term as they did is unclear, but it was probably done to make the Hebrew Old Testament coincide with current Greek thought, which followed Egyptian and Babylonian cosmologies.[15] Also, even the Greek word does not *require* a solid sky, as respected scholars have noted.[16]

It is likewise difficult to understand why translators of the King James and Revised Standard versions felt compelled to put so much emphasis on Latin and Greek renderings, rather than returning to the meaning in the original Hebrew. As Haines has noted, " 'firmament' is a most unfortunate mistranslation. 'Firmament' means something firm and seems to imply a sky something like a solid vault in which the sun, moon, and stars are fixed like light bulbs. . . . The true meaning of the Hebrew original here is that of something 'stretched out' or 'extended' . . . and the better translation is 'expanse'. . . . The error had its beginning in the translation of the . . . Septuagint. The ancient Greeks conceived of the sky as a solid, crystalline sphere. It was their false science which determined the Greek word used in this verse."[17] From these observations, it is obvious that Septuagint translators often tried to mold biblical ideas into concepts that were consistent with current Greek thought.[18]

If Greek and Latin translations are suspect, then what is the true meaning of "firmament"? More and more scholars are coming to the conclusion that the term is best translated by the English word *expanse* or the phrase *that which is spread out.* It is so rendered in the New American Standard and New International Versions and by Kohlenberger in *The NIV Interlinear Hebrew-English Old Testament.*[19]

Finally, Vine notes that while the "English word 'firmament' is derived from the Latin *firmamentum* which signifies firmness or strengthening (like the Greek *stereoma*), the Hebrew word *raqia* has no such meaning, but denoted the 'expanse,' or that which is stretched out." He concludes, "There is nothing in the language of the original to suggest that the writers were influenced by the imaginative ideas of heathen nations."[20]

From a linguistic standpoint, the evidence that "firmament" is used generically is persuasive because the Hebrews had "no comprehensive term for the universe" and "heaven" is used to denote both the place of the stars and the constellations and the clouds.[21]

If the term for heaven is applied equally to both the atmosphere and the universe, as Newman and Eckelmann argue, then the charge that "firmament" implies a solid, metallic dome is false—for the "birds are said to fly 'upon the face of the firmament' (Gen. 1:20, literal Hebrew). The preposition *al* used here means 'upon' not 'below' suggesting that the birds are flying upon the air rather than beneath a dome."[22]

The use of this particular preposition requires that the birds be either in or on the *raqia* (firmament) and it is certainly doubtful that the little creatures could fly "in" a metallic dome or that they could be seen from the earth if they were flying above a solid dome. This is also consistent with the earlier concept of an expandable universe since modern science certainly admits the capability of the atmosphere to expand or contract under certain conditions.

A Solid Dome?

The same biblical writers who are accused of referring to a solid dome around the earth actually make very clear statements that dictate the exact opposite. The psalmist speaks of heaven as being stretched out "like a curtain" (Ps. 104:2, KJV), a phrase also used by Isaiah (40:22), who similarly describes the heavens as being capable of being rolled back like a scroll (34:4). As Gaenssle asks, "Can anyone with these texts before him seriously and honestly believe that the writers of these words entertained the crude, inept notion of a metallic canopy above their heads?"[23]

The idea of an expansionistic heaven was also mentioned in the Book of Job, where it was referred to as "empty space" (26:7). In dealing with this idea, Maunder observes that the erroneous view required some type of water storage over the vault with appropriate "flood-gates" or "windows," and concludes that "the fantastic idea of solidly built cisterns in the sky furnished with sluices has no warrant in Scripture. There is also a very clear and concrete account of the atmospheric circulation"[24] in Job (36:27–28) and numerous other references that connect the clouds with rain (Judg. 5:4; Job 37:16; Ps. 77:17 and 147:8; Prov. 16:15; Eccles. 1:6–7; 12:2; Isa. 5:6; Jer. 10:13; Amos 9:6). On the basis of such evidences, it is not valid to charge the writers of the Bible with fostering Egyptian and Babylonian dogmas of a domed universe and a flat earth.

A Primeval Ocean?

Other areas of evidence in support of the view that the Bible depicts a primitive universe also lack persuasive appeal. For example, some assert that biblical writers imply an earth that is floating on some type of ocean. "Proof" is based on (1) the supposed meaning of the Hebrew word *tehom,* translated by the phrase "the deep," and (2) the perversion of two passages in the psalms (24:2; 139:9).

To make their point, it is important for critics to demonstrate conclusively the dependence of the biblical writers on Babylonian documents that describe the Babylonian goddess Tiamat as associated with a watery chaos under the earth. Though this has indeed been asserted, it has not been proven.

Critics make much of so-called similarities between the Hebrew and Babylonian terms. It is argued that "the Hebrew word *tehom* is the philological equivalent of Tiamat." The cumulative effect of the considerations "seems to warrant the conclusion that [the author of Genesis 1] . . . was not only dependent upon some version of the Babylonian creation myth; he was also . . . under the necessity of retaining its representations in recognizable form."[25]

Naturally, such speculations are intriguing, but the facts don't support them. Davidson comments, "The Hebrew word . . . (*tehom*) is thought by some scholars to be linked linguistically to *Ti'amat.* This is doubtful."[26] Kitchen elaborates: "The Hebrew word is linguistically a zero form (unaugmented by formative elements) and cannot be derived from the Babylonian word *Ti'amat* which is itself a derived form, principally a proper name and in any case shows different contextual usage."[27]

Further, Alexander Heidel declares, "The two words do not denote the same thing." He admits that the root from which both words are taken is the same, but points out that "root relationship does not itself prove identity in meaning."[28] For example, though the French word *actuellement* comes from the same root word as the English word *actually,* the French means "at the present time" and the English means "really" or "as a matter of fact."

In a similar vein, the German word *selig,* meaning "blessed," is from the same root as the English word *silly.* Even identical words can change their meanings drastically over the years. One scholar observed: "Names and words soon lose their meaning. In the process of years and centuries, the meanings die off them like the sunlight from the hills. The hills are there, the color is gone."[29] The French *marechal* once meant "one that dressed horses," but now it refers to one of the chief commanders of the armed services. The English term *alderman* at one time described someone in a position second only to the king. It certainly does not mean the same now! Further examples of lost meanings include the words *candidate* and *carping*. A candidate was once "a person who wore white," while carping was the same as "conversing with another." The original Greek-based meaning of the term *idiot* was "one who is opposed to holding public office."

The implications of such linguistic analysis become obvious in light of assertions that the biblical account of creation was written hundreds of years *after* the Babylonian document. Such critics are under obligation to show that the words in question—separated by hundreds of years, written in different languages, and carrying other linguistic differences—mean the same thing in both documents. They have failed to demonstrate this connection.

Heidel points out the real impossibility of deriving the Hebrew from the Babylonian when he writes, "To derive *tehom* from *Ti'amat* is grammatically impossible, because the former has a masculine, the latter a feminine ending. As a loan-word from *Ti'amat, tehom* would need a feminine ending, in accordance with the laws of derivation from Babylonian in Hebrew. . . . Had *Ti'amat* been taken over into Hebrew, it would either have been left as it was or it would have been changed to *ti'ama* or *te'ama,* with the feminine ending *a,* but it would not have become *tehom.*"[30]

Finally, *Ti'amat* is always associated with the mythical, while *tehom* is never so connected. That alone prompts a number of writers to argue that the Hebrew word came first and the Babylonian was derived from the Hebrew. Hasel notes that "*tehom* appears in connection with the subject of creation . . . in Ps. 33:7, 104:6; Job 38:16; Prov. 3:20, 8:24,27; in each case, however, without any mythological overtones."[31] Since the term appears elsewhere in perfectly natural settings, there is no reason to view it otherwise in the reference in Genesis, especially since many of the critics assign the composition and writing of the materials to the same time period. Thus, as Maunder adds, "If this resemblance proves any connection . . . it proves the Hebrew to be the original. The natural object, *tehom,* the sea, must have preceded the mythological personification of it."[32]

Still, old beliefs do not die easily. Two modern writers demonstrate how such erroneous beliefs can be held in spite of the facts. Ignoring the evidence, they write, "Were it not for the Tehom-Tiamat parallel, we should never guess that Tehom represents the formidable Babylonian Mother-goddess who bore the gods."[33] One might well ask, "Which parallel"? When one's mind is set, all the facts in the world will be of little use.

For two passages in the psalms, the basic objections that were noted above can be given here as well. Biblical authors nowhere mention an ocean "under" the earth, and Gaenssle concurs that a study of the Hebrew in the passages will force an admission that they are speaking "only of earthly waters on which the earth touches and over which it is elevated."[34] The phrases simply state that the earth (dry land) is higher than the ocean and nothing more.

A Supported Earth?

Finally, it is charged that passages referring to "pillars" of the earth (Job 9:6) suggest that the writers had in their minds something similar to a flat earth resting on the back of giant columns. Such a charge is preposterous. In the first place, the same writer who used that language also spoke of the earth's being hung on (suspended on or by) nothing (Job 26:7). He also wrote that the earth turns to produce sunrise and sunset. Both passages are sufficient to demonstrate that, whatever the author had in mind by "pillars," it was not the old Babylonian concept. In the second place, the Hebrew term translated "pillars" comes from the root *amad,* which literally means "to stand, remain, endure."[35]

Writers of the Bible often speak of the earth's "foundation," but such semantics surely do not force one into adopting the idea that the earth is flat. In fact, the earth does have a foundation[36] in the rocks that underlie its crust and provide it with stability.[37] There is no legitimate reason to read into the text any additional meaning.

16

Trouble at the Center

One erroneous doctrine that some critics say finds haven in the pages of the Bible is the geocentric theory popularized by Claudius Ptolemaeus and supported before his time by such intellectual heavyweights as Aristotle. The theory argues that the earth is the center of the solar system. In charging that the authors of Scripture were misled by such mistaken "scientific" thinking, it is asserted that "even a child" who reads Genesis 1 would reach such a conclusion.[1] Such criticism of the Bible's accuracy deserves an answer, which is summarized below.

A Summary of Genesis 1 and the Creation

An overview of the first chapter of Genesis reveals first that "in the beginning" (whenever that was) "God created the heavens and the earth" (Gen. 1:1). It further reveals that the sun would provide benefits to whatever would be living on earth and that stars could function as "timers" for the same inhabitants. (Gen. 1:14–17). The key point in our argument is that the facts are equally correct regardless of whether one adheres to the geocentric theory or Copernicus' heliocentric approach. To derive support for either from the chapter is to do the Scriptures injustice.

Those who press the issue argue that the biblical authors stress the importance of the earth and that such emphasis at least *implies* geocentrism. That is begging the question, for to be the center of attention does not mean the same as being the center of some geographical fixation. A lovely bride may be the center of attention at a wedding while the groom may be standing in the corner of the same room. That hardly means that one is more important than the other. It cannot be denied that references in the Bible give the earth center stage as far as the amount of divine attention afforded to it. These references, however, do not demonstrate biblical endorsement for the earth as center of the universe. Young aptly summarizes the point:

> . . . the first chapter of the Bible is indeed written from a geocentric standpoint. It does tell its story from the position of one who lives on this globe, and it also points out how the other heavenly bodies serve the earth. Is this, however, out of accord with the facts? Although the emphasis in Genesis 1 is geocentric, it is clear that this emphasis is for a religious purpose. . . . What would be the purpose in emphasizing what took place on some other planet? . . . It does not teach that the earth is the center of the universe. . . . It teaches that the sun and moon serve this earth, and, in so teaching, it is perfectly correct. . . . Whatever other purposes they may have, the sun and moon do serve the earth. The geocentricity which is found in the first chapter of the Bible is perfectly in accord with scientific fact. Genesis does not claim to give a description of the relation of the heavenly bodies one to another, but to state that the earth on which we live is benefitted by the sun and moon.[2]

Was the Earth Created First?

It is further argued that the author of Genesis teaches that the earth was created first and that thus everything created afterward had to revolve around it. The position is interesting but faces several difficulties:

1. Why must everything revolve around the earth even if it was created first?

2. In which verse does the writer of Genesis speak specifically of the actual creation of our planet? The answer is that the Bible does *not* refer specifically to the creation of this planet at all (though it is certainly implied and assumed throughout the narrative), unless it is covered in the general statement of verse one. But, if that verse does refer to the earth's formation, it must

be noted that the creation of earth follows rather than precedes the forming of the heavens.

3. Many scholars believe the terminology found in Genesis suggests that the sun was made to function for the benefit of the earth during the fourth creative period (Gen. 1:14–16) and had been brought into existence with the "light" during the first creative period.[3] In short, no *prima facie* case has been offered showing biblical geocentrism.

Other Geocentric Proof Texts Denied

Other than Genesis, geocentrists also appeal to two passages in the Psalms. The King James Version translates one phrase from Psalms 93:1 as "the world also is stablished, that it cannot be moved" (cf. 96:10). But once again some objections are appropriate:

1. The entire thrust of Psalm 93 (and 96 as well) is that the earth and its inhabitants cannot be removed from God's attention and that no person or thing can take control of the earth or wrest it from his control. Of course, the verses would not preclude geocentrism, but neither do they demand such. Yet Kidner finds the verses are "best seen against the welter of raging nations and collapsing regimes depicted in e.g., 46:6. The first and last lines of verse ten [Ps. 96] make it additionally clear that this is a prophecy of perfect government, not a pronouncement on—of all things!—the earth's rotation."[4]

2. The passage does not specify from which location the earth "cannot be moved." Could not the passage simply mean that the earth cannot be moved from its particular orbit around the sun. To assert that the psalmist was saying the earth could not be moved from the center of the universe is to make a leap that is without logical inference. Those who adhere to heliocentrism today also believe that God has fixed the earth so that it cannot be "shaken."

3. To adopt the geocentric meaning in this passage would bring this Psalm in conflict with Job 38,[5] which—as we have seen in chapter 14—attests to the rotation of the earth. When this is noted, geocentrists try to harmonize the two by arguing that the earth can revolve and still be in the center of the universe. That ploy forces those who take such a position to admit

that the phrase "cannot be moved" is not absolutely literal. The earth moves (revolves) but it remains in only one place. The passage in psalms is *either* literal *or* symbolic. It cannot be both.

4. A study of the Hebrew words used in these passages establishes the fact that the writer did not intend to convey geocentricity. Numerous Hebrew words carry the English rendering "moved." The one actually used by the psalmist is *mot,* which—when prefixed with a negative, as it is in the specific passages involved—denotes "dependability and certainty."[6]

Other Hebrew terms far more appropriate could have been used if geocentrism was the intended meaning. The Hebrew *nastab* expresses the idea of "to be stationed, to be placed, to be planted, to establish boundaries,"[7] all of which, when prefixed with a negative, would imply the lack of movement implied by the geocentrists. That *mot* was chosen rather than another term suggests there was no attempt to claim the earth as immovable.

A quick notice of other passages where *mot* is found solidifies the argument. In speaking of the wicked, the psalmist says, "He hath said in his heart, I shall not be moved [*mot*] . . ." (Ps. 10:6, KJV). Surely the term was used in a figurative sense and was not intended to bind the wicked to a particular physical location. Similarly, *nastab* occurs in such passages as Exodus 7:15, where God orders Moses to station himself at a certain spot near the Nile River to confront Pharaoh.

Likewise, the word *stablished* fails to provide any reason to think the psalmist was a believer in the Ptolemaic theory. Again, the Hebrew language has several words that are translated by the English "stablish." The one used in the passage was *kun,* which literally involves the concept of bringing something into being. Thus, "the main idea is to bring something into an incontrovertible existence."[8] In fact, "evidence of the original etymology may be found in those occurrences where something is said simply to have been formed or fashioned (Judg. 12:6; Job 31:15; Ps. 119:73; Ezek. 16:7). In none of these is the idea of . . . firmness in view, but rather of basic formation" or a "fixity of what (God) has done."[9]

Two other passages occur wherein God is said to have "established" (*kun*) the earth (Isa. 45:18; Jer. 33:2). In both, the phrase containing "establish" (the earth) is aligned with another in couplet form. In those usages the purpose of the second part of the couplet is to amplify the meaning of the former.[10] Reading either couplet demonstrates that to "establish" the earth meant to prepare it, or to make it habitable for man. Neither deals with the earth's location in the universe.

Galileo's Controversy over Geocentrism

But, one might ask, why was there so much controversy between Galileo and the leadership of the Catholic Church over the former's support of the Copernican heliocentric view? Too often the implication is made that this battle was limited to a group of fanatical and error-prone, Bible-wavers on the one hand and a smaller-but-calmer truth brigade of telescope-packing and unbiased scientists on the other.

It is true that Galileo was forced by those in authority to recant his testimony that the earth orbited the sun, despite the evidence he presented. It is also true that theologians were deeply involved in that decision. Furthermore, it is true that the works of Galileo and Copernicus were placed on the list of forbidden books (*Index Liborium Prohibitorium*). Finally, it is true that one of the arguments advanced against Galileo by his accusers was that his teaching was contrary to the Bible. These facts are so well documented by historians that many today will dig no deeper. They will assume they have heard enough and conclude that the Bible is filled with mythical assertions and scientific blunders. Before the case is closed so abruptly, however, several lesser-known facts should be noted.

Geocentrism Came from Scientific Roots

True geocentrism emanated from scientific roots rather than theological dogma. The doctrine, insofar as it is visualized by the average reader today, was proclaimed by the philosopher-scientists Plato, Aristotle, and Ptolemy, who built their systems on foundations totally alien to the Hebrew Old Testament.

Why the Church Accepted Geocentrism

Even when Ptolemaic teaching was incorporated into church dogma by Clement of Alexandria and others, the arguments were more often symbolic and allegorical than scriptural.[11] Clement argued that proof for geocentrism was to be found in the placement of an altar in the Jewish tabernacle. This altar, he said, was "a symbol of the earth placed in the middle of the universe."[12] That such an idea was not based on Scripture but in his imagination should be obvious to anyone who reads the Bible. No such implication is ever suggested. Even White admits, "Wrought into this foundation, and based upon it, there was developed in the Middle Ages, mainly out of fragments of Chaldean and other early theories . . . a new sacred system of astronomy."[13]

Scientific Objections to Removing Geocentrism

Galileo's ideas were in conflict with the widely respected sciences of Plato and Aristotle and would have had difficulty in gaining acceptance even if the Catholic Church had not opposed them.[14] After all, authorities of the day were unfamiliar with experimental methods and had all been trained in the deductive approach to knowledge, which Aristotle had popularized. Since geocentrism had been basically unquestioned for two thousand years, it was hard for the authorities to believe the theory was wrong. That Aristotelian teachings were used to refute Galileo often goes unnoticed. Over and over, historical records that are available to any who will study them note that Galileo's accusers argued against his position on the grounds that "Aristotle knew nothing of these revelations."

White blatantly asserts concerning Galileo that "semi-scientific professors, endeavoring to curry favor with the church, attacked him with sham science."[15] He totally ignores, however, that "reputable professors opposed the Copernican theory on legitimate [whether correct or not] scientific grounds; for example, the great astronomer, Tycho Brahe, did not espouse the . . . theory."[16]

Theologians Used Their Own Ideas

Theologians of the day also declared as "non-biblical" the idea that Jupiter had moons. After all, they argued, the Bible referred to "seven candlesticks" and "seven churches." Therefore, they reasoned, there must only be seven planets and these planets couldn't possibly have moons. That such a doctrine is supposedly found in the Bible is news to anyone who has read the Scriptures. It was conceived and nurtured by fertile imaginations and not out of fact. And, it should be remembered that these were the same theologians who were claiming that Bible authors taught geocentricity. Even White admitted that attacks on Galileo were made with "perverted Scripture."[17]

Key Theologians Supported Galileo

Records also show that several theologians sided with Galileo and that there was not nearly as much controversy as is often assumed.[18] Remember also that two hundred years before the telescope's appearance, theologians such as Cardinal Nicholas de Cusa argued that Bible writers did not teach geocentrism. His arguments, coming as they did before there was any hard scientific facts to support his position, were based on the Scriptures themselves.

The Banning of Books

While it is loudly proclaimed that the writings of Galileo and Copernicus were placed on the *Index Liborium Prohibitorium* of the Catholic Church, it is seldom noted that those writings shared a place on the *Index* with the Bible itself, which was forbidden in the common language of the people[19] by the Councils of Valencia (1229), Toulouse (1229), Terragona (1234), and Trent (1563). The Bible remained on the list until 1721.[20] For several hundred years prior to Galileo, church authorities had put more emphasis on theology than on the Bible. It is no surprise, therefore, that these theologians often misinterpreted the Scriptures. That which is not studied carefully is often misunderstood.

The Possibility of a Hidden Motive

In recent years another intriguing possibility has surfaced. Pietro Redondi has argued, on the basis of the discovery of some previously unknown documents, that a major reinterpretation of the entire Galileo story is now in order.[21] According to Redondi, "advocacy of Copernicanism was not the main teaching that caused him to be vehemently suspect of heresy; rather, it was the atomism he advanced in *The Assayer* which conflicted with Tridentine doctrine on the Eucharist."[22] In other words, the charges against Galileo regarding geocentrism were a convenient way to avoid an even more embarrassing situation in another and more sensitive area.

In summary, the Galileo case did not prove the Bible to be in error. Although it did show that many theological interpretations of the Scriptures were erroneous, discovering an error of interpretation is not the same as finding a corruption in the text itself.

17

Answering the Critics

Brief attention should be given to a few other biblical statements that some critics have categorized as errors in the sacred astronomy.

In several passages, Old Testament authors inform their readers that stones fell from the sky (as in Joshua 10:11). Descriptions of these events are given in detail, but no mythical interpretations are ever imbedded in the accounts. One generally accepted suggestion in regard to such phenomena was advanced by Aristotle. He held that "mineral veins, when they are exposed at the surface of a rock, slowly evaporate and rise into the air where, after they condense to form meteorites, they later fall down to earth, usually in storms."[1] When that idea was shown to be flawed (in the seventeenth century), scholars quickly proposed the idea that no stone could ever fall from the sky. If they were right, true, the Bible was obviously in error. Copernicus, Galileo, Kepler, Newton, the Royal Academy of Science in Paris, and numerous other authorities strongly asserted the truthfulness of the idea. It was not until the city of Paris was itself bombarded with such a shower of meteorites at the opening of the nineteenth century that the French Academy began to accept the fact that stones can indeed fall from the sky.[2] The biblical writer was correct once again.

Another so-called mistake in biblical astronomy is said to be found in Genesis 1:3, where "light" is said to have been created prior to the existence of the sun. While it might be true that such a statement found itself in conflict with theories of eighteenth-century science, such is certainly not the case today. Every major theory of science that deals with the origin of the universe testifies to the validity of the Genesis account. That light could have existed prior to the existence of the sun is both scientifically feasible and widely accepted today. Again the error is not in the Bible but in the shortsightedness and ignorance of man. The more we learn about the universe, the more correct becomes the biblical account in the eyes of scientists who study the Scriptures.

In every way, the astronomical references in the Scriptures are true and advanced far ahead of their times. Such accuracy certainly deserves an explanation. Where, then, must one turn for this explanation? In reality, there are no more options available here than there were in earlier discussions. One can attempt to account for both the lack of error and the advanced knowledge by claiming (1) that biblical writers copied from earlier sources; or (2) that the books were written later than previously estimated, at a time when such was common scientific knowledge; or (3) that the writers were just plain lucky; or (4) that there must be a supernatural explanation.

The same objections that were voiced earlier[3] are even more appropriate when applied to the first three "explanations" listed above. What ancient source could possibly have avoided all the errors of the day? What astronomer in that era of primitive tech-

Avoiding Astronomical Errors

Pitfalls biblical writers managed to avoid

1. Incorrect understanding of sun and moon
2. Deification of the natural universe
3. A flat earth
4. Incorrect understanding of the size of the universe
5. Astrology
6. A limited number of stars
7. Geocentricity
8. Magic and omens

nology could have known that the stars were innumerable, or that stars emit sound, or that the universe was capable of expansion? These ideas and many more biblical concepts were unique and without a champion in the times when the Bible was written. And to do as some would and shove the biblical materials to dates of origin some five hundred years later would accomplish nothing. Even if one so manipulated the chronolgy, the doctrines recorded are still centuries ahead of their time. Even Greek and Roman ideas, advanced though they were, had not pushed knowledge as far as the biblical authors. To invoke "luck" as an answer is to rely on chance against insurmountable odds. The probabilities of simply avoiding the errors of antiquity would be beyond reasonable expectations. We must therefore conclude that the Bible writers were truly "inspired"!

Part Three

The Earth Beneath

Sacred Revelations and Earth Science

18

What on Earth Is This?

Man's fascination with his own planet stretches back to the dawn of history. People of ancient times observed the good earth and the water surrounding it and found that it was filled with magnificence and splendor, though it was equally foreboding and mysterious. Rainbows arched through the heavens, lightning slashed across darkened skies, and the earth itself trembled and shook. Its human inhabitants stood in awe, searching for an explanation of the natural wonders. Of course, they proposed their own answers for the questions that troubled them, and those answers somewhat satisfied their curiosity. At best, the answers were evidence of their interpretive genius—a proof that mankind has always been creative. At worst, they were misleading, erroneous gibberish that disrupted the pace of scientific inquiry and fed superstitions and fear.

Once again, this review of man's early attempts at explaining the world around him is not made to disparage our ancestors. They made commendable progress in the search for knowledge, considering the limited materials and technologies available to them. It would be absurd to belittle them as unintelligent or ignorant, for if the best minds of the 1980s were planted in such cultures, they would probably fare no better. And that is precisely the point. We expect those ancient errors. It is only when they are not found that eyebrows are raised and we question why.

Errors Regarding the Earth

On many occasions, our globe has been labeled "the good earth"—"good" because its thin mantle of soil nourishes an abundance of life forms and "good" because in this vast universe of ours, it gives every indication of uniqueness. For a time, at the beginning of man's latest burst of discovery, that uniqueness was in doubt. But with the accumulation of time and evidence, the recognition of earth's special place is again asserting itself.[1] Scientists, though still hoping to find extraterrestrial life elsewhere in this galaxy, have become more and more aware that these forms may not be able to exist under the myriads of circumstances found on other planets. With all its resilience, "life" is proving remarkably well-adapted to this earth, and what we know about the rest of the observable universe seems remarkably sterile in comparison.

Further, much has been written recently regarding what has come to be known as the anthropic principle. This concept also argues for the uniqueness of the earth and life, noting that many of the structures taken for granted in our universe—galaxies, stars, planets, the various elements, water, atoms, even life itself—owe their very existence to numerous finely tuned "coincidences" in the values of the constants of physics. Even minute alterations in certain factors would make such entities as life, or the earth, or water, impossible.[2]

Ancient man knew the earth was "exclusive" and he was right in that vague generalization. When he tried to explain the "how" and "why," he stumbled. Sometimes he made the earth too important as far as its physical place in the universe was concerned.[3] He visualized the physical universe surrounding the earth as similar to the spokes of a wheel revolving around a hub. In reality, our earthly habitat is no more than a tiny speck in the infinity of space, and it moves through that space like any other object.[4] But until man's fertile imagination had instruments of science to restrain it, some rather unusual theories were planted and watered.

The Living Earth

Perhaps the earliest of humanity's earth-concepts was the idealization of the world as a living, breathing entity. Along the banks of the Nile, premier mathematicians and builders concluded that all things partook of a common life-form.[5] Even parts of the universe that today are thought of as inanimate—stones, minerals, air, water, and fire—were said to be impregnated with life. To the thinkers of the great dynasties of Egypt, an abundance of evidence seemed to authenticate the idea. The tides of the sea rose and fell, suggesting a slow but steady breathing process. Earthquakes shook the terrain. Islands appeared in the sea.

To the "dwellers by the Nile," only living things moved—and such obvious movements of the earth suggested to them that it was truly a living creature. And while the belief in a living earth would not go unchallenged, it was still dominant centuries later when Plato appointed a soul to the earth.[6] This soul, Plato reasoned, was both capable of self-movement[7] and possessed intelligence.[8] It was alive!

The Growing Earth

A natural outgrowth of the "living earth" doctrine was that the earth and all the objects it contained were capable of growth in the same manner as all other forms of life. Such doctrines were taught and popularized not only by Plato and his disciples but by almost every branch of Greek society.[9] So embedded were these ideas that they were seriously defended as truth as late as the eighteenth century, when mountains were said to grow like plants.[10]

The Earth as Deity

Since the earth was considered alive and growing, it was easy to view it as deity. Available evidence suggests that the Egyptians were the first civilization to make the transition to this line of thought. In their oldest-surviving religious literature—the Pyramid Texts—the earth, sky, and moisture were deified.[11] The Nile itself was said to be a god's bloodstream. This was a belief that more or less pervaded the entire globe.[12]

1. *Sacrifices to the Earth.* Since the earth was understood to be divine, or at least alive, it was thought dangerous to disturb its crust (or hide). Plowing, digging foundations or wells, mining, and other activities required propitiation by sacrifice. That sacrifice was occasionally human.[13] Even the gathering of certain

plants necessitated offerings to appease any injury incurred during the process,[14] and customs went so far as prohibiting plowing on certain days because the earth was then asleep.[15]

2. *Ancient Understanding of Earthquakes.* One common punishment for tampering with the earth, according to some of our forebears, was the sending of earthquakes.[16] Explanations of this terrifying natural phenomenon ran rampant.

Among some civilizations, earthquakes were said to be sent by earthquake deities. In other cultures, where the earth was said to be a living animal, quakes were assumed to be the result of bees or other insects stinging the earth. In other areas, earth movements were attributed to the dead as they fought in the underworld or struggled to reach the surface.[17] In most locations, however, earthquakes were ascribed to the animals that held the earth in place and kept it from falling endlessly through the void below. These earth-bearing animals differed from culture to culture, not only in type but also in number.

In Japan, the animal was usually a fish[18] or a spider.[19] In Slavic countries, four whales were given the job.[20] In India, one account cited a snake as charged with the responsibility, while another listed an elephant. Still another account assigned eight elephants to the task.[21]

Of course, before too long some inquisitive soul ventured to ask what held the elephants in place. By what reasoning process it was decided that the elephants were on the back of a large mud turtle might provide some interesting speculation. At any rate, an infinite series of such questions was averted by having the turtle swim about in a sea of milk. No one seemed worried abut what contained the milk. In Ceylon, the scheme of things was even more elaborate, with a giant holding the earth while standing on the back of a serpent. In turn, the serpent was coiled on the back of a turtle, which was sitting on a frog that was cushioned by air.[22] Why the earth itself could not have simply rested on a cushion of air no one seems to have wondered.

Each ancient culture explained earthquakes by the movement of these large creatures, and they moved for every conceivable reason. The Indian serpent, which coiled around the flat, silver-dollar—shaped earth, was said to have its tail in its mouth. Evidently, a good bite on its tail was enough to cause it—and the earth—to tremble.[23]

According to Epiphanius, the Manichaeans believed that the earth rested on the shoulders of a giant who transferred the burden from one shoulder to another every thirty years.[24] Near the end of each such interval, it was necessary for someone to yell at the giant (as in Dr. Seuss's *Horton Hears a Who*) to inform the kindly oaf that the earth was inhabited.

In Egypt and Arabia, the worst earth tremors were explained as the result of a bull playfully tossing the earth from one horn to another. One other group envisioned the earth as an egg that cracked to let something out,[25] while others blamed a giant mole or subterranean demons.[26]

Even the Greeks, who struggled fiercely to rid themselves of such metaphysical fancies, invented only slightly more natural fancies in their place. Aristotle and the Greeks blamed the *pneuma*—or breath of the earth—for quakes, which they said could be caused by such things as an eclipse of the moon, drought, or a heavy rain.[27] This breath, or subterranean wind, was accused of producing disasters by another Greek writer, Theophrastus,[28] who added that thunder might also be involved. Democritus claimed that rain caused movements in the earth, and Ovid suggested nearness to the sun as the culprit. Lucretius nominated the collapse of huge underground caverns.[29] In the latter half of the first century, Pliny wrote, "Tremors of the earth never occur except when the sea is calm and sky so still that the birds are unable to soar because all the breath that carries them has been withdrawn; and never except after wind, doubtless because the blast has been shut up in the veins and hidden hollows of the sky."[30]

It comes as no surprise that modern science spurns such undocumented beliefs. And, while modern cultures still lack the expertise of perfect prediction or control of earthquakes, there is a basic understanding of the phenomenon.[31]

Errors Regarding Materials Within the Earth

Another problem for earth scholars surfaced with the discovery of gems, fossils, and other materials buried within the earth. Since the earth was said to live and grow, substances found inside it were given similar characteristics. Thus, it was believed that metals grew and propagated themselves with the help of the stars. By the time of the Greeks, the doctrine was firmly established, and gold was said to "spread itself through the earth's crust like the roots of trees," metals were explained as "subterranean plants," and minerals and ores were supposedly born from seed.[32]

The Influence of Astrology

The original explanations of how such objects grew were usually couched in astrological terms. It was said these earth substances were formed by the occult influences of the sun, planets, and fixed stars. The brilliance and radiance of certain gems no doubt reminded the ancients of the dazzling spectacle of a glittering sky. Since any correlation found in those days so often meant causation, the link was easily established in the imagination of the ancients.

The Different Elements

Once two elements were "wed," it was necessary to account for the location of various ores and precious stones in certain areas and their absence in others. Obvious differences in the materials themselves also had to be explained. An elaborate system was soon concocted, attributing various influences to certain planets, constellations, and other astral occurrences. For example, the element mercury in some ways resembled the swiftness of the planet of the same name and was thus said to be produced by the influences of that body. Similarly, the moon's soft color resembled silver and was said to influence the formation of that element. In the thirteenth century, a classic medieval work noted, "No bodies, animal, vegetable, or mineral can be generated on or within the earth by a mere association of the elements, but there must be in addition an infusion of the influences of the heavens."[33] One historian of the geological sciences observed that "the Aristotelian theory of the origin of stones and metals through the radiation of celestial influences upon the earth, became the commonly accepted doctrine . . . and was accepted by almost all writers . . . down to the end of the sixteenth century."[34]

The Sun and the Making of Gold

The main catalyst in all these productions was said to be rays from the sun, and—though it was supposed to assist in all processes—the sun was said to be the sole influence in the making of gold.[35] The belief persisted well into the eighteenth century, during which one author wrote (in 1759): "Thus we see that gold which is the most perfect of all metals comes most abundantly in hot climates, silver, copper, and lead require less heat in their formation and come in cooler lands."[36]

Many sources went so far as to suggest that it was useless to look for gold in colder regions.[37] In fact, the theory was so widely accepted that the cultural makeup of the entire hemisphere was altered. As George Godwin relates, the Spanish relinquished all claims to American waters north of the Gulf of California, including the entirety of British Columbia, because Spain was "preoccupied with the quest for gold and the commonly held theory that the nearer the equator, the better the chances of finding it."[38]

Further, not only did the sun or planets purportedly influence the formation of elements buried in the earth, they were also presumed to implant in these elements certain virtues that could be passed to their owners. To the emerald was ascribed potent curative powers, and Julius Caesar built up a collection of the gems for that purpose.[39] In similar unknown ways, coral was said to promote abundant harvest, and amethysts were claimed to preserve individuals from intoxication. The onyx was said to produce hate, strife, and bloodshed (wearing a sardonyx at the same time counterbalanced that influence), while sapphires supposedly promoted vast medicinal, magical, and spiritual powers. Every stone, ore, and fossil was said to influence its owner in some way.[40] The addition of engravings (or sigils) on the gems was supposed to magnify their virtues.[41]

The Role of Water in the Formation of Stone

Ancient teachings regarding stones reveal an almost universal belief that water or some other liquid was responsible for their formation. This theory was followed earnestly by such men of science as Thales, Strabo, Van Helmont, and Boyle. It was not disproved until 1770.[42] In the days prior to its demise, its proponents could point to such "evidence" for the concept as water dripping from the ceiling of caves and islands rising from the sea. Those who could not accept water as the source of stone formation believed there was some type of coagulating fluid within the earth that solidified into stone.[43] Another theory proposed that there were male and female stones within the earth and that infant rocks were the seed of parent stones.[44]

There were always some thinkers who shed light in the darkness, and any good history of science will trumpet their achievements. But it should be understood that no one came close to our modern concepts. Even the greatest minds made multitudes of errors. Sarton describes it well: "We must not be surprised when we come across some irrational sayings."[45]

The Description of the Mountains

Other features of the earth also drew the attention of early thinkers. Mountains tower majestically into the skies, as if daring to touch the fabric of heaven. Many peaks or ranges are enshrouded in mist or clouds and covered with snow. Some belch forth fire and smoke. Mountains fill men's hearts with the mysterious—the sound of boulders dancing down canyon sides, the eerie noise of winds rushing through the crevices or racing up and down the rocky heights. Both danger and beauty give an aura of life to mountain formations.

In antiquity, like the earth itself, mountains were regarded as living entities, deities, or dwelling places of gods and spirits.[46] It was common for worship and reverence to be offered either to the mountain or to a spirit supposedly dwelling on its heights. Like the stones found on or below the earth's surface, these huge edifices were believed to possess certain virtues that could be passed along to those who lived in their shadows. In some instances, magically acquired blessings were said to come to anyone who merely looked at these peaks.

In addition to these beliefs, most ancient writers also believed in the existence of super mountains (usually found at the center of the flat earth), which were said to tower thousands of miles into the sky. Some societies even taught that night was caused by the sun's movement behind one of these giant peaks.

Errors Regarding Water

Even today, the great oceans of our planet remain shrouded in darkness and mystery. In many respects more is known about a satellite 240,000 miles away than is known about the depths of the earth's oceans. It is thus not surprising that our ancestors found these untamed depths foreboding. The awesomeness and immensity of the "great waters," coupled with their seemingly capricious moods, swept many an ancient thinker into error.

The Living Water

Early civilizations saw in the oceans the same evidence of life they attributed to the solid portions of earth. The rhythmic rise and fall of the tides seemed similar to the breathing process in animal life.[47] The variableness of the seas suggested changes that were visible in other life forms. Some cultures elevated water to the pedestal of deity. To the Babylonians, "water was divine and holy, and . . . was worshiped as a god. . . . It acted as a divine power in decisions by ordeal, and in it flowed the blood of the gods."[48] Water was also sacred to the Egyptians and was granted the characteristics of a deity.

Sacrifices were offered to this "living" water; though the usual gifts were bulls and horses, it was not uncommon for humans to be sacrificed.[49] Old records of human sacrifices to rivers, lakes, springs, and seas testify to the almost universal nature of these beliefs in antiquity. Accounts of such offerings to the Tiber, the Ganges, the Yellow, and the Nile rivers abound in early literature.[50]

The Origin of Water

The origin, or source, of water was also of great interest to the ancients. To the Egyptians, water was the eternal element that had always existed. In their mythologies, water gave birth to the gods, the heavens, and the earth.[51] Babylonian philosophers agreed.[52] Even later, when the answer to the question of water's origin became more "scientific," the proposals were nothing more than fables couched in natural terms. The Persians held that all water, including that which was in the heavens, originated at the head of the Persian Gulf.[53] Aristotle gave no better explanation than that all water originated in the high mountains "in the north" and flowed downhill into Europe and Asia.[54]

Misconceptions About the Ocean Floor

Sea floors were thought to be smooth, sandy, and lacking any unusual geographical features. As Corliss explains, "Prior to 1900,

In antiquity human sacrifices were offered to the gods or spirits of rivers. One of those who received such offerings was the Spirit of the Yellow River, shown here. Courtesy, C. A. S. Williams, *Outlines of Chinese Symbolism and Art Motives,* Dover Publications, Inc.

most geologists had conceived the ocean floor to be featureless."[55] Aristotle (in the *Meteorologica*) and other Greek philosophers thought of the oceans as relatively shallow, sterile bodies. Still others chased the other extreme and asserted that the great depths were infinite. Seemingly there was no middle ground. Cultures that believed the oceans to be relatively shallow usually thought of them as a giant river, Oceanus, which encircled the earth and was itself enclosed by a ring of mountains at the edge of the world.[56]

Finally, throughout antiquity, the oceans were envisioned as homogeneous entities. The underwater characteristics of the oceans were thought to be identical, whether five feet or five hundred miles from the shoreline, and whether two feet or two thousand feet beneath the surface. The presence of currents was totally unknown.

Errors Regarding Weather Phenomena

Of all the natural phenomena, lightning was perhaps the most terrifying to ancient cultures. Accompanied by loud, booming noises, it streaked from one part of a stormy sky to another. Often it darted from heaven's portals to strike the earth with blinding, unpredictable destruction. Even in modern times, lightning inspires awe and fear. Not surprisingly, records from earlier civilizations indicate that these "magic" thunderbolts were ascribed to non-naturalistic causes. It was believed that each thunderbolt was deliberately prepared for a specific act or purpose.

Lightning as Missiles from the Gods

In Egypt, Babylon, Canaan, Persia, Assyria, India, Greece, Rome, and the Scandanavian countries, these bolts were always assumed to be missiles hurled by the gods. Seemingly the only difference between the diverse cultures was the name of the fireballer. In Egypt, he was called Seth; in Canaan, Baal-Hadad; in India, Indra; in Greece, Zeus; in Rome, Jove or Jupiter; in Scandanavia, Thor. But in every culture lightning was said to be either a sign of a god's displeasure or a specific punishment.[57] Earlier Chinese cultures believed the lightning itself to be divine. There, lightning was seen as the female counterpart of the god of thunder, and its purpose was to find the targets of the god's displeasure and flash light on them so the god's wrath would not be wasted on the wrong subject. The god of thunder presumably lacked either intelligence or good vision! In any case, lightning was said to assist mankind by preventing the god of thunder from indiscriminately blasting everything in the vicinity.[58]

Magical Control of Lightning

Some ancient civilizations believed they could control lightning through magical charms and ceremonies,[59] while others believed it could be produced—or commanded—by imitating its appearance on a smaller scale. Hence, sticks and flints were rubbed together to produce sparks, which were supposed to summon lightning.[60] On the other hand, some cultures considered anything that imitated thunder or lightning to be sacrilegious; Virgil and others tell of those who supposedly lost their lives for such incursions into the realms of the gods.[61]

Objects struck by lightning were almost universally set apart by early man. Some believed these objects to be sacred and made them places of worship and sacrifice. The Greeks, for instance, regularly marked off areas struck by lightning as consecrated to Zeus and erected altars to offer sacrifices at these locations.[62]

Others viewed such sites with dread and attempted to remove all evidence that lightning had struck the area. These places were then taboo and were avoided at all cost. Roman tradition, for instance, did not permit the repairing of houses damaged by

Belief that storms could be produced through magic persisted almost unscathed well into the Middle Ages. This illustration appeared on the title page of Ulrich Molitor's *De lanijs et Phitonicis Mulieribus* in 1489. It shows witches brewing up a hailstorm. Courtesy, Ernst and Johanna Lehner, *Devils, Demons and Witchcraft,* Dover Publications, Inc.

lightning.[63] Portions of the Roman Empire believed that laurel prevented one's being struck, so even non-religious emperors like Tiberius wore laurel wreaths during storms.

Lightning as an Omen

Importance was also attached to thunderbolts as signs or omens. Among the Babylonians, Assyrians, Persians, Romans, and (to a lesser degree) the Greeks, there was a widespread belief that lightning was sent to deliver a message to mortals from the gods. And, as was true with the practice of divination in regard to health, detailed traditions emerged that categorized and explained the meaning of various strokes of lightning.[64] Lightning in the east was regarded as a favorable sign; in the west it was considered unfavorable. Its appearance on certain days of the week was said to bring warnings to specific classes of people. Lightning on the day of Roman elections was sufficient to cancel them.[65]

Greek Explanations Fall Short

Greek thinkers advanced theories relating to lightning that were at best "crude" and "inadequate."[66] Xenophon traced the origin of lightning to "glowing clouds."[67] Aristotle believed that exhalations from the earth caused the aerial fireworks and confidently proclaimed that movement of the bolts was "always downward."[68] He also argued that thunder occurred prior to lightning.[69] Other Greek naturalists, Empedocles and Anaxagoras, argued that lightning escaped from clouds that were on fire. They disagreed only on the mechanism that supposedly produced these "fire clouds."[70]

One of the more interesting incidents of antiquity centers around the claim of at least one ruler, Salmoneus of Elis, to be equal or superior to Jupiter, the god of lightning. This regal wit ordered the construction of machines capable of producing loud noises and bright flashes of light. He then ordered his soldiers to bang their swords and shields during thunderstorms to prove that he could make more noise than the actual celestial events. He died early in his reign—after being struck by lightning.[71]

Theories Regarding Rain

Usually associated with the aerial fireworks display was the cooling rain that brought life to the parched earth below. Nourishing the earth with its water, the rain left in its path trees, flowers, and crops that seemed greener and stronger, an atmosphere that was cleansed of haze and smoke, and a smell of freshness in the air. After the summer rains, all life forms seemed to venture into the open in numbers and variety much larger than before. It is no wonder the ancients worshiped the rain.

Through centuries of recorded history, many theories were forwarded to explain the great miracle of rainwater and how it reached the living forms that required its presence for their very survival. Unfortunately, as one of the great surveys of the theories of rain has shown, no theory prior to the seventeenth century even approximated the truth.

One historian of science has recorded, "Probably everything written . . . before the seventeenth century ought to be classified as speculation rather than theory. . . . the mental constructions in antiquity were . . . often very superficial."[72] He concluded that all the earlier theories could be totally ignored without any loss to scholarship. A complete list of the items, events, and personages believed capable of magically producing rain is far beyond the scope of this work. Perhaps a representative sample will suffice.

1. *Producing Rain Through Mimicry.* Imitating rain, clouds, and the elements of storms was commonly thought to be effective in rainmaking. Water was sprinkled on the ground or even tossed in the air, clouds of dust and smoke were manufactured in hopes of bringing real clouds, loud noises were made by beating on drums or rolling rocks down hillsides and mountains, and bright flashes of light were concocted by whatever means available.[73] All this was done to prompt the real thing to leave the skies and join its likeness on the earth.

2. *Oriental Ideas Regarding the Production of Rain.* Oriental ideas were equally magical in their approach. One concept declared that spirit creatures, while not necessarily able to produce rain, were able to prevent its occurrence. The argument ran something to the effect that the spirits' bodies were unburied and therefore would be uncomfortable in rainy weather. Spirits were said to block rainfall until their bodies were properly interred.[74]

Others believed that certain rules and/or other gods prevented rain, and they had to be punished by being locked up or sent

In ancient times many superstitions prevailed regarding the cause and production of rainfall. Some people believed it could be produced through magic. Others used mimicry and tried to "stab" holes in the clouds with spears to allow the rain to fall, as pictured here. Courtesy, Hart Pictorial Archives.

into exile until rain fell. Presumably the gods could be punished in a physical way by man.[75] Other ideas regarding the production of rain ranged from tossing impurities into springs,[76] to tying a frog to a stake with its mouth open, to forcing young women to plow fields at night *aux naturelle.*[77]

3. *Greek Theories of Rain.* When Greek scientists attempted to explain air, wind, and rain on a natural basis, they, too, failed. The crucial mistake that doomed their theories was their belief that earth, fire, air, and water were the only elements of nature and that these elements were, to a degree, interconvertible.

Based on such a belief, clouds were easily perceived as thickened air, and rain that fell from the skies was believed to change into earth.[78] The importance of precipitation in producing streams was minimized. Aristotle argued that mountains soaked up air and transformed that air into underground water. This noted philosopher also believed that winds and air were different entities altogether.[79]

Those who disagreed with such theories usually argued for more outlandish ones. The illustrious Seneca submitted to his readers that wind was, in fact, air in motion. He then proposed, however, that the wind was expelled from the interior of the earth by a literal breathing process.[80]

Summary

It is little wonder that modern readers are informed that "classical meteorology did not get very far."[81] Hindered by the lack of meaningful instruments and equipment, our forebears ventured forth into the unknown without a light. It was only natural that so often they were hopelessly lost in a wilderness of error.

19

The Magic of the Rocks

Having generally charted the course of the physical sciences throughout antiquity, examination of the sacred literature in that regard is now appropriate. The issue again will be whether these non-biblical writings contain "proof" that imply supernatural guidance is hidden behind their pronouncements or whether the musings therein suggest that their authors were driven solely by fallible human intelligence and imagination. The evidence continues to point to the latter hypothesis.

Errors in the Hindu Writings

Perhaps the most obvious errors are incorporated into the *Vedas* and *Upanishads* of the Hindu religion. Indeed, the very foundation of these sacred writings is that "all the objects and phenomena of nature with which man is surrounded, are animate and divine."[1] Building on this belief, these books record that the earth, clouds, rain, rivers, seas, and rocks are alive. Since these features were alive (and, to an extent, divine), they were also viewed as legitimate objects of worship or sacrifice. The rituals ranged from a simple prayer or its equivalent to the supreme offering of life itself—human life, in some cases. This was sometimes considered necessary, for "it was believed that the Earth-spirit needed to be refreshed with human blood."[2]

That spirit, thus refreshed, was considered able to give life to others. For example, the custom of cremating dead children and burying their ashes was followed because it was believed the Earth-spirit could give new life to the remains.[3] Similar teachings are found regarding other aspects of nature.[4] Although such beliefs might not exactly be labeled as pantheism,[5] the failure to differentiate between life and non-life has made the Hindu books espouse, at the very least, a close cousin of that doctrine.

In addition, Hindu writings abound with mistakes in their conception of the physical sciences. The earth is described as wheel-shaped[6] with four continents radiating outward from a giant central mountain. This earth is said to be eternal as well[7] and to have produced most of the universe.[8] Actual rivers are said to flow in the atmosphere and celestial areas just as they do on the earth,[9] and they are supposedly able to protect their worshipers and aid in conquering enemies.[10] Clouds are spoken of as the literal fortresses of aerial demons[11] that are made of metal[12] or stone,[13] as are thunderbolts,[14] whereas the ocean is supposed to be the source of lightning.[15]

Hindu authors also subscribed to the idea that certain stones or gems passed along valuable characteristics to those that possessed them (see previous chapter). Owners of "pressing stones" were supposedly brought much wealth and offspring by keeping these powerful stones around their person. The stones were also said to be able to repel demons.[16] The *Rig-Veda* proclaimed these stones to be "immortal" and "unaging,"[17] a concept that is demonstrably false, even as to weight, size, and other measurable physical properties.

All told, Hindu scripture writers fell victim to most of the errors common to the physical sciences at their time of compilation. Before leaving the Sanskrit writings, one other doctrine deserves attention—the preoccupation of these books with the belief that humans can control the natural world by magic. These beliefs were so entwined in Hindu culture that the magician's thread seems woven into the fabric of their scriptures. The *Upanishads,* according to learned authorities, "are charged with magical notion."[18] Image-filled hymns of the *Rig-Veda* openly teach "belief in magical power independent of the gods."[19] The *Yayur-Veda* instructs priests to be magicians by "influencing the powers of nature by the use of spells and other expedients of sorcery."[20] The *Atharva-Veda* contains an entire compendium of "maleficent spells," and the *Code of Manu* is equally magical in its approach.[21]

Magical Rainmaking

Rain is said to be guaranteed through sacrifice, whether or not the gods wish it.[22] It can be produced by imitation, such as pouring water on the ground or by mimicking clouds through the production of smoke.[23] It is also said that life-giving waters can be demanded through the medium of certain aquatic plants and animals.[24] One example occurs in the *Rig-Veda,* where readers are told that rain can be produced by tying a frog, with its mouth propped open, to a rod or branch of a certain tree while singing, "Send, O frog, the jewel of water!" The rationale seems to be that the gods would take pity on the poor creature roasting in the sun and cover it with rain.[25]

Should both sacrifice and the big-mouthed frog prove ineffectual, other magical inducements were available. The followers of Krishna, for example, sent 108 young maidens to milk 108 holy cows in the temple of Govindji and then requested the same females to plow the fields in the dead of night wearing nothing but a smile.[26]

Magical Control of Storms and Lightning

Instructions found in the *Atharva-Veda* direct priests to confront approaching storms "armed to the teeth with a bludgeon, a sword, and a firebrand" while chanting a magical formula.[27] If that method failed, or if the priest was blown over or struck by lightning, an offering of homage was suggested as appeasement.[28]

The naive imperfection of these methods is aptly illustrated in a declaration that if objects were still struck by thunderbolts, any object so struck became magical and served as protection against further bolts. We can conclude that in this regard the Hindu books are no more accurate than is the myth that lightning never strikes twice in the same place.

Magical Use of Stones

As mentioned above, a belief that magical attributes of stones and gems may be transferred to their owners also surfaced in Hindu scripture. For example, the pearl was said to ward off

The Lord of the Rain, the Parjanya of the Vedas, was also believed by the Chinese to control rainfall. Courtesy, C. A. S. Williams, *Outlines of Chinese Symbolism and Art Motives,* Dover Publications, Inc.

demons, disease, and poverty,[29] and gold was thought to secure a long life.[30]

Errors in Buddhist Doctrines

Buddhist writings are as error-prone as the Hindu texts and, like the *Vedas,* show extreme misconceptions of the earth, which is flat, according to these documents. Earth is said to have a mountain 84,000 leagues high at its center. Eight rings of mountains and seven circular oceans surround this super mountain, and humanity is supposed to reside on four continents in the outermost ocean. These continents float freely on the waters of the ocean.[31] One sacred book espouses the commonly held mistake that animals shake the earth to produce earthquakes—at least the big ones. Small tremors are said to be caused by underground beings who knock on their roofs because they are lonely.[32]

Writers of the Buddhist canon ascribe life to numerous nonliving objects. Lightning is animated,[33] as are mountains[34] and possibly the oceans.[35] The rainbow is said to be a rain-dragon.[36] In these texts, unique abilities and influences are attributed to objects that do not possess such traits. One reference informs readers that the willow is capable of causing rain and adherents are provided with proper methods to use in time of drought.[37]

Errors in Taoist Literature

The *Tao-Te-Ching* and other sacred literature of the Taoist practitioners are equally lacking in accuracy. Taoist references to mountains use the designation *shen,* a term reserved for benevolent deities[38] and indicating that mountains were regarded as living entities. Since evil spirits, demons, and other malign beings were believed to dwell in these mountain regions, they were not crossed except on certain ritual days.[39]

Like their contemporaries, Taoist writings ascribed magical influences, both good and bad, to almost every inanimate object. Hills and mountains supposedly deflected the evil influences that were borne on the winds or carried to earth through other mediums.[40] They also allowed benevolent influences to reach the population. Lightning, thought to be a work of evil, was given the characteristics of life.[41] As mentioned, Taoist teachings regarded the rainbow as a deadly rain-dragon, and the literature informed their readers that merely pointing a finger at a rainbow was dangerous and could incur the spirit's wrath.[42]

Errors in Confucian Texts

Similar errors fill the Confucian writings. They postulate that many inanimate objects were alive and later deified those objects

Lei Kung, the god of thunder, assisted by Tien Mu, the goddess of lightning. It was believed that Tien Mu flashed light on intended victims to enable her colleague to launch his deadly bolt with accuracy. Courtesy, C. A. S. Williams, *Outlines of Chinese Symbolism and Art Motives,* Dover Publications, Inc.

as worthy of worship. Confucian texts also speak of sacrifices to "Heaven and Earth, to all the famous hills and great streams under the sky, the five mountains and the four rivers . . . to the spirits of the land and grain, to the famous hills and great streams." The books also record that Confucius "extended his worship to a host of spirits."[43] This literature speaks of so many inanimate objects as being alive that a mere listing would be sufficient for a pamphlet in itself. Like other ancient texts already considered, these writings impart magical influences to a variety of items in the environment. Records abound stressing the need to build houses and cities in locations where the influences of these magical materials occur.[44]

In discussing meteorological information in the Confucian (and Taoist) writings, Needham agrees with eminent Oriental scholars that such knowledge "never advanced beyond the stage of peasant proverbs."[45] A significant part of the *I Ching*, the "omen text," abounds in examples of homey wisdom. That some of the proverbs contain a germ of truth might be expected. That many do not could be equally anticipated. Elsewhere, references in both the *Shu Ching*[46] and the *Shih Ching*[47] imply that heaven (the area where the stars are located) causes rain. Other so-called religious materials trudge off into the same darkness. Time after time, statements are brought to light that show the authors to have been mere men, entrapped by their own foibles and frailties and by the primitive state of technology at the time.

Errors in Zoroastrian Writings

Other Oriental scriptures that fall prey to erroneous concepts are the writings of the Zoroastrian faith, which contain many statements imputing life to non-living materials. Fire, for example, is considered sacred and worthy of worship.[48]

In these writings, descriptions of other natural phenomena such as mountains are nothing more than reflections of the prevailing views of that day and demonstrate no evidence of their authors' ability to sift the valid from the absurd. All mountains, it is said, have their roots in one great mountain, Alburz, which stands at the center of the earth. There is no scientific validity for this contention, of course.

Also included are statements that mountains ward off the wind and demons, provide a resting place for rain clouds, and supply numerous influences for good to humanity. Presumably, it is the belief in all these influences that led composers of the Zoroastrian scriptures to teach that mountains themselves were sacred. They were so highly regarded that after childbirth women were forbidden to look at one.[49]

To a limited extent, the sun, moon, and earth are also held worthy of worship and praise, as they are in other Oriental religions.[50] Zarathustra notes in passing that the hope of a future resurrection hinges on committing the body to the divine earth-spirit.[51] The thesis that there was some type of special, supernatural knowledge behind the Zoroastrian scriptures is easily refuted by noting their obvious inaccuracies.

Errors in Shinto Scriptures

Shinto texts recommend magical tricks to produce rain. In one reference, pouring water on a certain stone is said to bring rainfall.[52] Elsewhere, the writings advise that rain will develop if an artificial dragon constructed of straw, weeds, bamboo, and magnolia leaves is marched behind a priest to a specified waterfall and thrown in.[53] The books also provide a way to ward off an eclipse of the sun. During such events, jewels are to be hung from branches of the sacred *cleyera,* fires are to be lit, and roosters are to be coerced into crowing. Such activities, the readers are advised, will reverse the eclipse.[54]

Of even greater significance than these errors is the underlying belief that the many facets of nature are animated and divine. As one scholar observed, the "national religion of Japan is not, as was for a long time believed, a cult of ancestors, accompanied secondarily by a vague nature-worship; it is essentially a cult of nature, complete and precise, to which a much less important cult of ancestors only gradually came to be added. . . . The nature-gods constitute almost the whole pantheon of the ancient Shinto."[55]

Thus, storms, wind, rain, thunder, and fire are all seen as living entities.[56] In a similar vein, the sea, land, mountains, and rivers were ascribed life as well.[57] To see that the earth was viewed as a living creature, one must look no further than the *Ji-matsuri* ("earth-festival"), which instructs that it is necessary to placate the earth before disturbing the surface of the ground in any way. Even the name *Ohi-kuni-dama* means "great-land-spirit."[58]

Likewise, Shinto teachings on the cause of earthquakes were fashioned after those of other Far East cultures, though altered slightly to bring them in line with Japanese culture. Movements of the earth are said to be caused by a great monster that resides in the nether world. Only through rituals and sacrifice can this monster be appeased.[59]

Errors in Mormon Documents

Even the supposedly inspired Mormon revelations of the nineteenth century blunder into at least one of the same mistakes committed in antiquity: the earth is spoken of as living. On November 8, 1857, Heber C. Kimball, who claimed to speak with God's authority and by divine revelation, declared, "I live on an earth that lives. . . . Well, it is truth. . . . If a woman will not produce when she is dead, then the earth cannot produce living things if it were dead. . . . Where did this earth come from? From its parent earths."[60] Later and more current teachings from other Mormons, also claiming divine revelation, have backed up, rather than contradicted, the testimony. "The earth was created first as a spirit," one prophet added, while the tenth president of the Latter-Day Saints said: "The earth is living and must die."[61]

Summary

In summary, all the non-biblical scriptures fail to avoid the erroneous concepts common to their time regarding knowledge of the earth sciences. Through these texts runs a thread of animism that imputes life to the earth and to virtually every physical object associated with it. There is also an almost universal tendency toward overestimating the value of physical objects and their influences on other objects, including mankind. Magical rituals are rampant. Rain is misunderstood, as are most weather-related phenomena. On and on the list goes. While the specific indictments may vary, the overall verdict is the same—there was no supernatural guidance behind the writing of the non-biblical scriptures.

20

Quite a Foundation

After combing the pages of other documents for evidence that their writers received guidance from a supernatural source and finding no substantiation for such a thesis, we must now make the same demands of the writers of the Judeo-Christian Bible. What evidence, if any, implies that they had divine guidance when they speak regarding the earth? Do they commit the typical errors made by scientists and philosophers of the era in which these texts were written? Are there statements within the Bible that were unknown and unknowable by men at the time they were composed?

Biblical Writers Avoid Errors of Their Contemporaries

Amazingly, Bible writers do not follow their peers in perpetuating the mistakes of their day. That itself is significant. Only the biblical writings—like a towering, solitary mountain peak in the middle of a vast plain—refuse to ascribe life or deity to nature. Isolated in an era of misconceptions about the physical world are authors who avoided the cultural errors regarding earthquakes, mountains, rain, and lightning.

Anyone who searches the Bible carefully will be amazed at the rationality of the material. One scholar who did so came away from his study concluding, "There is a chaste, wholesome, refreshing view of nature in the Bible. . . ."[1] An earlier author was impressed by the lack of "animal mythology, plant mythology, superstitions, and fantastic notions in the Scriptures at a time when such were 'characteristic' of all the peoples surrounding Israel.'[2] Not one of the errors in the earth sciences described in previous chapters was allowed to grow in the biblical text. Some will find this to be yet another coincidence or lucky guess. But, realistically, how far can one push the "luck theory" before it loses credibility?

Any good text on statistical probability will note that the more "coincidences" one must utilize to defend a position, the greater the likelihood that the position is bogus. There is an upper limit beyond which luck cannot explain the evidence. To avoid reaching that limit, one must be able to explain not only why biblical writers did not play follow-the-leader with their peers in medicine and astronomy, but why they were "free from the grotesque absurdity which disfigures the . . . geology of their contemporaries."[3]

The Correct Understanding of Nature

An overview of the biblical text reveals its writers to be far in advance of humanly discoverable scientific knowledge when speaking of the physical universe. Nature was viewed by Bible writers as a purposed, meaningful entity. That is, it was understood as operating according to certain inexorable laws and, at the same time, was conceived of as incapable of self-existence.

Further, by attributing the existence of nature to a higher force, the biblical writers avoided the magical beliefs of others and argued vehemently against the worship of nature. Finally, through these authors man is encouraged to take control of nature, not by means of spells, potions, and hocus-pocus, but by using intelligent management.

Such a view is basically the modern concept, though some would deny that nature is "purposed" or created. Most, however, do find nature to some extent "meaningful," and all but a few errant philosophers are aware that it does operate according to set patterns or laws. All of modern science is predicated upon the regularity of nature and the belief that an event that happened once will happen again, with faithful replication of the same conditions. Or, as one author has noted, "science depends on the assumption that the arm of coincidence is *not* long, but quite short; that no explanation which falls back on highly improbable coincidence . . . can claim to be scientific."[4] Penicillin—along with other great miracle drugs, advances in medical technology, vast promises of future research in such areas as DNA, genetics, microbiology, space travel, and electronics—were all made possible because nature is orderly, not restive. Progress in physics, chemistry, biology, and astronomy has been possible simply because the natural world *is* predictable.

Modern society sometimes finds it difficult to believe there was ever a time when such was not the predominant worldview. Unfortunately, such a time did exist, for when early Bible writers prepared their records for posterity, "nature" was viewed as highly unpredictable and prone to fits of madness and irrationality. All features in the world were thought of as living entities, and many were seen as vacillating and capricious deities. Centuries passed before the first Greek scientist-philosophers planted the seeds of current secular understanding. Once planted, those first seeds required nearly two centuries before they took root.[5]

Yet, in that milieu, the biblical writers consistently avoided the errors of the ancients and matter-of-factly described nature in a way consistent with modern knowledge.[6] In the first book of the Bible, notice is drawn to the regularity of natural occurrences (Gen. 8:22; 9:1–17). Weather-related phenomena, the sea, the mountains, and the heavens are alternately described as abiding by preset regulations (Job 28:25–26; 38:8–11; Ps. 104; Prov. 8:29; Jer. 5:22–24; 8:7; 31:35–36; 33:20). It is that conception that provides the basis for scientific investigations.

The Foundation of Modern Science

As one author realized, "Belief in the fundamental stability of the universe contributed significantly to the rise of modern science." He then listed the attitude that biblical writers expressed toward nature as one of six keys necessary for the birth of the scientific principle.[7]

Other modern-day historians of science agree. One suggests:

> The confrontation of Graeco-Roman culture with biblical religion engendered, after centuries of tension, a new science. This science preserved the indispensable parts of the ancient heritage (mathematics, logic, methods of observation and experimenta-

> tion), but it was directed by different social and methodological conceptions, largely stemming from a biblical world-view. . . . whereas the ingredients of science may have been Greek, its vitamins and hormones were biblical.[8]

A well-known physicist adds, "The concept of strict and generally valid laws of nature could hardly have arisen without the Christian concept of creation. . . . I called modern science a legacy, I might even have said a child, of Christianity."[9]

Thus, there is evidence that the foundations of modern science are based on biblical doctrines. As we have already seen, those doctrines are amazingly advanced for the times in which they appeared. Truly, "When we read in Psalm 19 'the heavens declare the glory of God, and the firmament showeth his handiwork,' we hear a voice which mocks the Egyptians and Babylonians[10] [because] in total contradiction to pagan religion, nature is not a deity to be feared and worshiped, but a work of God to be admired, studied, and managed. . . . In the Bible, God and nature are no longer both opposed to man, but God and man together confront nature. The denial that God coincides with nature implies the denial that nature is god-like."[11]

Craigie adds, "The Babylonian hymns to Shamash, the Egyptian hymns to various sun-gods, even the glorious hymn to Aten, differ in one remarkable respect from Psalm 19. In those psalms, nature itself is deified. . . . Yet, in Psalm 19, nature is personified, not deified."[12] In a similar vein, Kidner writes regarding Psalm 19: "If it glances at mythology, it refutes it!"[13]

Avoiding Errors in Earth Science

Pitfalls biblical writers managed to avoid

1. Belief in a living earth
2. Deification of nature
3. Astrological influences regarding nature
4. Magical control of nature
5. Demonological influences in nature
6. Incorrect understandings of earthquakes, storms, oceans, mountains, lightning, and other physical phenomenon

21

Waste Not, Want Not

Biblical directions charged man with the responsibility of taking control of nature and using it wisely for his own good. In the first chapter of the Bible, God is recorded as saying that man was to have dominion over all the earth (Gen. 1:26). Later, the psalmist acknowledged God's power and purpose: "Thou madest him [man] to have dominion over the works of thy hands: thou hast put all things under his feet" (Ps. 8:6, KJV). There can be no question of what is meant in either passage. The writers plainly declare that man has supremacy over the earth and that which is found in it.[1]

Although current thinking recognizes the validity of such a concept, the idea was absolutely in opposition to the beliefs of the era in which it first originated among the Bible writings—and even later. Babylonians, Egyptians, Assyrians, Chinese, and the early Greeks were far more interested in pacifying what they believed was an animate, deified nature than in controlling an inanimate, impersonal one. The sacred literature of other prescientific religions stands in marked contrast to the biblical statements. In non-biblical writings one reads of a fickle, changeable nature rather than an environment governed by laws,[2] of the deification of nature rather than studying it,[3] and of the natural world's eternity rather than its limited existence.[4] Societies paid little heed to texts that foreshadowed the enormous opportunities of seizing dominion over nature because "it was not obvious before the days of science that man could ever exert dominion of this scale, but we are realizing that the language is not exaggerated."[5]

Side by side with man's ability to use nature to his advantage were far more numerous admonitions regarding the responsibility to use nature wisely.[6] Biblical authorities repeatedly reminded humanity that it did not own nature and, though given dominion over it, mankind was always to remember that nature belonged to another.

"The earth is the LORD's and everything in it . . ." wrote the psalmist (Ps. 24:1). Though this dictum was popularized by its place in the Jewish book of praise, it merely echoed what had already sounded for hundreds of years (Exod. 9:29 and Deut. 10:14).

The strongest voice for ecological responsibility was raised by Moses centuries before any other.[7] In Exodus, Leviticus, and Deuteronomy, the Israelites were instructed to allow their land to lie uncultivated for one year out of every seven (Exod. 23:10–11; Lev. 25; Deut. 15:1–11). As scholars have observed, this Sabbatical Year, as it came to be known, accrued a "great physical advantage" to the people of Israel in that "the land lay fallow, thus increasing the fruitfulness of the six years of cultivation, especially in that ancient period when the artificial use of fertilizers was unknown."[8]

Though the practice of "resting" the land is not used often in modern times because of the availability of artificial fertilizers, it is scientifically valid. One modern author explained, "If in a wheat-growing country crops are raised year after year and forests and grassland turned into cornfields over a very wide area, the region becomes desiccated, rain ceases, or only falls in great storms that wash away the soil, and the area is blown over with dust and sand. Reclamation is difficult. It was therefore a very wise provision . . . that the land should keep her Sabbaths."[9]

The Sabbatical Year was coupled with the equally unique Year of Jubilee (celebrated on the fiftieth year, or after seven times seven years), which extended the time of release for the soil and added provisions to benefit the poor and release the servants of the Hebrews. These were "remarkable provisions"[10] in the Judeo-Christian heritage, were mentioned "in all Semitic literature, only in the Bible,"[11] and, in comparison to all other laws, show "a unique regard for natural resources."[12] Specific requirements for the Year of Jubilee added immensely to the ecological advancement of the Jewish people. The precepts emphasized caring for the soil and fostered a reverence for life and a sense of dignity and humility unique in ancient days.

Few would argue that these scientifically advanced ideas were rooted solely in the principles of soil chemistry. They had a deeper, religious significance that taught, for instance, that "man is not the sole owner of the soil, and he does not hold property in perpetuity but possesses it in trust with God."[13] As a result, adherence to these laws would preclude any family from becoming perpetually poor. It is this humanitarian aspect of the law that has impressed many authors and seems to be the dominant thrust of the precepts. At the same time, however, it does not detract from their importance to find that viable scientific benefits accrue from adherence to the same commands.[14]

One commentator observed, "The earth was to be saved from the hand of man exhausting its power for earthly purposes as his own property. . . . Israel . . . was to learn . . . that although the earth was created for man, it was not merely created for him to draw out its powers for his own use. . . ."[15] He concluded, "There are perhaps in the ancient world no institutions bearing comparison with the Hebrew year of release and of Jubilee, either in comprehensiveness or loftiness of principle."[16]

Another commentator suggested that the customs arose in Egypt,[17] though frankly admitting that he "can produce no specific evidence on the subject."[18] An exhaustive examination of Egyptian culture failed to uncover any information linking either idea to the Egyptian nation. One may safely infer that Bible writers have once again described scientifically valid concepts far in advance of their later discovery by secular scientists and at a time when such concepts were unknowable by physical means to any of their contemporaries. In this area, too, one is confronted by the big question. Why is the Bible so unique—why do the biblical writers seem to have such vision and foresight?

22

The Pieces of a Puzzle

Humanity's understanding of the great land masses, or continents, has undergone a radical metamorphosis during the twentieth century, a discovery similar in philosophical scope to the one forced on society by the travels of Christopher Columbus nearly a half-millennium ago. Throughout the pre-Columbian era, it was believed that all the great land masses (except Australia) were joined together and had always been so. The mere existence of separate and yet-unknown land masses was not seriously considered. Columbus's voyage in the late fifteenth century wiped the slate clean on that score, and new theories were proposed to try to explain why the Americas were located so far from the other continents. The simplest answer seemed to be that there was no explanation!

It was not until Alfred Wegener published his epochal work in 1912[1] that scientists began to realize that there was evidence that the great land masses were, indeed, at one time shoved together, that the seas were once unified, and that the land had been divided into its current geography after life had appeared.

One popular author explains the newness of the idea:

> . . . the scientists who study the earth have for centuries climbed and poked about with rock hammers, sampling and cataloguing endless varieties of rocks. Until a few years ago, the state of the earth sciences was comparable to the state of chemistry before the theory of the atom or to biology before evolution or genetics.

> In less than a decade, the earth sciences have been altogether shaken by one of the most rapid, thorough, and potentially practical revolutions in the history of science.[2]

Wegener's theory, now known as "plate tectonics," postulates that the earth's original land mass was unified into one continent, usually refered to as Pangaea. That continent divided into Laurasia and Gondwanaland and then into the continents as we know them today. Though Wegener's work was remarkable, the time was ripe for this discovery. Millions of man-hours of research had preceded his thesis, and the seed of truth had been germinating for some time. It is the rest of the story that becomes fascinating.

At least three millennia *before* Wegener, another writer had accurately described the world in its original state. The seas, he wrote, were "gathered to one place" (Gen. 1:9). Several chapters later in the account, casual mention is made that "the earth was divided" (Gen. 10:25), at a time *after* life had first appeared. Such a description fits nicely with the theory of ancient Pangaea, which has become the favorite son of modern geology. It seems as if this ancient writer accurately described the original appearance of the earth. And, keep in mind, these references occurred without millions of man-hours of scientific research and multitudes of facts at the author's disposal.

Though the scientific community generally accepts the major aspects of this land-mass theory, there does seem to be sufficient reason for questioning the validity of the time frame.[3] Creationists who believe the earth is relatively "young"—geologically speaking—would not accept the section of the continental drift theory that incorporates uniformitarian standards which require millions of years for the separation of the continents to occur.[4] Still, the major concept of the splitting of the earth's land mass seems to be supported by the available evidence.

23

Into the Depths

Although 70.8 percent of the earth's surface, or some 139,400,000 square miles, consists of the great oceans, the undersea realm is still described by oceanographers as "virgin territory" and a "great hinterland."[1] The reason is obvious.

Hampered until the modern era by the lack of suitable equipment and know-how, man's exploration of the great depths was generally limited to the ebb and flow of creative imagination or reasoned guesswork. With no solid facts upon which to anchor his creativity, man's efforts to understand the earth's bodies of water were thwarted. Even relatively simple coastal soundings were not carried out with any degree of precision until Juan de la Costa's efforts in 1504. In short, as a direct result of the inability to investigate them firsthand, man believed the ocean bottoms were

> . . . flat, sandy beds like the deserts. Explorers and traders crisscrossed the major oceans for over three hundred years without making an effort to chart the topography over which they travelled. . . . Since those sailors had no navigational need for a knowledge of the water depth in the open sea, the topographic panorama of the ocean bottom remained unknown. It was just assumed that the ocean was deepest in the middle, resembling a saucer or soup dish.[2]

Submarine Canyons

Not until the voyage of H.M.S. *Challenger* in 1873 was the existence of underwater canyons documented by scientific research, though even the scientists aboard the *Challenger* were unaware of what they found. All they passed down to later efforts was an obscure reference to one isolated oceanic depth finding of 4500 fathoms. Perhaps these marine explorers were merely cautious; they may have been afraid that human error was the cause of the one unusual sounding. Perhaps they were afraid that their finding would be rejected for lack of confirmation, or perhaps they were merely unwilling to buck the generally held view of the ocean's flat, sandy bottom. At any rate, the official report of the expedition, which covered some thirty thousand pages in almost fifty volumes, chose to ignore the implications of the finding. It was merely reported in passing as some type of anomaly.

Another quarter-century followed the publication of the *Challenger's* notes before oceanographers finally began to understand what the sea bottom was like.[3] Still, science writers admitted of the ocean floor that "until the 1940s it remained virtually a terra incognito."[4]

Although knowledge of the oceanic depths was almost nonexistent before the modern era, the Bible contains numerous statements in remarkable accord with later discoveries. Scriptural writers made at least three references to the canyons[5] or recesses of the deep (2 Sam. 22:16; Job 38:16; Ps. 18:15) at a time when informed opinion held that the ocean bottoms were flat, sandy, and bowl-like.[6] As in other references to the nature of the universe, no attempt was made to force the concept into the common acceptance of people living in the pre-scientific era. The real purpose of the Scriptures was not to provide scientific enlightenment but to teach spiritual truth. Consequently, the remarks were inserted without discussion or argument. One is simply informed that the seas have canyons.

Modern discoveries provide conclusive proof that deep valleys or canyons cut across the continental shelf in all parts of the globe. These cuts, or canyons, occur in such diverse areas as the Arctic and the Mediterranean as well as in the major oceans.

Many underwater canyons are associated with mouths of rivers such as the Congo, the Indus, the Ganges, the Columbia, the Hudson, the Mississippi, and the Yukon. Still others are totally unconnected with river systems. Some are small. Others are gigantic. Some are short, measuring less than twenty kilometers.

Others, like the ones assocated with the Congo and the Hudson river systems, reach outward for hundreds of kilometers.[7] One mid-ocean canyon winds southward from its origin in the western North Atlantic near Greenland for more than 2,500 kilometers. It averages two to four miles in width and maintains a depth of from fifty to two hundred meters.[8] Such are the canyons or recesses spoken of by biblical writers.

In addition, there are some eighteen trenches sunk into the ocean floors. These trenches have depths in excess of six thousand meters below the level of the ocean.[9] Some have walls steeper than the Grand Canyon. Biblical authorities were certainly accurate when they wrote of the recesses of the deep. Once again, we find valid statements in literature some 2,500 to 3,500 years older than the actual scientific discoveries that verified their existence.[10]

Seamounts

At least one Bible writer also refers to the existence of seamounts or guyots (Jonah 2:3, 6). No other ancient author made any mention that such underwater mountains were located under the waves, though their presence has been widely authenticated in the twentieth century. One scholar added that there "are 10,000 seamounts and guyots in the Pacific alone, some of which rise 10,000 feet above the adjacent ocean floor."[11] Can one merely say that these biblical references are yet more lucky guesses and coincidences? It hardly seems possible.

Springs of the Sea

Bible writers also mention "springs of the sea" (Job 38:16, "springs of the great deep" (Gen. 7:11; cf. 8:2), and "fountains of the deep" (Prov. 8:28). These references predate the earliest nonbiblical source of such statements by almost one thousand years.[12] During the periods when Moses, Job, and Solomon first wrote of such springs, the authoritative voices of the day, whether in China, Babylon, Assyria, or Egypt, were asserting that only rain and rivers filled the oceans. The idea of underwater fountains seems to have eluded the average thinker of the era. Today the presence of such springs is taken for granted by the scientific establishment.

Undersea outlets of fresh water are found near every major continent. They are common in the Mediterranean off the coast of Greece, Italy, Syria, and Israel. Immense freshwater springs are also located near Australia and several South Sea islands. The United States Geological Survey has charted their presence in the Atlantic off New England near the Georges Bank and near the Georgia coastline. How much water flows from these giant springs? Estimates vary, but the latest measurements indicate that as much as 30×10^{19} tons (30 million trillion tons) of water are trapped in the rocks of the earth. A sizable percentage of this vast storehouse seeps into the seas via these submarine springs each year.[13] Again, Bible writers were correct in their statements regarding the oceans.

Ocean Currents

Old Testament writers described the existence of oceanic "paths" or currents long before equipment to verify such statements had been invented (Ps. 8:8 and 107:23f; Eccles. 1:7; Isa. 43:16). From the earliest days of recorded history, man had been infatuated by the seas and constructed boats and ships in which to explore the great waters and discover their secrets. As early as the Egyptian dynasties, the Phoenicians, according to Strabo, had circumnavigated the African continent. Still, the ancient record speaks only of "near-shore" sailors who cautiously limited their adventures in the foreboding waters, choosing to skirt the coastlines rather than tempt the monsters and terrors of the open seas. For those first seafaring adventurers, the most significant movements of the oceans were the tides. Perhaps that is why early men of science took so long to recognize the existence of the great "ocean rivers." They may never have observed them, or they may have been so preoccupied with the tides that everything about the ocean depths was interpreted in that framework.

Over two millennia passed between the days of the Phoenician navigators and their adventuresome Norsemen counterparts. From the travels of these Viking sailors came more knowledge of the seas. Still, though their long ships plied the waves and their historians recorded their discoveries, there is no evidence that even these hearty travelers were aware of the currents.[14]

Another five centuries passed between the Vikings and Prince Henry and his navigators of Portugal, who are generally credited for first recognizing the existence of the oceanic currents. Once identified, information regarding these phenomena increased substantially. For example, in the fifteenth century, Christopher Columbus confirmed the presence of westward-moving currents in the Atlantic. However, the understanding of these great channels of water was generally inaccurate for at least another three centuries.

In 1575, Thevet argued that currents were merely the outflow of great rivers and eventually dissipated in the oceans. Others believed they were attributable to the pull of the moon. As late as 1667, one writer concluded that the sun caused water immediately underneath the solar orb to evaporate, causing a giant hole in the ocean into which all the waters rushed.[15] Two historians of oceanography, viewing such explanations from the vantage point of twentieth-century technology mused, "Many years were to pass before the great Atlantic circulation of salt waters became known as it is today when we can follow its course on the printed surface of a chart."[16]

Matthew Fontaine Maury, an American naval officer with an

Matthew Fontaine Maury based his belief in the existence of ocean currents on a passage from Psalm 8:8 that spoke of "the paths of the sea." Courtesy, The National Archives.

unrelenting confidence in the Bible, was a pioneer in providing us with an accurate understanding of the great "paths" in the sea. With the Psalms as his guiding inspiration, Maury used his appointment in 1842 as superintendent of the Navy's Depot of Charts and Instruments to gather information about the oceans on a global scale. He compiled the world's first textbook on oceanographic physics—*Physical Geology of the Sea.*[17] It was published in 1855, twenty-five hundred years after the Psalms were written. "There is a river in the ocean," Maury wrote—and the reason he searched for this "river" was not physical evidence but a reference in the Bible.

Much has been learned about the great oceanic currents since Maury's day. The currents show a great deal of variation. They can exist at the surface, below the surface, and even in the ocean depths. It is not uncommon for submarine currents to be found in layers, with one directly underneath another, and simultaneously moving in opposite directions.[18]

Because of the fluidity of their environment, currents are also able to alter their courses to some degree, though reasons why they do so are still uncertain. Why there should be so much diversity in their size and rate of flow is equally obscure. The Florida Current, for instance, flows northward at a rate of seventy million cubic feet of water per second or the equivalent flow of four thousand Mississippi Rivers.[19] Others, like the Cromwell Current, stretch across thirteen thousand miles of the Pacific.[20]

At least one feature of the currents is stable: their association with life forms in the ocean. In ancient times, the generally accepted thesis was that all parts of the oceans were equally habitable by living organisms, since there was no reason to suspect otherwise. Yet, at the time when this was a universally held belief, the psalmist implied that living things were somehow associated with the currents (Ps. 8:8). Modern scholarship confirms that idea.

Over the last century, data from the oceans has inundated labs of marine biologists around the globe. As the data has been examined and analyzed, the connection between the ocean rivers and life in an underwater environment has become more and more obvious.

Currents are responsible for a continual mixing of warm and

cold waters. This "turbulent mixing of waters provides the proper conditions of temperature and food for an outburst of plankton growth."[21] Plankton is the key to life in the seas and has been called the "pasturage and corn land of the sea," a "miniscule botanical garden and zoo," and "nursery of the ocean."[22]

Under the peering eyes of giant microscopes, these miniature life forms burst into an infinite universe of their own. Without sufficient power of movement to swim against the currents, these rapidly multiplying creatures move with the oceanic circulation. As they move, so do the larger forms of ocean life, following the currents to obtain their daily food. Quite literally, plankton has become the true life flow of the ocean river, "for in it there float baby crabs with projecting spines many times the length of their bodies, and the young of spiny lobsters, flat, transparent, and leaflike, with spider-like legs and eyes on stalks. Drifting helplessly along with them are large-eyed, transparent, newly-hatched fishes."[23] Larger schools of fishes and sea life come to these rich feeding stations, and it is here that they find their best chance of survival.

In addition to the temperature control promoted by the currents, the flow of the ocean river provides the turbidity necessary to continually refertilize the vast fisheries that truly swim through the "paths of the seas" (Ps. 8:8). The cold and deep submarine currents constantly bring to the surface waters the chemical nutrients necessary for living organisms to thrive. The upwelling of these underwater rivers serves as a giant pump that drains from the depths the much-needed nourishment for sea life.

These two factors prime the ocean river until it becomes crowded with life. Currents create a beneficial habitat for the great ocean fisheries, while the center of the ocean, devoid of all but minimal circulation, becomes a watery wasteland where there is truly "water, water everywhere" but little life to see. The contrast is striking. Fishing fleets crowd the currents, where thousands of ships fill their holds with the catch—a fisherman's delight. Yet, in the central ocean—the Sargasso Sea—there is no great fleet of trawlers to be found. The sea is calm, undisturbed by currents or the hum of propellers, a calmness betokening death—or at least the absence of most life.

24

Rain, Rain, Go Away, Come Again Another Day

Prior to the seventeenth century, theorizing about the origin of rainfall was drenched either in magic, ridiculous speculation, or false science. It was said that rain originated in response to good-luck charms, amulets, and incantations. It was also said that rain fell when sluice gates were opened in the solid vault of heaven, allowing water to fall from a celestial ocean that encompassed the globe. Another idea argued that plain, simple air (*not* water vapor) was transformed into rainwater. Perhaps the universal lack of agreement among secular scientists of much-earlier time periods explains the difficulty sensed by modern historians of science when they encounter biblical passages on the subject.

Historians document that no correct scientific understanding of rainfall and the water cycle existed prior to the days of French scientists Pierre Perrault and Edme Mariotte. They are aware, of course, that all authors and thinkers during the times when most of the Old Testament was penned put forth nothing but fallacies. While recognizing the errors of our ancestors, they are in sympathy with their lack of adequate equipment with which to make better judgments.

In the middle of this confusion are set numerous biblical references to rainfall, including its source and its origin, that are so simple as to be disarming. Yet, they are also so sublime that experts are sent scampering in all sorts of unlikely directions in an attempt to avoid the obvious—that Bible writers were painstakingly accurate about rain when others of that era were not.

The Bible's earliest recorders correctly note what is obvious to modern man: that rain comes from the clouds, not from magical charms. Now from the simple to the sublime. Where do clouds originate?

The Origin of Rainfall

Amos, writing in the eighth century B.C., explains rainfall on two separate occasions: "Seek the LORD . . . (he who calls for the waters of the sea and pours them out over the face of the land—the LORD is his name . . .)" (Amos 5:6–8; cf. 9:6). Because no one else in those days made such statements, some scholars try to explain them away. One typical explanation suggests, "It is very probable that the passages in the book were inserted much later. . . . If not, it is a most interesting passage."[1]

"Most interesting" indeed, if it was written prior to the modern era—and the evidence strongly suggests that it was. Over two centuries before Amos, Solomon wrote, "All the rivers run into the sea; yet the sea is not full; unto the place from whence the rivers come, thither they return again" (Eccles. 1:7, KJV). Faced with more than one isolated statement in the scriptural record, one historian of science is forced to admit grudgingly, "it may just be possible that about the fifth century B.C. someone in Palestine had at least as clear an understanding . . . as anyone else before A.D. 1750."[2]

In addition to the water cycle, references to lightning and its relation to rainfall are accurately reported by biblical writers centuries before the technology of twentieth-century scientists reached the same conclusions. One of the Scriptures' oldest books reads, "Who hath divided a watercourse for the overflowing of waters, or a way for the lightning of thunder; To cause it to rain on the earth . . ." (Job 38:25–26, KJV). The psalmist later concurred: "He [God] causeth the vapours to ascend from the ends of the earth; he maketh lightnings for the rain . . ." (Ps. 135:7, KJV). A minimum of two basic principles seems to emerge from these passages. First, lightning travels in a "way" or "path." Second, lightning is somehow involved in causing rain. Neither concept is to be found in any other writing prior to the modern era. Current lightning research concurs with both of these biblical observations.

The Movement of Lightning

Within the past few decades, research into the origin and behavior of lightning has been nothing short of brilliant. The current wealth of knowledge is especially impressive when one realizes that: "Modern lightning research began in the latter part of the nineteenth century."[3] Certainly there were some experiments with bolts from heaven prior to that time, as is evidenced by Benjamin Franklin's kite-and-key experiences. But those efforts were scattered and of little importance for the purposes of science. Much is still unknown, naturally, but the state of knowledge in the field is expanding rapidly. And ever-accumulating evidence points toward the validity of biblical statements made thousands of years earlier.

Realization that the flight of "hot thunderbolts" (Ps. 78:48, KJV) was inexorably linked to electrical charges paved the way for verification of Job's observation that lightning follows a set course or path or channel. It was known for many years in the modern era that electricity needed a conductor, and Franklin's experiments demonstrated the electrical nature of lightning. But what "kite strings" in the atmosphere carried the energy from the skies toward its targets below? For nearly two centuries after Franklin's research, lack of suitable technology hampered efforts to find the answer.

Then, in the 1930s, investigators Schonland, Malan, Collens, and Hodges utilized a special camera that made possible time-resolution photographs of an electrical discharge in the skies. By taking additional measurements of electric field intensity charges, they soon isolated their "kite string." It was in the form of a streamer or leader of charged particles that dangled from a cloud.[4] When the streamer came in close proximity (fifty meters) to particles of an opposite charge, the mutual attraction was sufficient to form a conducting medium of charged particles in the air and produce what is commonly called lightning.

That atmospheric "kite string" is now called a channel because electrical current literally runs along a line of particles where currents "may range from a few thousand to 200,000 amperes. Temperatures in the channel are on the order of 30,000 degrees K (50,000 degrees F)."[5] Lightning does travel in paths, just as the biblical writers had implied.

The Link Between Lightning and Rain

Confirmation of lightning's role as rainmaker is not as clear because the meteorological technology has not progressed far enough to isolate the primary cause of rainfall. Scientists have made enough progress, however, to realize that electrification is one necessary ingredient. One key text on cloud formation points out that "the electrical and precipitation processes are indissolubly linked."[6] One of those links is demonstrated by the well-known phenomenon that rainfall intensifies significantly within a minute or so following lightning flashes.[7] Though such has been recognized in part for years, the causative agent was long held to be the thunder and not the lightning. "As long ago as 58 B.C., Lucretius wrote that such gushes of rain were caused by thunder."[8] The idea persisted well into the current era.

As recently as one hundred years ago there were numerous attempts by American rainmakers throughout the western and midwestern states to "sound out" the rain on the parched, dusty fields.[9] A particular type and intensity of noise, the rainmakers averred, would produce significant rainfall. And so artificial noisemakers—cannons, gongs, and whistles—were rolled into place and set into action.

Seldom was there any rain produced by these efforts, and (more likely than not) the rainmakers were chased out of town by another fearful noise—the angered voices of skeptical locals. Still, many believed that earthquakes, volcanic rumblings, and cannonade or artillery made such concussions in the air that rain droplets would be jarred from the skies to fall toward the parched land below.

The "boom-boom theory" of rain, as Spence describes it, was very popular. Napoleon believed it. So did many soldiers who remembered the numerous battles fought during the American Civil War in constant downpours. Soon after those hostilities ceased, civil engineer Edward Powers published a widely read document, *War and the Weather: or, The Artificial Production*

One of America's most famous rainmakers, Charles Hatfield prepares his rainmaking supplies prior to a 1916 attempt in California. His famous tower served as a focal point in many of his efforts. Rather than using artillery or sound, Hatfield attempted to produce rain by chemical mixtures. Courtesy, San Diego Historical Society—Ticor Collection.

of Rain, in which he argued favorably for such a theory, noting that some two hundred battles during the conflict had been fought in the rain. The large number fought in nonrainy weather, however, was conveniently overlooked.

Not until this century did Schonland's ground-breaking study in South Africa push the scientific theory of rain in line with the Bible. Thunder was ruled out. "Agglomeration by acoustic shock is not an efficient process. . . . The acoustic energy available in thunder is not considered sufficient to make a significant contribution," one authority noted. Lightning *is* "sufficient," however:

> Large electrically charged drops in the base of the cloud are considered to be prevented from falling by electrostatic attraction between them and oppositely charged droplets and ice particles higher up in the cloud. . . . When a lightning flash takes place . . . the sustaining electrostatic force is annihilated and the drops start falling to reach the ground after a minute or two.[10]

Additional studies utilizing Centimetric Radar at Grand Bahama Island further supported this position in the 1960s. Scholars today readily admit the need for some electrification in the rainmaking process.

Once more the Bible writers are proven correct centuries after they recorded their observations about the universe. And how is such accuracy to be explained? Must one suffer through the charges of coincidence yet anther time? Is one forced to believe that the Bible was written *after* science discovered these bits of information? Surely no one can argue that the passages were inserted into the Scriptures after the twentieth century!

25

Putting the Pieces Together

The long search for truth goes on, but numerous pieces of our gigantic puzzle have been assembled. As each piece has been carefully examined and placed on the table, an obvious pattern began to emerge. We have seen how the biblical materials are unique. They are no run-of-the-mill religious writings, but—quite the contrary—reveal a remarkable understanding of the universe.

Our simple glimpse into the past revealed man's blurred attempt to understand his world and his own place in the cosmos. That brief glimpse kindled our imagination through a deeper comprehension of the worldviews with which our ancestors wrestled.

We marvel at their imagination and creativity, but we recoil at the absurdity of their creative spirit, unanchored as it was by the stability of modern scientific discoveries.

We chuckle at their misinterpretations, but we sympathize with their intense desire to understand.

Perhaps, above all, we sense the commonality of man. It has become obvious that no one culture is superior to another or ever was. Scientists in ancient Egypt were no less intelligent than those in China. Authors in Arabic cultures were equal in ability to their counterparts in the western world. "Scientific" mistakes have known no boundaries. Furthermore, just as errors were common to all, secular advances in the sciences (when they came) were conceived in every major world setting.

After carefully uncovering and examining the pieces of our

puzzle, we can breathe a sigh of relief. As we saw how the medical, earth, and astronomical sciences yielded their findings, we understood that our generation is blessed to live in an age far more enlightened than the times of our ancestors. We realize that—given their limited technology—we would have fared no better in the search for answers. We are the lucky ones, we can say, as we examine the intriguing mosaic of ancient times that pictured humanity's simple imperfections.

Until there were modern laboratories bustling with expensive and sensitive equipment, the secrets of medical science were locked away from those physicians of old, awaiting the correct key that could unlock mysteries of disease processes. Until there were microscopes, the marvels of a miniscule universe were never witnessed. Until there were telescopes, the immensity of the vast cosmos was not grasped. In effect, because our ancestors lacked the proper equipment, their human weaknesses were revealed in exaggerated degrees.

The broader picture gradually fell into place. As the outer boundaries of the puzzle were completed, the task shifted to filling in the remainder of the pieces. These details added another dimension. When writings of most of the world's great religious leaders are examined in light of the times in which they were written, it becomes quickly apparent that they were merely a miniaturization of the overall picture. They are the smaller icons that fit within the larger picture.

As the scientific borders were laid down, they interlocked with the prevailing worldviews, converging so nicely that it is obvious they were cut from the same mold. No one had to force the pieces together. No one had to alter the edges. They seemed to fit. If the worldview current when the sacred texts of Hinduism, Islam, Buddhism and other non-biblical religions were written envisioned a flat earth, so did their writers. If they wrote during the ages when demons were believed to be the cause of all disease, most religious giants, too, spoke of demons in the same way. The writings fit.

No matter what the common error might have been, the writings interlocked perfectly in the puzzle. The pieces fit. The picture was complete—or so they assumed.

Curiously, however, there were always a large number of pieces left to the side of the main puzzle. Those pieces never seemed to fit. The colors differed markedly from the rest of the puzzle. The points where those pieces ought to interlock with the rest of the puzzle were oddly shaped. Their texture was wildly divergent. Because humanity is disturbed by such dissonance, we still seek a sensible explanation for their divergence and uniqueness.

Why are these strange pieces—these unexpected bits of information found in the Bible—so different from the rest?

How did biblical writers manage to avoid the erroneous world views of their contemporaries?

What made these men capable of producing painstakingly accurate scientific statements far in advance of their actual discovery?

We want answers to those important questions.

Could it be that these strange pieces were provided by humans from an intellectually superior culture or race? There is no evidence that they were. And we have seen that non-biblical sacred writings and secular texts by ancient Hebrew and Christian writers blundered into the identical mistakes committed by their contemporaries.

No, culture and even religious fervor do not provide the answer. Could it be that the unusual pieces were later additions to the puzzle? That, too, is highly unlikely. Even if the scientifically advanced sections of Scripture were written hundreds of years later than we think, the basic problem would remain. Had the entire Bible been composed five centuries into the Christian era, it would still be impossible to explain the numerous scientific accuracies found in the Scriptures.

An answer to our questions must lie elsewhere.

One answer has been suggested by the biblical authors themselves. If their materials are so radically different from other sources, surely we must listen to their explanation. Rather than finding confusion or uncertainty in their ranks, we find calm unanimity.

They refused to be called geniuses and scorned personal glory. Even more significant, they denied having figured it out for themselves. In fact, there is reason to believe that they never really understood the far-reaching implications of the words they wrote.

Humbly, without a dissenting voice, these writers gave credit to a superior being. One of their favorite phrases was: "This is the Word of God." They sensed a far-greater intelligence behind this universe than that of any mortal. They stood in awe before that wisdom and power. They even wrote words on their papyri and scrolls that made little earthly sense. *"All Scripture is given by inspiration of God."* It was the only answer they ever gave.

Is that answer reasonable? The evidence of those extra pieces of the puzzle suggests that it is.

Our study has forced us to recognize that the Bible is pregnant with gems of wisdom buried within its pages. Physicians are amazed by the rationality of its dictums. Its commands for daily living provide a rational basis for preventive medicine. Even unbelievers often heap accolades on its moral codes. Astronomers must admit to the accuracy of its simplistic, yet moving description of the heavens. Geologists have been stunned as they stumble across modern concepts hidden within its pages. The biblical writers demonstrate a careful, quiet avoidance of the faulty doctrines outlined by others who wrote in those times. But those unexpected pieces of insight apparently don't fit the picture puzzle completed by other great minds of the past.

How, then, must these pieces be explained except by recognizing their real source?

It is the thesis of this study that one must simply look at the trademark, the signature of authorship. The extra pieces don't fit humanity's mold. Rather, they claim to be provided by a supernatural intelligence. Our lines of evidence converge on that end truth. Unless we can devise a more suitable explanation, it seems reasonable to believe that the seemingly incongruous wisdom was placed in the Bible by an intelligence far greater than that of man. That intelligence is God's alone.

Some may wonder how it was possible for these fingerprints of God's inspiration to remain hidden from humanity's view for so long. Surely the answer is obvious. They were there all along but just didn't fit with the rest of the puzzle, constructed as it was by fallible, mortal humans.

The real problem was that we wanted so desperately for everything to fall neatly in place that we ignored the evidence. Our concept of the universe and our place within it will remain an incomplete puzzle until God provides the final missing pieces. Until then, we have good reason to believe that the Bible is Number One—the best source of eternal truth.

Appendix

The World's Scriptures

RELIGION	FOUNDER	SACRED OR AUTHORITATIVE WRITINGS	OPENLY CLAIM INSPIRATION	CLAIM SPECIAL IMPORTANCE	ADHERENTS VIEW AS SACRED	WHEN WRITTEN
Buddhism	Gautama, Buddha	Tripitaka		•	•	550 B.C.
Christianity	Jesus	New Testament	•	•	•	30–70 A.D.
		Church Fathers				100–500 A.D.
Christian Science	Mary Baker Eddy	Science & Health		•	•	1875 A.D.
Confucianism	Confucius	Five Classics		•	•	550 B.C.
		Analects				550 B.C.
		Works of Mencius				300 B.C.
Hinduism	none	Vedas	*	•	•	1500–1000 B.C.
		Brahamas		•	•	1000–800 B.C.
		Upanishads		•	•	800–400 B.C.
		Laws of Manu		•	•	250 B.C.
		Bhagavad-Gita		•	•	1 A.D.
		Puranas		•	•	1–250 A.D.
Islam	Mohammed	The Qur'an	•	•	•	550 A.D.
Jainism	Vardhamana	Angas		•	•	600 B.C.
Judaism	Moses	Old Testament	•	•	•	1500–400 B.C.
		Talmud		•		200–280 A.D.
		Mishnah		•		200 A.D.
		Apocrypha				400–100 B.C.
Mormonism	Joseph Smith, Jr.	Book of Mormon	•	•	•	1830 A.D.
		Pearl of Great Price	•	•	•	1840 A.D.
		Doctrine& Covenant	•	•	•	1835 A.D.
Shintoism	none	Ko-ji-ki		•	•	650 B.C.
		Nihon-gi		•	•	650 B.C.
Sikhism	Nanak	Granth		•	•	1500 B.C.
Taoism	Lao-tze	Tao-te-Ching		•	•	600 B.C.
Zoroastrianism	Zoroaster	Avesta	•	•	•	650 B.C.

* Only the Rig Veda claims inspiration.

Notes

Introduction

1. Generally speaking, the issues regarding hermeneutics and science have centered on creation-evolution issues. Yet, there are a number of worthwhile materials that relate to hermeneutical issues as they are presented in this study. See, for instance, F. Furman Kearley, Edward P. Myers, and Timothy D. Hadley, eds., *Biblical Interpretation: Studies in Honor of Jack Pearl Lewis* (Grand Rapids: Baker, 1986); Norman L. Geisler, ed., *Inerrancy* (Grand Rapids: Zondervan, 1979); R. C. Sproul, John Gerstner, and Arthur Lindsley, *Classical Apologetics* (Grand Rapids: Zondervan, 1984); Earl D. Radmacher and Robert D. Preus, eds., *Hermeneutics, Inerrancy and the Bible* (Grand Rapids: Zondervan, 1984); and Larry Chouinard, *The Current Debate on Biblical Inerrancy* (Montgomery: Apologetics Press, n.d.).

2. This is not to imply that primary meanings regarding moral doctrines are not understandable. The basics of Scripture are very understandable. See Jody L. Apple, *Hermeneutical Agnosticism* (Media, Penn.: New Testament Christian Press, 1985).

3. Philip B. Payne, "The Fallacy of Equating Meaning with the Human Author's Intention," *JETS* 13 (1970): 243–252.

Chapter 1

1. For a more detailed account of the glory of ancient Egyptian medicine, see E. Vidal, "*Les idees des Assyriens et des Egyptiens sur la vie et la mort, le sant et la maladie, 3000 ans avant* Jesus Christ," *SGAB* 7 (1912): 569–596. Though not complete, its general comments are still valid. A somewhat shorter but more recent study is George Steindorff and Keith C. Seele, *When Egypt Ruled the East,* 2d ed. (Chicago: Univ. of Chicago Press, 1957), pp. 129–137.

Note also Roderick E. McGrew, "Egyptian Medicine," *EMH* (New York: McGraw-Hill, 1985), pp. 105–106, and Guido Majno, *The Healing Hand: Man and Wound in the Ancient World* (Cambridge: Harvard Univ. Press, 1975).

2. Physicians in antiquity developed surgical arts to commendable levels, and acupuncture was in wide use in China. There were numerous achievements. But it would be a travesty to paint the medical arts as free from the ignorant, the erroneous, and the grotesque. The times were primitive and mistakes were the order of the day.

3. R. K. Harrison, "Healing, Health," *IDB,* vol. 2, p. 542.

4. Chauncey D. Leake, *The Old Egyptian Medical Papyri* (Lawrence: Univ. of Kansas Press, 1952), p. 13. See also George Sarton, A History of Science, vol. 1 (Cambridge: Harvard Univ. Press, 1959), p. 45, and H. E. Sigerist, *History of Medicine,* vol. 1 (Oxford: Oxford Univ. Press, 1951), p. 311.

5. Sigerist, *History of Medicine,* p. 342. See also Alexander Badawy, "Egypt, Ancient: Science and Technology," *EA* (1985), vol. 10, pp. 60–62, and Douglas Guthrie, *A History of Medicine* (Philadelphia: J. B. Lippincott, 1946), p. 25. Some of today's more enthusiastic cheerleaders for the ancients are quick to point out that some of our modern miracle drugs, such as aureomycin, are derived from some rather bizarre substances. Though that is true, these scholars conveniently fail to mention that the drug must be in the pure state to be of any real value. They also neglect informing their readers of the many substances in bile and urine that effectively mitigate against effective healing.

6. Otto L. Bettmann, "Prescriptions Come on Papyrus," *A Pictorial History of Medicine* (Springfield, Ill.: Charles C. Thomas, 1956), p. 17.

7. Sigerist, *History of Medicine,* p. 247. See also C. P. Bryan, *The Papyrus Ebers* (London: Geoffrey Bles, 1930).

8. Jurgen Thorwald, *Science and Secrets of Early Medicine,* tr. Richard and Clara Winston (New York: Harcourt, Brace and World, 1963), p. 86.

9. C. H. LaWall, *Four Thousand Years of Pharmacy* (Philadelphia: J. B. Lippincott, 1927), p. 8.

10. Guenter B. Risse, "Medicine: History," *EA* (1985), vol. 18, p. 625. Sigerist (*History of Medicine,* p. 247) labels it "purely magical."

11. Samuel Leff and Vera Leff, *From Witchcraft to World Health* (New York: Macmillan, 1957), p. 32.

12. R. H. Major, *A History of Medicine* (Springfield, Ill.: Charles C. Thomas, 1954), p. 50.

13. Brian Inglis, *A History of Medicine* (New York: World, 1965), p. 121.

14. See James G. Frazer, *The Golden Bough: A Study in Magic and Religion,* 3rd ed, vol. 1: *The Magic Art and the Evolution of Kings* (London: Macmillan, 1955).

15. E. A. Wallis Budge, *Archaeologica,* 2nd ser., *II* (1890), p. 428.

16. The author accepts the older, more conservative view that attributes the Pentateuch to Moses, though, as far as the argument is concerned, the issue is irrelevant.

17. E. H. Ackerknecht, *A Short History of Medicine* (New York: Ronald Press, 1955), p. 26. See also A. Leo Oppenheim, *Ancient Mesopotamia,* rev. ed. (Chicago: Univ. of Chicago Press, 1977), p. 204, and H. W. F. Saggs, *The Great-*

ness That Was Babylon (New York: New American Library, 1962), pp. 290f, 442.

18. Major, *History of Medicine,* p. 30.

19. R. Campbell Thompson, "Medical History," *PRSM* 17 (1924): 2–22. See also M. Civil, "Prescriptions *medicales sumeriennes,*" *RA* 54 (1960): 57–72, and R. D. Biggs, "Medicine in Ancient Mesopotamia," *HS* 8 (1969): 94–105. The largest text from Mesopotamia, "The Treatise of Medical Diagnosis and Prognoses," comprises three thousand entries on forty tablets, yet has "no modern medical significance at all" and has been labeled "a sorcerer's handbook" (Roderick E. McGrew, "Medicine in Mesopotamia," *EMH* [1985], p. 186).

20. Saggs, *Greatness That Was Babylon,* p. 307.

21. Sigerist, *History of Medicine,* p. 462. See also Oppenheim, *Ancient Mesopotamia,* pp. 213f, 372 n. 46, and Rencontre Assyriologique Internationale, *La Divination en Mesopotamie Ancienne et dans les Regions Voisines* (Paris: Presses Universitaires de France, 1966). Also note J. P. Vernant et al., *Divination et Rationalite* (Paris: Editions du Seuil, 1974). Auguste Bouche-Le Clerq's *Histoire de la Divinatione dans l'Antiquite,* 4 vols. (Paris: E. Leroux, 1879–1882), though dated, is still excellent, as is Cicero's *De Divinatione,* ed. A. S. Pease (Urbana: Univ. of Illinois Press, 1920).

22. Thorwald, *Science and Secrets,* p. 153.

23. Ibid., p. 154. Oppenheim, *Ancient Mesopotamia,* p. 212.

24. F. W. Geers, "A Babylonian Omen Text," *AJSLL* 43 (1926–1927): 29–33. Also, Oppenheim, *Ancient Mesopotamia,* pp. 209–211.

25. Saggs, *Greatness That Was Babylon,* p. 308.

26. LaWall, *Four Thousand Years,* pp. 15–16; Sigerist, *History of Medicine,* pp. 441–472. A. J. Sachs, "Babylonian Horoscopes," *JCS* 6 (1952): 49–75, and D. Pingree, "Astronomy and Astrology in India and Iran," *Isis* 54 (1963): 229–246, provide an excellent overview of the omen-texts.

27. "Science vs. Astrology: New Battle, Old War," *Science News* 108 (1975): 166. See also Lawrence Jerome, *Astrology Disproved* (Buffalo: Prometheus, 1977).

28. B. L. Gordon, *Medicine Through Antiquity* (Philadelphia: F. A. Davis, 1949), p. 166.

29. Cited in Jack Lindsey, *The Origins of Astrology* (New York: Barnes and Noble, 1971), p. 149.

30. Major, *History of Medicine,* p. 31.

31. This does not imply there was no good in Babylonian medicine. There were achievements (see Saggs, *Greatness That Was Babylon,* pp. 290f). The advances were what one would expect from human intelligence.

32. Saggs, *Greatness That Was Babylon,* p. 292f.

33. Ibid., p. 291.

34. Ibid., p. 296.

35. Ibid., pp. 297–298.

36. Thorwald, *Science and Secrets,* p. 157.

37. J. J. M. de Groot, *The Religious System of China* (1901; rprt. Taipei: Literature House, 1964), vol. 4, p. 396.

Chapter 2

1. *Atharva-Veda Samhita,* tr. W. D. Whitney, rev. by C. R. Lanman, Harvard Oriental Series (Cambridge: Harvard Univ. Press, 1905), vols. vii–viii.

2. B. L. Gordon, *Medicine Through Antiquity* (Philadelphia: F. A. Davis, 1949), p. 318.

3. Julius Jolly, "Disease and Medicine (Hindu)," in James Hastings, ed., *ERE,* vol. 4, p. 754. *Atharva-Veda,* ii, 31–32; v. 23. See also G. M. Bolling, "Vedic Literature," *EA* (1985), vol. 27, pp. 925–928; and A. L. Basham, "Hinduism and Hindu Medicine," in W. T. Reich et al., eds., *EBE* (1978), vol. 2, p. 661.

4. *Atharva-Veda,* i,12.

5. G. M. Bolling, "Disease and Medicine (Vedic)," *ERE,* vol. 2, p. 768.

6. *Atharva-Veda,* i, 25.

7. Jolly, "Disease and Medicine," p. 754.

8. George B. Walker, "Medicine," *Hindu World,* vol. 2 (London: George Allen & Unwin, 1968), p. 56.

9. Gordon, *Medicine Through Antiquity,* pp. 319–340. Walker (p. 367) adds that the Hindu contribution to science in Vedic times was "negligible."

10. Ibid., p. 323. It is true that Hindu doctors made great strides in surgical techniques. However, as noted earlier (see note 3 above), advances in this area would be expected of highly intelligent people. In other areas, Hindu writers fell far short. They accepted the validity of omens and believed a connection existed between gold and long life.

11. David L. Johnson (*A Reasoned Look at the Asian Religions* [Minneapolis: Bethan House, 1985], p. 120) notes that a "negative assessment of human life is fundamental to the Buddhist teaching" and any attempt at restoring or prolonging life only postpones the inevitable.

12. Gordon, *Medicine Through Antiquity,* p. 325.

13. Great advances in Chinese medicine, and they were considerable, were gained outside the sphere of religion. It is impossible to discover any intimations of "breakthroughs" in the *Tao.*

14. Joseph Needham, *Science and Civilization in China,* vol. 2, *History of Scientific Thought* (Cambridge: Cambridge Univ. Press, 1956). Alchemy was not limited to the Taoist religion. Its adherents may be found in the sacred writings of both Buddhist (E. T. Fenner, "Rasayana Siddhi: Medicine and Alchemy in the Buddhist Tantras," Ph.D. diss., Univ. of Wisconsin, Madison, 1978) and Jaina religions (J. C. Sikdar, "Jaina Alchemy," *IJHS* 15 [1980]: 6–17).

15. A. K. Seidel, "Taoism," *EB-MAC* (1975), vol. 17, p. 1040.

16. See P. U. Unschuld, "Concepts of Illness in Ancient China: The Case of Demonological Medicine," *JMP* 5 (1980): 117–132.

17. Gordon, *Medicine Through Antiquity,* p. 361.

18. Ibid., p. 303.

19. *Pahlavi Texts, Sad-Dar,* 7:1–7, tr. by E. B. West, *SBE,* 24 (London: Clarendon, 1910). See also pp. 265–266.

20. *Vendidad,* 1:13. See also *The Zend-Avesta,* tr. by James Darmesteter and L. H. Mills, vol. 4, *SBE* (1880; rprt. Delhi: Motilal Bonarsidass, 1965).

21. Gordon, *Medicine Through Antiquity,* pp. 392–397.

22. A. Rendle Short, *The Bible and Modern Medicine* (Chicago: Moody, 1953), p. 35.
23. Josephus, *Antiquities of the Jews*, II, 5.

Chapter 3

1. Frederick Eby and Charles F. Arrowood, *The History and Philosophy of Education: Ancient and Medieval* (New York: Prentice-Hall, 1942), p. 58.
2. Ibid., p. 57.
3. James Bowen, *A History of Western Education*, vol. 1 (New York: St. Martin's, 1972), p. 39.
4. Eby and Arrowood, *History and Philosophy of Education*, pp. 97–98.
5. Ibid., p. 79.
6. James Mulhern, *A History of Education*, 2d ed. (New York: Ronald Press, 1959), p. 71.
7. R. C. H. Lenski, *The Interpretation of the Acts of the Apostles* (Minneapolis: Augsburg, 1961), p. 275.
8. Chauncey D. Leake, *The Old Egyptian Medical Papyri* (Lawrence: Univ. of Kansas Press, 1952), p. 13.
9. Harry Wain, *A History of Preventive Medicine* (Springfield, Ill.: Charles C. Thomas, 1970), p. 7.
10. See the prophecy found in Zech. 13:1–2.
11. Max Neuberger, *History of Medicine* (London: Oxford Univ. Press, 1910), vol. 1, p. 38.
12. Roderick E. McGrew, "Hebrew Medicine," *EMH* (New York: McGraw-Hill, 1985), p. 130.
13. Sir M. Monier Williams, cited in Sidney Collett, *All About the Bible* (Old Tappan, N.J.: Revell, 1933), pp. 314–315.

Chapter 4

1. Fielding Garrison, *History of Medicine*, 4th ed. (Philadelphia: W. B. Saunders, 1961), p. 67.
2. B. L. Gordon, *Medicine Through Antiquity* (Philadelphia: F. A. Davis, 1949), p. 255.
3. Robert P. Hudson, *Disease and Its Control: The Shaping of Modern Thought* (Westport, Conn.: Greenwood, 1983), p. 63.
4. D. T. Atkinson, *Magic, Myth and Medicine* (New York: World, 1956), pp. 30–31.
5. R. K. Harrison, "Health, Healing," *IDB*, vol. 2, p. 546.
6. Arturo Castiglione, *A History of Medicine*, 2d ed. (New York: Alfred A. Knopf, 1958), p. 71.
7. Harry Wain, *A History of Preventive Medicine* (Springfield, Ill.: Charles C. Thomas, 1970), p. 11.
8. See Imre Zoltan, "Ignaz Philipp Semmelweis," *EB-MAC* (1975), vol. 16, p. 529.

9. Gordon, *Medicine Through Antiquity,* p. 260.

10. R. J. Thomsen, *The Bible: Book of Medical Wisdom* (Old Tappan, N.J.: Revell, 1974), p. 24.

11. John E. Heinze, "Bar Soap and Liquid Soap," *JAMA* 251 (June 22/29, 1984): 3223. Other materials relating to the value of handwashing include: E. A. Bannan and L. F. Judge, "Bacteriological Studies Relating to Handwashing," *AJPH* 55 (1965): 915–922; K. Sprunt, W. Redman, and G. Leidy, "Antibacterial Effectiveness of Routine Handwashing," *Ped* 52 (1973): 264–271; and Walter J. Hierholzer, Jr., "Nosocomial Bacterial Infections," in *Bacterial Infections of Humans: Epidemiology and Control,* ed. A. S. Evans and H. A. Feldman (New York: Plenum, 1982), p. 383.

12. A. C. Steere and G. F. Mallison, "Handwashing Practices for the Prevention of Nosocomial Infections," *AIM* 83 (1975): 683–690.

13. S. I. McMillen, *None of These Diseases,* rev. by David E. Stern (Old Tappan, N.J.: Revell, 1984), p. 26.

14. Estimated casualties since 1500 are in the tens of millions.

15. Castiglione, *History of Medicine, p. 70.*

16. *"Quarantine," EA* (1985), vol. 23, pp. 56–57. See also Abram S. Berenson, ed., *Control of Communicable Diseases in Man* (New York: American Public Health Association, 1970).

17. Wain, *Preventive Medicine,* p. 9.

18. Roderick E. McGrew, "Contagion," *EMH,* p. 77.

19. H. E. Sigerist, *A History of Medicine* (Oxford: Oxford Univ. Press, 1951), p. 446. E. H. Ackerknecht, *A Short History of Medicine* (New York: Ronald Press, 1955) p. 83, adds that the OT "is far more contagion-minded than the Greek classics."

20. A. B. Christie, "Infectious Diseases," *EB-MAC* (1975), vol. 9, p. 549.

21. Garrison, *History of Medicine,* p. 187.

22. George Rosen, *History of Public Health* (New York: M D Publications, 1958), pp. 62–63.

23. Ibid., pp. 63–65.

24. E. E. Hume, *The Military Sanitation of Moses in the Light of Modern Knowledge* (Carlisle Barracks, Penn.: Medical Field Service School, 1940).

Chapter 5

1. R. K. Harrison, "Health, Healing," *IDB,* vol. 2, p. 544.

2. A. Rendle Short, *The Bible and Modern Medicine* (Chicago: Moody, 1953), pp. 45–46.

3. Harry Wain, *A History of Preventive Medicine* (Springfield, Ill.: Charles C. Thomas, 1970), p. 11.

4. A. Rendle Short, *Modern Discoveries and the Bible* (London: Inter-Varsity, 1942), p. 85.

5. Harrison, "Health, Healing," p. 544.

6. R. H. Major, *A History of Medicine* (Springfield, Ill.: Charles C. Thomas, 1954), p. 63.

7. W. F. Albright, *Yahweh and the Gods of Canaan* (Garden City: Doubleday, 1968), p. 180.

8. R. K. Harrison, "Heal," *ISBE-REV,* vol. 2, p. 642. See also Gerhard F. Hasel, "Health and Healing in the Old Testament," *AUSS* 21 (1983): 195–196.

9. R. K. Harrison, *Leviticus* (Downers Grove, Ill.: Inter-Varsity, 1980), pp. 124–126; and R. E. Clements, "Leviticus," *Broadman Bible Commentary* (Nashville: Broadman, 1970), p. 34.

10. Albright, *Gods of Canaan*, p. 175.

11. See Sonja L. Connor, et al. "The Cholesterol Saturated Fat Index: An Indication of the Hypercholesterolaemic and Atherogenic Potential of Food," TL 08492 (May 31, 1986): 1229–1232.

12. R. J. Thomsen, *The Bible: Book of Medical Wisdom* (Old Tappan, N.J.: Revell, 1974), p. 100.

13. D. I. Macht, "An Experimental Pharmacological Appreciation of Leviticus 11 and Deuteronomy 14," *BHM* 27 (1953): 444–450.

14. W. R. Vis, in American Scientific Affiliation, *Modern Science and the Christian Faith* (Wheaton, Ill.: Van Kampen, 1948), p. 191. Note Harrison, "Health, Healing," p. 544.

15. Many diseases, including infectious and serum hepatitis are transmitted directly through the blood. See D. K. Grissom, *Communicable Diseases* (Dubuque, Iowa: William C. Brown, 1971), p. 29.

16. See, generally, James G. Frazer's *The Golden Bough*; also Pliny, *Naturalis Historia*, ed. D. Detlefsen (Berlin, 1866–1882), xxviii, 147.

17. James G. Frazer, *The Golden Bough: The Magic Art and the Evolution of Kings*, vol. 2., 1890 (rprt. New York: St. Martin's, 1980), p. 239. Further, see the *Grihya Sutras*, tr. by H. Oldenberg, *SBE*, vol. 29, part I, pp. 81, 141.

18. Ibid.

19. Pliny, *Naturalis Historia*, xxviii, 19.

20. Frazer, *Magic Art*, p. 118.

21. Edward Konig, "Defilement and Purification," *SHERK*, vol. 3, p. 388.

22. Julius Jolly, "Food (Hindu)," *ERE*, vol. 6, pp. 63–65.

23. A. F. R. Hoernle, *The Bower Manuscript* (Calcutta: Superintendent of Government Printing, 1893).

24. Gordon J. Wenham, *The Book of Leviticus* (Grand Rapids: Eerdmans, 1979), pp. 166–185.

25. See J. H. Hertz, *Leviticus*, (London: Oxford Univ. Press, 1932), p. 93.

26. Wenham, *Leviticus*, p. 166.

27. Martin Noth, *The Laws in the Pentateuch and Other Studies* (Edinburgh: Oliver and Boyd, 1966), pp. 56ff.

28. Wenham, *Leviticus*, p. 167.

29. Origen, *Contra Celsum*, 4:93.

30. See, for example, Mary Douglas, "Deciphering a Meal," *Dae* 101 (1972): 61–81.

31. Wenham, *Leviticus*, p. 170.

32. Peter C. Craigie, *The Book of Deuteronomy* (Grand Rapids: Eerdmans, 1976), pp. 230–231.

33. Don DeWelt, *Leviticus* (Joplin, Mo.: College Press, 1975), p. 171.

Chapter 6

1. Evelyn Zamula, "Syphilis and Gonorrhea: Old-Fashioned VD Still Flourishing," *FDA Consumer* 20 (April, 1986): 6. A discussion of the international

problems associated with STDs can be found in Miriam Ryan, "Venereal Diseases Increase in the Third World," *NS* 106 (May 16, 1985): 18.

2. Morbidity and Mortality Weekly Report, "Gonorrhea—United States, 1983," *JAMA* 252 (August 10, 1984): 751–752.

3. Morbidity and Mortality Weekly Report, "Syphilis—United States, 1983," *JAMA* 252 (August 24/31, 1984): 992.

4. Nancy J. Binkin, Jeffrey P. Koplan, and Willard Cates, Jr., "Preventing Neonatal Herpes," *JAMA* 251 (June 1, 1984): 2816.

5. Sana Siwolop, "New Drugs for Herpes," *Discover* 5 (July, 1984): 31–33.

6. A. Eugene Washington, Willard Cates, Jr., and Akbar A. Zaidi, "Hospitalizations for Pelvic Inflammatory Disease," *JAMA* 251 (May 18, 1984): 2529–2533.

7. Jurgen Thorwald, *Science and Secrets of Early Medicine* (New York: Harcourt, Brace and World, 1963), pp. 163–167.

8. Otto L. Bettmann, *A Pictorial History of Medicine* (Springfield, Ill.: Charles C. Thomas, 1956), p. 12.

9. R. H. Major, *A History of Medicine* (Springfield, Ill.: Charles C. Thomas, 1954), p. 369.

10. Bettmann, *Pictorial History,* pp. 98–99.

11. Ibid., pp. 100–101.

12. R. Campbell Thompson, "Assyrian Prescriptions for Stone in Kidneys, for the 'Middle,' and for Pneumonia," *Arch. Orientforschung* 11 (1936–1937): 336–340.

13. H. E. Sigerist, *A History of Medicine* (Oxford: Oxford Univ. Press, 1951), p. 483.

14. B. L. Gordon, *Medicine Through Antiquity* (Philadelphia: F. A. Davis, 1949), p. 264.

15. P. Ruutu et al., "Septicemia Caused by Penicillinase-producing Gonorrhea," *JAMA* 251 (April 13, 1984): 1836; R. Z. Rinaldi, W. O. Harrison, and Peng Thim Fan, "Penicillin-resistant, Gonococcal Arthritis," *AIM* 97 (1982): 43–45; M. I. Leftik, J. W. Miller, and J. D. Brown, "Penicillin-resistant Gonococcal Polyarthritis," *JAMA* 239 (1978): 134; and Morbidity and Mortality Weekly Report, "Disseminated Gonorrheal Infections and Meningitis—Pennsylvania," *JAMA* 251 (April 20, 1984): 1943.

16. S. I. McMillen, *None of These Diseases,* rev. ed. (Old Tappan, N.J.: Revell, 1985), p. 60.

17. S. I. McMillen, *None of these Diseases* (Old Tappan, N.J.: Revell, 1963), pp. 39–42.

18. Siwolop, "New Drugs," p. 31f.

19. Binkin, Koplan, and Cates, "Preventing Herpes," p. 2816.

20. Siwolop, "New Drugs," p. 31f.

21. See note 6 above.

22. Melvin Zelnik and John F. Kantor, "Sexual Activity, Contraceptive Use and Pregnancy among Metropolitan Teenagers, 1971–1979," *FPP* 12 (1980): 230–237; Melvin Zelnik and John F. Kantor, "Sexual and Contraceptive Experience of Young Unmarried Women in the United States," *FPP* 9 (1977): 55–71; Washington, Cates, and Zaidi, "Hospitalizations," p. 2532.

23. McMillen, *None of Theses Diseases,* rev. ed., pp. 77–85; Frank M. du

Mas, *Gay Is Not Good* (Nashville: Nelson, 1979); Allen Clifford, *A Textbook of Psychosexual Disorders* (New York: Oxford Univ. Press, 1969); I. Bieber, ed., *Homosexuality—A Psychoanalytic Study* (New York: Basic Books, 1962).

24. McMillen, *None of These Diseases,* rev. ed., p. 78.

25. Cited in Anne C. Lewis, "A Dangerous Silence," *Phi Delta Kappan,* January, 1987, pp. 348–349.

26. Otis Bowen, "Epidemic Predicted," *USA Today,* January 30, 1987: 4A.

27. W. G. Aston, "Shinto," *ERE,* vol. 11, p. 469.

28. A. B. Keith, "Marriage (Hindu)," *ERE,* vol. 8, p. 454.

29. T. J. De Boer, "Ethics and Morality (Muslim)," *ERE,* vol. 5, p. 505.

30. B. C. de Vaux, "Family (Muslim)," *ERE,* vol. 5, p. 742.

31. A. H. Gardiner, "Ethics and Morality (Egyptian)," *ERE,* vol. 5, p. 482.

32. Alfred Jeremias, "Ethics and Morality (Babylonian)," *ERE,* vol. 5, p. 447.

33. Masahar Anesaki, "Ethics and Morality (Buddhist)," *ERE,* vol. 5, p. 452.

Chapter 7

1. For a complete discussion of the stress theory, see Hans Selye, *The Stress of Life* (New York: McGraw-Hill, 1956). Selye's *The Physiology and Pathology of Exposure to Stress* (Montreal: Acta Press, 1950) is the technical work on which the popular version is based. See also *Stress of Life* (New York: McGraw-Hill, 1978).

2. Many texts deal with the relationship between stress and disease. See G. R. Elliott and C. Eisdorfer, eds., *Stress and Human Health* (New York: Springer, 1982); L. A. Bieliauskas, *Stress and Its Relationship to Health and Illness* (Boulder, Colo.: Westview Press, 1982); C. B. Dobson, *Stress: The Hidden Adversary* (Hingham, Md.: Kluwer Academic Publications, 1983); and Robert Friis, *Stress and Physical Health: A Bibliography,* vol. 4, (Irving, Calif.: Human Behavior Research Group, 1984).

3. Charles Seabrook, "Stress," *The Atlanta Journal and Constitution Magazine,* (July 8, 1979), p. 15.

4. N. Herbert Spector, cited in Jean L. Marx, "The Immune System 'Belongs in the Body,' " *Science* 227 (March 8, 1985): 1190.

5. Elliott and Eisdorfer, *Stress and Human Health;* also M. R. Zales, ed., *Stress in Health and Disease* (New York: Brunner-Mazel, 1984); H. Ursin and R. Murison, eds., *Biological and Psychological Basis of Psychosomatic Disease* (Oxford: Pergamon, 1980); T. P. Almy, "Therapeutic Strategy in Stress-Related Digestive Disorders," *CG* 6 (1977): 709–722; W. G. Thompson, *The Irritable Gut: Functional Disorders of the Alimentary Canal* (Baltimore: University Park Press, 1979); M. D. Esler and K. T. Goulston, "Levels of Anxiety in Colonic Disorders," *NEJM* 288 (1973): 16–20, and "An Irritable Mind or an Irritable Bowel?" *TL* 8415 (December 1, 1984): 1249–1250.

6. Meyer Friedman and R. H. Rosenman, *Type A: Behavior and Your Heart* (New York: Alfred A. Knopf, 1974); David Wheatley, ed., *Stress and the Heart,* 2d ed. (New York: Raven, 1981); Gail Armstrong and Robert Friis, *Stress-Heart Disease Connection* (Irving, Calif.: Human Behavior Research Group, 1981); J. Bahlmann and H. Liebau, eds., *Stress and Hypertension* (New York: S. Karger,

1982); John E. Deanfield et al., "Silent Myocardial Ischaemia Due to Mental Stress," *TL* 8410 (November 3, 1984): 1001f; Thomas B. Graboys, "Stress and the Aching Heart," *NEJM* 311 (August 30, 1984): 594–595; T. P. Hackett and J. F. Rosenbaum, "Emotion, Psychiatric Disorders and the Heart," in E. Braunwald, ed., *Heart Disease* (Philadelphia: W. B. Saunders, 1984), pp. 1826–1946; and J. H. Medalie, et al., "Angina Pectoris Among 10,000 Men: 5 Year Incidence and Univariate Analysis," *AJM* 55 (1973): 583.

7. See David V. Perkins, "The Assessment of Stress Using Life Events Scales," in Leo Goldberger and Schlomo Breznitz, eds., *Handbook of Stress: Theoretical and Clinical Aspects* (New York: Raven Press, 1982), pp. 319–331; R. R. Solomon and R. H. Moos, "The Relationship of Personality to the Presence of Rheumatoid Arthritis in Asymptomatic Relatives of Patients with Rheumatoid Arthritis," *PM* 27 (1965): 350.

8. J. J. Groen et al. *Psychosomatic Research: A Collection of Papers* (New York: Macmillan, 1964); Sir McFarlane Burnet, *Natural History of Infectious Disease,* 4th ed. (Cambridge: Cambridge Univ. Press, 1972).

9. Kurt Bammer and B. H. Newberry, eds., *Stress and Cancer* (Lewiston, N.Y.: C. J. Hogrefe, 1981); G. A. Taff and Robert Friis, *Stress and Cancer: An Annotated Bibliography* (Irving, Calif.: Human Behavior Research Group, 1983).

10. "Conquering the Quiet Killer," *Time,* January 13, 1975, pp. 60–62. See also Bahlmann and Liebau, *Stress and Hypertension.*

11. Seabrook, "Stress," p. 15.

12. Walter McQuade and Ann Aikman, *Stress* (New York: Bantam Books, 1975), pp. 8–9.

13. Herbert Sorenson and Margurite Malm, *Psychology for Living* (New York: McGraw-Hill, 1957). p. 96.

14. J. T. Fisher and L. S. Hawley, *A Few Buttons Missing* (New York: Lippincott, 1951), pp. 273–274.

15. William Sadler, *Practice of Psychiatry* (St. Louis: C. V. Mosby, 1953), p. 1008.

16. C. G. Jung, *Modern Man in Search of a Soul* (New York: Harcourt, Brace and World, 1933), pp. 260–262.

17. Leo Madow, *Anger* (New York: Charles Scribner's Sons, 1972), pp. 73–91.

Chapter 8

1. See Lewis Spence, "Circumcision (Introductory)," in *ERE,* vol. 3, pp. 664–666.

2. L. H. Bachman, "The Statistics on Circumcision and Penile Cancer," *CA* 34 (July/August, 1984): 238.

3. R. J. Thomsen, *The Bible: Book of Medical Wisdom* (Old Tappan, N.J.: Revell, 1974), p. 17.

4. See Fetus and Newborn Committee, Canadian Pediatric Society, "Benefits and Risks of Circumcision: Another View," *CMAJ* 126 (1982): 1399; Committee on Fetus Newborn, "Report of the Ad Hoc Committee on Circumcision," *Ped* 56 (1975): 610; Edward Wallerstein, *Circumcision: An American Health Fantasy* (New York: Springer, 1980).

5. Lawrence Garfinkel, letter in *CA* 33 (September/October, 1983): 320.

6. E. Warner and E. Strashin, "Benefits and Risks of Circumcision," *CMAJ* 125 (1981): 967–976.

7. R. Dagher, M. L. Selzer, and J. Lapides, "Carcinoma of the Penis and the Anticircumcision Crusade," *JU* 110 (1973): 79–80. When results were reported by Garfinkel in 1983 (see note 5 above), the text erroneously reported that the studies showed no cases in uncircumcised males. That error was corrected in Bachman, "Statistics," p. 238.

8. E. Leiter and A. M. Lefkovits, "Circumcision and Penile Cancer," *NYSJM* 75 (1975): 1520–1522.

9. G. W. Kaplan, "Circumcision—An Overview," *CPP* 7 (1977): 10.

10. Cited in S. I. McMillen, *None of These Diseases*, rev. ed. (Old Tappan, N.J.: Revell, 1985), p. 90. See also M. Kochen and S. McCurdy, "Circumcision and the Risk of Cancer of the Penis," *AJDC* 134 (1980): 484–486.

11. Spence, "Circumcision," p. 665f.

12. Ibid., p. 671f. See also B. L. Gordon, *Medicine Through Antiquity* (Philadelphia: F. A. Davis, 1949),p. 237; and H. E. Sigerist, *A History of Medicine* (Oxford: Oxford Univ. Press, 1951), p. 244.

13. L. Emmett Holt, Jr., and Rustin McIntosh, *Holt Pediatrics*, 12th ed. (New York: Appleton-Century-Crofts, 1953), pp. 125–126. Note also, C. W. McMillan, A. E. Weis, and A. M. Johnson, "Acquired Coagulation Disorders in Children," *PCNA* 19 (1972): 1034, and McMillen, *None of These Diseases*, rev. ed., pp. 90f.

14. McMillen, *None of These Diseases*, rev. ed., p. 21.

15. Modern technology allows the artificial introduction of extra vitamin K and prothrombin through injections; consequently, the requirement is no longer as necessary as it used to be.

16. Joseph Katz, "The Question of Circumcision," *IS* 62 (1977): 490–492.

17. McMillen, *None of These Diseases*, rev. ed., pp. 91–92.

18. Spence, "Circumcision," p. 665.

Chapter 9

1. Sir W. C. Dampier, *A History of Science*, 4th ed. (London: Cambridge Univ. Press, 1948), p. xiii.

2. Franklyn Branley, "Conceptions of the Universe," *NH* 79 (December, 1970): 30.

3. H. W. F. Saggs, *The Greatness That Was Babylon* (New York: New American Library, 1962), p. 428f, and A. H. Sayce, "Babylonia," *EB*, 9th ed., vol. 3, p. 191.

4. Isaac Asimov, *The Universe: From Flat Earth to Quasar* (New York: Avon, 1966), p. 14.

5. Saggs, *Greatness*, pp. 428f.

6. George Sarton, *A History of Science*, vol. 1 (Cambridge: Harvard Univ. Press, 1959), p. 120. Sarton says much of the praise of Chaldean astronomy is unmerited. Many have attributed later materials (of the period *circa* 200 B.C.) to periods of 1000 to 2000 years earlier. See also M. J. Costelloe, "Astral Religion," *EDR*, vol. 1, p. 296, and "Astrology," pp. 296–297.

7. For problems in astrology, see Mark A. Graubard, *Astrology and Alchemy: Two Fossil Sciences* (New York: AMS, 1953); Lawrence Jerome, *Astrology Disproved* (Buffalo: Prometheus, 1977); and A. E. Thierens, *Astrology in Mesopotamian Culture* (New York: Gordon, 1977).

8. Xenophon, *Memorabilia,* tr. by E. C. Marchant, Loeb Classical Library (Cambridge: Harvard Univ. Press, 1923), I, 1; IV, 3, 12; IV, 7, 10.

9. Cicero, *De divinatione,* A. S. Pease, ed. (Urbana: Univ. of Illinois Press, 1920).

10. G. W. Gilmore, "Stars," *SHERK,* vol. 11, pp. 68–69. See also J. M. Plumley, "The Cosmology of Ancient Egypt," in Carmen Blacker and Michael Loewe, eds., *Ancient Cosmologies* (London: George Allen & Unwin, 1975), pp. 40–41; Erik Hornung, *Concepts of God in Ancient Egypt,* tr. by John Baines (Ithaca: Cornell Univ. Press, 1982), pp. 80–81.

11. Antonie Pannekoek, *A History of Astronomy* (New York: Interscience Publishers, 1961), p. 84. Also, Plumley, "Cosmology," pp. 21–33; Costelloe, "Astral Religion," p. 296; Barbara Watterson, *The Gods of Ancient Egypt* (New York: Facts on File, 1984), pp. 44–71. An older but still useful work is E. A. Wallis Budge, *Gods of the Egyptians* (London: Peter Smith, 1904).

12. Branley, "Conceptions of the Universe," p. 30.

13. R. A. Proctor, "Astronomy," *EB,* 9th ed., vol. 2, p. 745. See also R. A. Parker, "Ancient Egyptian Astronomy," in F. R. Hodson, ed., *The Place of Astronomy in the Ancient World* (London: Oxford Univ. Press, 1974), pp. 51–66.

14. Dampier, *History of Science,* p. 6. Pannekoek (*History of Astronomy,* p. 84) agreed: "There is in Egypt no trace of a development of astronomy to scientific stature."

15. Proctor, "Astronomy," p. 756. Also Clive Kilmister, *The Nature of the Universe* (New York: E. P. Dutton, 1971), p. 26; John L. E. Dreyer, *A History of Astronomy,* 2d. ed., rev. by W. H. Stahl (Mineola, N.Y.: Dover, 1952), pp. 11–13.

16. Proctor, "Astronomy," p. 746; Dreyer, *History of Astronomy,* pp. 31–32; and the excellent discussion by D. R. Ricks, *Early Greek Astronomy to Aristotle* (Ithaca: Cornell Univ. Press, 1970), pp. 55–59.

17. Sarton, *History of Science,* p. 243.

18. Ibid., p. 178.

19. Proctor, "Astronomy," pp. 747–748. Empedocles also followed the theory that the heavens were made of glass (crystal). The lengthy coverage in Ricks (*Early Greek Astronomy,* pp. 151–189) is among the best available.

20. Cicero, *Academicorum priorum liber* II, 39, 123, ed. James S. Reid (London, 1885), p. 322.

21. Hippolytus, *Philosophumena,* I, 11, tr. F. Legge (London: Society for Promoting Christian Knowledge, 1921), vol. 1, p. 48.

22. For a more complete analysis of *Timaeus,* see Francis M. Cornford's *Plato's Cosmology* (London: Kegan Paul, 1937). Likewise, Gale E. Christianson, *This Wild Abyss* (New York: Free Press, 1978) notes, "In the *Timaeus* . . . Plato freely mingles myth with science" to the point that it has become almost impossible to determine Plato's real beliefs (p. 41).

23. Sarton, *History of Science,* p. 420. Dreyer's discussion (*History of Astronomy,* pp. 71–81) is also very helpful.

24. Sarton, *History of Science,* pp. 509–537. Much of Aristotelian astron-

omy is contained in his *Meteorologica, Metaphysics lambda, Physics,* and *De caelo.*

25. Proctor, "Astronomy," p. 745. Likewise, Pannekoek (*History of Astronomy*) notes that "Astronomy in China . . . had no perceptible influence on the progress of science" (p. 94).

26. Carl Sagan and Ann Druyan, *Comet* (New York: Random House, 1985), pp. 16, 18.

27. Ibid., p. 16.

28. F. von Oefele, "Sun, Moon, and Stars (Introduction)," in *ERE,* vol. 12, p. 48.

Chapter 10

1. *The Koran,* tr. by George Sale (London: Frederick Warne, 1909), pp. 5, 541, 544, 555, and 567.

2. Ibid., p. 567.

3. Ibid., p. 545.

4. Ibid., p. 252.

5. Ibid., p. 318.

6. Ibid., p. 571.

7. Ibid., p. 577.

8. Ibid., p. 294.

9. Ibid., p. 551. If the redshift interpretation can be correctly applied to the heavens, then the size of the universe far exceeds the estimate given in *The Koran.* If the Doppler effect cannot be applied, Mohammed's estimate is probably too large. In either case, the estimate is incorrect.

10. Ibid., p. 196.

11. Sukumar Ranjan Das, "Scope and Development of Indian Astronomy," in George Sarton, ed., *Os,* vol. 2 (Bruges, Belgium: Saint Catherine Press, 1936), pp. 197–219. John L. E. Dreyer (*A History of Astronomy,* 2d. ed. [Mineola, N.Y.: Dover, 1952], p. 240) adds that "early Hindu astronomy seems to have been chiefly astrology" and concludes that even later materials of the period from 300–1300 A.D. "though supposed to be derived from divine sources, are strongly influenced or simply borrowed from Greek authors." W. R. Kloetzli ("Maps of Time—Mythologies of Descent: Scientific Instruments and the Puranic Cosmograph," *HR* 25 [1985]: 117) notes that "the cosmologies . . . present us with representations of the universe that . . . are incongruous with reality."

12. Louis Renou, *The Nature of Hinduism,* tr. by Patrick Evans (New York: Walker, 1962), p. 6.

13. A. S. Geden, "Sun, Moon, and Stars (Hindu)," in *ERE,* vol. 12, p. 83. A more complete discussion is found in A. Berriedale Keith, "Indian," in *MAR,* vol. 6, pp. 15–40.

14. Geden, "Sun, Moon, and Stars," p. 84.

15. L. Gaussen, *The Divine Inspiration of the Bible* (1841; rprt. Grand Rapids: Kregel, 1971), pp. 253–254; Charles-Albert Reichen, *A History of Astronomy,* (New York: Hawthorn, 1963), p. 10.

16. Franklyn Branley, "Conceptions of the Universe," *NH* 79 (December 1970): 30f.

17. E. J. Thomas, "Sun, Moon, and Stars (Buddhist)," in *ERE,* vol. 12, p. 71.
18. *Jataka,* no. 450; *Digha,* ii.259.
19. Thomas, "Sun, Moon, and Stars," p. 71. See also *Anguttara,* i.227.
20. J.J.M. deGroot, *The Religious System of China* vol. 4, (1901; rprt. Taipei: Literature House, 1964), vol. 4, p. ix.
21. John C. Ferguson, "Chinese," in *MAR,* vol. 8, pp. 61–63.
22. M. J. Costelloe, "Astral Religion," *EDR,* vol. 1, p. 296.
23. Reuben Kaufman, "Astrology," *UJE,* vol. 1, p. 570.
24. Ibid.
25. Ibid., p. 571.
26. W. H. Blumenthal, "Astronomy," *UJE,* vol. 1, p. 572.

Chapter 11

1. E. M. Fallaize, "Sun, Moon, and Stars (Primitive)," in *ERE,* vol. 12, pp. 62–63.
2. W. Corswant, *A Dictionary of Life in Bible Times,* tr. by A. Heathcote (Bungay, Suffolk: Hodder and Stoughton, 1960), pp. 262, 187.
3. C. F. Whitley, *The Genius of Ancient Israel* (Amsterdam: Philo Press, 1969), pp. 61–62.
4. E. W. Maunder, "Astronomy," in *ISBE,* vol. 1, p. 302.
5. Fallaize, "Sun, Moon, and Stars," p. 64.
6. Pliny, *Naturalis Historia,* ii, 81. See also Frederic Golden, *The Trembling Earth* (New York: Charles Scribner's Sons, 1983), p. 21; D. S. Halacy, Jr., *Earthquakes* (Indianapolis: Bobbs-Merrill, 1974), p. 12; and W. D. Wallis, "Prodigies and Portents," in *ERE,* Vol. X, p. 367.
7. W. D. Wallis, "Prodigies and Portents," *ERE,* vol. 10, p. 371. See also Mark Littman and Donald K. Yeomans, *Comet Halley: Once in a Lifetime* (Washington: American Chemical Society, 1985), pp. 3–7.
8. Carl Sagan and Ann Druyan, *Comet* (New York: Random House, 1985), pp. 3–24. See also H. A. Giles, *Confucianism and Its Rituals* (London: Williams and Northgate, 1915), p. 180. T. Fu, "Sun. Moon, and Stars (Chinese)," in *ERE,* vol. 12, p. 77.
9. Wallis, "Prodigies," p. 368.
10. George Benjamin Walker, *Hindu World II* (London: George Allen & Unwin, 1968), pp. 67–68; Fu, "Sun, Moon, and Stars," p. 77.

Chapter 12

1. See April Lawton, "From Here to Infinity," *Science Digest* 89 (January/February, 1981): 98–105.
2. Rene Taton, for example (*History of Science: Ancient and Medieval Science* [New York: Basic Books, 1963], p. 315), cites sources that put the catalog at around 800 stars, while Rudolf Tiel (*And There Was Light* [New York: Alfred A. Knopf, 1957], p. 46) refers to other sources that say Hipparchus counted 1080 stars.
3. Joseph Needham, *Science and Civilization in China* (Cambridge: Cambridge Univ. Press, 1956), vol. 3, pp. 263–271.

4. Ibid., p. 265.

5. R. Laird Harris, Gleason L. Archer, Jr., and Bruce Waltke, eds. *TWOT* (Chicago: Moody, 1980), pp. 296–297; Francis Brown, S. R. Driver, and Charles A. Briggs, *BDB,* 1907 (rprt. with corrections. Oxford: Clarendon, 1958), pp. 328–329; G. W. Gilmore, "Sun and Sun Worship," in *SHERK,* vol. 9, p. 137.

6. *BDB,* pp. 328–329. See G. W. Gilmore, "Hebrew Conceptions of the Moon," in *SHERK,* vol. 7, pp. 492–494.

7. D. R. Ricks, *Early Greek Astronomy to Aristotle* (Ithaca: Cornell Univ. Press, 1970), p. 68.

8. Ibid., p. 74.

9. Ricks, *Early Greek Astronomy.* p. 71.

10. Ibid. p. 46.

11. Ibid., pp. 47–48.

12. Gertrude Jobes and James Jobes, *Outer Space: From the Emergence of History to the Present Day* (New York: Scarecrow, 1964), p. 287.

13. W. H. Blumenthal, "Astronomy," *UJE,* vol. 1, p. 572.

14. See, for example, *BDB,* p. 465; *KB,* p. 434. Likewise, Hans Walter Wolff (*Joel and Amos,* tr. by Waldemar Janzen, S. Dean McBride, Jr., and Charles A. Muenchow [Philadelphia: Fortress, 1977], p. 241) accepts the designation.

15. George Abell, *Exploration of the Universe,* 2d ed. (New York: Holt, Rinehart and Winston, 1969), p. 548. Interestingly, of all clusters in existence, the Pleiades is considered among the most stable. See Stanley Wyatt, *Principles of Astronomy,* 2d ed. (Boston: Allyn and Bacon, 1971), pp. 483–484.

16. Cecilia Payne-Gaposchkin, *Stars and Clusters* (Cambridge: Harvard Univ. Press, 1979), p. 13. See also, T. C. Lyon, *Witness in the Sky* (Chicago: Moody, 1961), pp. 103–104.

Chapter 13

1. R. Laird Harris, Gleason L. Archer, Jr., and Bruce K. Waltke, eds. (*TWOT* [1980], vol. 2, p. 862) note that the Hebrew term is more correctly rendered "expanse."

2. A. O. Schnabel, *Has God Spoken?* (San Diego: Creation-Life, 1974), p. 10.

3. Gale E. Christianson, *This Wild Abyss* (New York: Free Press, 1978), p. 41. Also George Sarton, *A History of Science* (Cambridge: Harvard Univ. Press, 1959), vol. 1, p. 450.

4. Sarton, *History of Science,* p. 517.

5. Isaac Asimov, *The Universe: From Flat Earth To Quasar* (New York: Avon, 1966) p. 39.

6. George Mulfinger, "Our Degenerating Universe," in Walter Lang, ed., *A Challenge to Education* (Caldwell, Idaho: Bible-Science, 1972), p. 53.

7. Cited by Martin J. Klein, "Thermodynamics in Einstein's Universe," *Science* 157 (1967): 509.

8. P. W. Bridgman, "Reflections on Thermodynamics," *AS* 41 (October, 1953): 549. Likewise, John B. Fenn (*Engines, Energy, and Entropy* [San Francisco: W. H. Freeman, 1982], p. 241) observes: "This perhaps bold generalization has never been found wanting."

9. Lincoln Barnett, *The Universe and Dr. Einstein* (New York: New American Library, 1957), p. 102. A. B. Pippard (*Elements of Chemical Thermodynamics for Advanced Students* [Cambridge: Cambridge Univ. Press, 1966], p. 100) adds that "no evidence has ever been presented that the Second Law breaks down under any circumstances."

10. S. W. Angrist, "Perpetual Motion Machines," *SA* 218 (1968): 120–121.

11. Mulfinger, "Our Degenerating Universe," p. 54. See also E. N. Parker, "The Solar Wind," in Owen Gingerich, ed. *Frontiers in Astronomy* (San Francisco: W. H. Freeman, 1970), p. 106, and Robert H. Koch, review of *Mass Loss from the Stars* in *Science* 167 (February 13, 1970): 971. For recent controversy over the rate at which the sun is losing its mass, see John A. Eddy and Aram A. Boornazian, "Analyses of Historical Data Suggest Sun Is Shrinking," *PT* 32 (September, 1979): 17–19; and David W. Dunham et al., "Observations of a Probable Change in the Solar Radius between 1715 and 1979," *Science* 210 (1980): 1243–1245.

12. Mulfinger, "Our Degenerating Universe," p. 56. See also Halton C. Arp, "The Evolution of Galaxies," in Owen Gingerich, ed. *Frontiers in Astronomy* (San Francisco: W. H. Freeman, 1970), p. 222.

13. Isaac Asimov, "In the Game of Energy and Thermodynamics You Can't Even Break Even," *SIJ* 4 (June, 1970): p. 6.

14. Harold Morowitz, "Biology as a Cosmological Science," *Main Currents in Modern Thought* 28 (1972): 151.

Chapter 14

1. Frederic Golden, *The Trembling Earth* (New York: Charles Scribner's Sons, 1983), pp. 18–21. Likewise, Bruce A. Bolt (*Earthquakes: A Primer* [San Francisco: W. H. Freeman, 1978], p. 3) writes that "in many countries" it was believed there were "grotesque monsters that supported the earth."

2. Elmer B. Smick ("Mythology and the Book of Job," *JETS* 20 [1970]: 102) cogently points out: "No one has ever satisfactorily explained how verse 7 fits into any primitive cosmology."

3. John Clayton, *The Source* (Mentone, Ind.: Superior, 1976), p. 102. See also *TWOT* (vol. 1, pp. 266–267), where the authors note specifically that the term "may refer to sphericity of the earth."

4. Fred Hoyle, *Astronomy* (New York: Doubleday, 1962), p. 83. For a visual depiction, see H. F. Tozer, *History of Ancient Geography*, 2d ed. (Cambridge: Cambridge Univ. Press, 1935), map II.

5. W. H. Guier and R. R. Newton, "The Earth's Gravity Field—Doppler Tracking of Five Satellites," *JGR 70* (September 15, 1965).

6. *TWOT*, vol. 1, p. 334; *BDB*, p. 368. See also D. M. Edwards, "Seal," *ISBE*, vol. 4, p. 2708.

7. *BDB*, pp. 245–246.

8. W. E. Vine, *An Expository Dictionary of Biblical Words*, rev. ed., Merrill F. Unger and William White, eds. (Nashville: Nelson, 1985), pp. 269–270.

Chapter 15

1. Each area has been dealt with elsewhere in the text. The biblical conception of the earth and universe is described in previous chapters in this

section. For a thorough discussion of miracles, see C. S. Lewis, *Miracles* (New York: Macmillan, 1947); Norman L. Geisler, *Miracles and Modern Thought* (Grand Rapids: Zondervan, 1982); Ninian Smart, *Philosophers and Religious Truth* (London: SCM, 1964); and Richard Swinburne, *The Concept of Miracle* (London: Macmillan, 1970).

2. W. R. Bowie, "The Book of Genesis," *IB*, vol. 1 (Nashville: Abingdon, 1952), p. 472.

3. See Alexander Heidel, *The Babylonian Genesis*, 3d ed. (Chicago: Univ. of Chicago Press, 1963).

4. A. R. Millard, "A New Babylonian 'Genesis' Story," *TB* 18 (1966): 3–18.

5. Gerhard F. Hasel, "The Polemic Nature of the Genesis Cosmology," *EQ* 46 (1974): p. 83. See also S. N. Kramer, *Mythologies of the Ancient World* (Garden City, N.Y.: Doubleday, 1961), p. 120; Nahum M. Sarna, *Understanding Genesis* (New York: Schocken Institute, 1970), p. 7.

6. W. G. Lambert, "A New Look at the Babylonian Genesis," *JTS* 16 (1965): 288.

7. Millard, "New Babylonian Genesis," p. 17. An excellent compendium of the differences in the two accounts is presented by John J. Davis, *Paradise to Prison: Studies in Genesis* (Grand Rapids: Baker, 1975), pp. 67–71.

8. Ibid.

9. Ibid., p. 18.

10. C. F. Whitley, *The Genius of Ancient Israel* (Amsterdam: Philo Press, 1969), pp. 45, 46, 48.

11. L. I. J. Stadelmann, *The Hebrew Conception of the World* (Rome: Pontifical Bible Institute, 1970), p. 13.

12. Hasel, "Polemic Nature," p. 84.

13. Claus Westermann, *Genesis 1–11* (Minneapolis: Augsburg, 1984), p. 105f.

14. *TWOT,* vol. 2, p. 862. Also Thomas Whitelaw, "Genesis," in *The Pulpit Commentary,* ed. by H. D. M. Spence and Joseph S. Excell, vol. 1, 1881, (rprt. Grand Rapids: Eerdmans, 1952), p. 15.

15. *TWOT,* vol. 2, p. 862.

16. H. Torczyner ("The Firmament and the Clouds," *ST* 1 [1948]: 188–196) argues that the term refers to the clouds, not a solid vault. See Robert Baker Girdlestone, *Girdlestone's Synonyms of the Old Testament,* ed. Donald White, 3d ed. (Grand Rapids: Baker, 1983), pp. 293–294; Clyde T. Francisco, *Genesis,* rev. ed. (Nashville: Broadman, 1969), p. 123.

17. Lee Haines, "Genesis and Exodus," *WBC* (Grand Rapids: Eerdmans, 1967), vol. 1, p. 26.

18. An excellent short discussion is F. F. Bruce, *The Books and the Parchments,* 3d ed. (Old Tappan, N.J.: Revell, 1963).

19. John R. Kohlenberger, III, ed., *The NIV Interlinear Hebrew-English Old Testament* (Grand Rapids: Zondervan, 1979), p. 1. Among the recent commentaries adopting "expanse" are F. F. Bruce, *International Bible Commentary* (Grand Rapids: Zondervan, 1986), p. 115; George Herbert Livingston, *BBC,* vol. 1 (Kansas City: Beacon Hill, 1969), p. 32; C. C. Crawford, *Genesis* (Joplin, Mo.: College Press, 1985), p. 141; and Howard F. Vos, *Genesis* (Chicago: Moody, 1983), pp. 14–15.

20. W. E. Vine, *An Expository Dictionary of Old Testament Words,* F. F. Bruce, ed. (Old Tappan, N.J.: Revell, 1978), p. 67.

21. Ibid. See also A. H. Cremer, "Heaven," *SHERK,* vol. 5, pp. 180–181.

22. R. C. Newman and H. J. Eckelmann, Jr., *Genesis One and the Origin of the Earth* (Downers Grove, Ill.: Inter-Varsity, 1977), p. 75. See also U. Cassuto, *A Commentary on the Book of Genesis,* tr. by Israel Abrahams (Jerusalem: Magnes, 1961), p. 49.

23. C. Gaenssle, "A Look at Current Biblical Cosmologies," *CTM* 23 (1952): 738–749 (cited in Bernard Ramm, *The Christian View of Science and Scripture* [Grand Rapids: Eerdmans, 1954], p. 99).

24. E. W. Maunder, "Astronomy," ISBE, vol. 1, p. 315.

25. C. A. Simpson, "Genesis," in *IB,* vol. 1, p. 467.

26. R. Davidson, *Genesis 1–11, CBC,* vol. 1 (Cambridge: Cambridge Univ. Press, 1973), pp. 15–16.

27. K. A. Kitchen, *Ancient Orient and the Old Testament* (Downers Grove, Ill.: Inter-Varsity, 1966), p. 89. See further J. V. Kinnier Wilson, "The Epic of Creation," in *Documents from Old Testament Times,* D. W. Thomas, ed. (New York: Harper and Row, 1958), p. 14.

28. Heidel, *Babylonian Genesis,* p. 99.

29. George Marsh, *Lectures on the English Language,* p. 255, cited in M. C. Kurfees, "Change of Meaning in the History of Words," *Instrumental Music in the Worship* (1911; rprt. Nashville: Gospel Advocate, 1969), p. 28.

30. Heidel, *Babylonian Genesis,* p. 100.

31. Hasel, "Polemic Nature," p. 83.

32. Maunder, "Astronomy," p. 316.

33. Robert Graves and Raphael Patai, *Hebrew Myths: The Book of Genesis* (Garden City, N.Y.: Doubleday, 1965), p. 26.

34. Gaenssle, "Current Biblical Cosmologies," p. 747 (cited in Ramm, *Science and Scripture,* p. 100).

35. *TWOT,* vol. 2, pp. 673–674.

36. See sections on earth sciences in Part Three.

37. Ramm, *Science and Scripture,* p. 101.

Chapter 16

1. Walter Van Der Kamp, "I Make Its Pillars Firm." *BSN,* 14 (January, 1976): 3.

2. Edward Young, *Thy Word Is Truth* (Grand Rapids: Eerdmans, 1957), pp. 168–169.

3. Controversy over the length of the creative "periods" has raged for centuries. The arguments are lengthy and have been cogently presented elsewhere. See Arthur F. Williams, "The Genesis Account of Creation," in *Why Not Creation?,* Walter E. Lammerts, ed. (Grand Rapids: Baker, 1970), pp. 28–33; Henry M. Morris, "The Day-Age Theory Revisited," in *The Decade of Creation,* Henry M. Morris and Donald H. Rohrer, eds. (San Diego: Creation-Life, 1981), pp. 15–22; and R. C. Newman and H. J. Eckelmann, *Genesis One and the Origin of Earth* (Downers Grove, Ill.: Inter-Varsity, 1977), pp. 61–66.

4. David Kidner, *Psalms 73–150* (Downers Grove, Ill.: Inter-Varsity, 1975), p. 349.

5. See earlier discussion of passages relating to the revolution of the earth in chapter 14.

6. *TWOT,* vol. 1, p. 493.

7. Spiros Zodhiates, "Lexical Aids to the Old Testament," *The Hebrew-Greek Key Study Bible* (Grand Rapids: Baker, 1984), p. 1615.

8. Zodhiates, "Lexical Aids," p. 1600.

9. *TWOT,* vol. 1, p. 433.

10. These elements of Hebrew poetry, known as parallelisms, involve "one statement followed by another, done with art, style, and image (where) by saying the same thing in slightly different words, the total impression is enhanced . . ." (Ronald Barclay Allen, *Praise! A Matter of Life and Breath* [Grand Rapids: Zondervan, 1980], p. 51).

11. Edward Grant, *In Defense of the Earth's Centrality and Immutability: Scholastic Reaction to Copernicanism in the Seventeenth Century* (Philadelphia: American Philosophical Society, 1984).

12. Clement of Alexandria, *Miscellanies,* Book V, Chapter vi, English translation, ed. by Alexander Roberts and James Donaldson (Edinburgh: The Ante-Nicene Christian Library, 1869), vol. ii, p. 368.

13. Ibid., p. 111.

14. See George Grote, *Plato* (London: John Murray, 1885), vol. 3, p. 257.

15. Andrew Dickson White, *A History of the Warfare of Science with Theology* (New York: Free Press, 1965), p. 126.

16. Bruce Mazlish in Ibid., p. 126.

17. Ibid.

18. See James Broderick, *Galileo: The Man, His Work, His Misfortunes* (New York: Harper and Row, 1964); Louis Young, ed., *Exploring the Universe* (New York: McGraw-Hill, 1963), pp. 112–135.

19. Lorraine Boettner, *Roman Catholicism* (Philadelphia: Presbyterian and Reformed, 1962), pp. 97ff.

20. H. J. Schroeder, *Canons and Decrees of the Council of Trent* (St. Louis: Herder, 1950), pp. 273–278; William Edward Addis and Thomas Arnold, *Catholic Dictionary* (New York: Catholic Publication Society, 1887), p. 82.

21. Pietro Redondi, *Galileo Eretico* (Turin: Giulio Einaudi Editore, 1983).

22. William A. Wallace, "Galileo," *Isis* 76 (1985): 379–380.

Chapter 17

1. Robert E. D. Clark, *The Christian Stake in Science* (Chicago: Moody, 1967), p. 94.

2. For ancient beliefs regarding meteorites, see Fritz Heide, *Meteorites* (Chicago: Univ. of Chicago Press, 1964), pp. 63–67; Gerald Joseph McCall, *Meteorites and Their Origin* (New York: John Wiley, 1973), pp. 17–26; and Lincoln Lapaz and Jean Lapaz, *Space Nomads* (New York: Holiday House, 1961), pp. 147–157.

3. Clark, *Christian Stake in Science,* pp. 85–97.

Chapter 18

1. The uniqueness of the earth has been dealt with in a number of publications. See John Clayton, *The Source* (Mentone, Ind.: Superior Printing, 1976), pp. 77–88; Vincent Cronin, *The View from Planet Earth* (New York: William Morrow, 1981), pp. 304–309, 331–340; A. Creasy Morrison, *Seven Reasons Why a Scientist Believes in God* (Westwood, N.J.: Revell, 1963); Arthur Custance, *Evolution or Creation?* (Grand Rapids: Zondervan, 1976), pp. 27–33; Robert Kofahl and Kelly Seagraves, *The Creation Explanation* (Wheaton, Ill.: Shaw, 1975), pp. 14–19; and Stuart Nevins, "Planet Earth: Design or Accident?" in *The Battle for Creation,* Henry Morris and Duane Gish, eds. (San Diego: Creation-Life, 1976), pp. 215–223.

2. The most comprehensive coverage of the anthropic principle to date is found in John D. Barrow and Frank J. Tipler, *The Anthropic Cosmological Principle* (Oxford: Oxford Univ. Press, 1986). The principle is related to biblical teachings by W. G. Pollard, "Science and the Bible," *IDB-S* (Nashville: Abingdon, 1976), pp. 789–790.

3. Earlier civilizations often made the earth the center of the entire universe. (See Part Two, especially chapter 16.)

4. The antithesis of the ideas held by previous cultures is equally false. There is no difference in kind in granting this planet too much uniqueness or in granting it too little. Many modern scientists, rebelling against the geocentricity of earlier days, have moved too far in the other direction.

5. J. M. Plumley, "The Cosmology of Ancient Egypt," in *Ancient Cosmologies* (London: George Allen & Unwin, 1975), p. 24.

6. Plato, *Timaeus,* tr. by Francis Cornford (New York: Liberal Arts Press, 1959), pp. 23–29.

7. Ibid., p. 27. See further, Plato, *Laws,* E. B. England, ed. (1921; rprt. Salem, N.H.: Ayer, 1976), x. 896A.

8. I. F. Burns, "Cosmogony and Cosmology (Greek)," in *ERE,* vol. 4, p. 148.

9. Frank Dawson Adams, *The Birth and the Development of the Geological Sciences* (New York: Dover, 1954), p. 289.

10. Francois Marie-Pompee Colonna, *Historie Naturelle de l'Univers* (Paris: A. Cailleau, 1734), vol. 1, Part 2, p. 204.

11. For a more detailed account of the creation of the Egyptian pantheon, see Barbara Watterson, *The Gods of Ancient Egypt* (New York: Facts on File, 1984). See also, E. A. Wallis Budge, *Egyptian Religion* (1900; rprt. New York: Bell, 1959); Donald Mackenzie, *Egyptian Myth and Legend* (1907; rprt. New York: Bell, 1978).

12. J. A. MacCulloch, "Earth, Earth-Gods," in *ERE,* vol. 5, p. 127f.

13. Joseph Campbell, *The Masks of God: Oriental Mythology* (New York: Viking, 1962), p. 160. Note also James G. Frazer, *The Golden Bough,* Vol. 2, *The Magic Art and the Evolution of Kings,* (1890; rprt. New York: St. Martin's, 1980), pp. 155–159.

14. MacCulloch, "Earth," pp. 127f.

15. William Crooke, *Popular Religion and Folklore of Northern India* (Westminster: Archibald Constable, 1896), ii, p. 293. See also, i, p. 49.

16. While the Bible does note that some earthquakes were supernaturally induced, it nowhere claims all tremors are so caused.

17. MacCulloch, "Earth," p. 128.

18. Bruce Walker et al., *Earthquake* (Alexandria: Time-Life, 1982), pp. 36ff.

19. "The Taming of Earthquakes," *Time*, September 7, 1970, p. 46.

20. N. W. Thomas, "Animals," in *ERE*, vol. 1, p. 491.

21. Ibid. In China, the earth was said to be supported by giant tortoises. See Anthony Christie, *Chinese Mythology* (London: Paul Hamlyn, 1968), p. 65.

22. Ibid.

23. D. S. Halacy, Jr., *Earthquakes: A Natural History* (Indianapolis: Bobbs-Merrill, 1974), p. 12.

24. Epiphanius, *Adversus Haereses*, ii.2.23. in J. P. Migne, *Patrologia Graeca* (Oxford: Basil B. Blackwell, 1858), xlii.68.

25. Halacy, *Earthquakes*, p. 10.

26. William R. Gray et al., *The Powers of Nature* (Washington: National Geographic, 1978).

27. Halacy, *Earthquakes*, p. 13.

28. Marshall Clogett, *Greek Science in Antiquity* (New York: Abelard-Schuman, 1955), p. 412.

29. Halacy, *Earthquakes*, p. 16.

30. Ibid., p. 13.

31. Walker, *Earthquake*, pp. 74–101.

32. Adams, *Birth and Development*, p. 289.

33. Ristoro d'Arezzo, *La Composizione del Mondo* (Rome: Bibliotaca rara. 1859), p. 96.

34. Adams, *Birth and Development*, pp. 84–85.

35. The opinion was shared by such notables as Aristotle, Agricola, and Roger Bacon. See Adams, *Birth and Development*, p. 282.

36. Johann Gottlob Lehmann, *Traite de la Physique* (Paris: J. Herissant, 1759), vol. 1.

37. Gabriel Plattes, *A Discovery of Subterranean Treasure* (London: I. Okes for Jasper Emery, 1638).

38. George Stanley Godwin, *Vancouver, A Life, 1757–1798* (London: P. Allan, 1930), p. 27.

39. Ruth V. Wright and Robert Chadbourne, *Gems and Minerals of the Bible* (New York: Harper and Row, 1970), p. 57.

40. Adams, *Birth and Development*, pp. 149–151.

41. Joan Evans, *Magical Jewels of the Middle Ages and the Renaissance* (Oxford: Oxford Univ. Press, 1923).

42. Adams, *Birth and Development*, pp. 124–128.

43. Ibid., pp. 90–94.

44. Ibid., pp. 95–102.

45. George Sarton, *A History of Science* (Cambridge: Harvard Univ. Press, 1959), vol. 1, p. 560.

46. Christie, *Chinese Mythology*, pp. 60–72. See also J. A. MacCulloch, "Mountains, Mountain-Gods," in *ERE*, vol. 8, pp. 863f.

47. A. M. Rehwinkel, *Wonders of Creation* (Grand Rapids: Baker, 1974), p. 10.

48. S.A.B. Mercer, "Water, Water-Gods (Babylonian)," in *ERE*, vol. 12, p. 708.

49. Ibid., p. 710.

50. Ibid. See also Frazer, *The Magic Art*, Part I, vol. 2, pp. 155f. In early Greek civilization, water was worshiped as a god (Homer, *Iliad*, xiv, 201, 246; Hesiod, *Theogony*, 133–136). For Roman times, see E. A. Gardner, "Water, Water-Gods," in *ERE*, vol. 12, p. 713. In China, human sacrifice was offered to the god ("count") of the Yellow River (Christie, *Chinese Mythology*, pp. 79, 83).

51. Mercer, "Water, Water-Gods," p. 710; Naphtali Lewis, *Life in Egypt Under Roman Rule* (Oxford: Clarendon, 1983), p. 94.

52. Mercer, "Water, Water-Gods," p. 708.

53. Ibid., p. 709.

54. Aristotle, *Meteorologica*, Loeb Classical Library, No. 397 (Cambridge: Harvard Univ. Press, 1952), II, 1.

55. William R. Corliss, *Mysteries Beneath the Sea* (New York: Thomas Y. Crowell, 1970), p. 31.

56. Vincent H. Cassidy, *The Sea Around Them* (Baton Rouge: Louisiana State Univ. Press, 1968), p. 21.

57. W. D. Wallis, "Prodigies and Portents," in *ERE*, vol. 10, pp. 369–371. Note also B.F.J. Schonland, *The Flight of the Thunder Bolts* (Oxford: Clarendon, 1950), pp. 1–7.

58. J. Dyer Ball, "Light and Darkness (Chinese)," in *ERE*, vol. 8, p. 51; Mircea Eliade, *Patterns in Comparative Religion* (New York: New American Library, 1958), pp. 84–85; and *Rig-Veda*, vii,56.9,17; v,55.9; i,23.12.

59. Frazer, *The Magic Art*, Part I, vol. 1, pp. 309–310, 370.

60. Sir Edward B. Taylor, *Researches into the Early History of Mankind*, 3rd series (1878; rprt. London: Luzac, 1929), pp. 223–227.

61. Schonland, *Thunderbolts*, p. 4.

62. Pausanias, *Description of Greece*, Loeb Classical Library, No. 298 (Cambridge: Harvard Univ. Press, 1935), v.14.10. evidence that lightning had struck the location.

63. Schonland, *Thunderbolts*, p. 5.

64. See chapter 1.

65. Livy, *Roman History*, Loeb Classical Library, vol. 7, No. 301 tr. F. G. Moore (Cambridge: Harvard Univ. Press, 1943), p. 31. See also, Seneca, *Naturales Quaestiones*, Loeb Classical Library, No. 457 (Cambridge: Harvard University Press, 1972), pp. 32–34 and 39–49.

66. Sarton, *A History of Science*, vol. I, pp. 243–244.

67. D. R. Ricks, *Early Greek Astronomy to Aristotle* (Ithaca: Cornell Univ. Press, 1970), p. 47.

68. Aristotle, *Meteorologica*, i, 369a, 10.

69. Ibid., i, 369b, 10.

70. Ibid.

71. Schonland, *Thunderbolts*, p. 4; Frazer, *The Magic Art*, Part 1, vol. 1, pp. 309–310.

72. W. E. Middleton, *A History of the Theories of Rain and Other Forms of Precipitation* (Chicago: Univ. of Chicago Press, 1968), p. 2.

73. Frazer, *The Magic Art*, Part 1, vol. 1, p. 248. "The Magical Control of the Weather," pp. 217–230.

74. J. J. M. deGroot, *The Religious System of China* (1901; rprt. Taipei: Literature House, 1964), vol. 3, pp. 918ff.

75. Frazer, *The Magic Art,* Part 1, vol. 1, p. 298.

76. J. Biddulph, *Tribes of the Hindoo Koosh* (Calcutta: Office of the Superintendent of Government Printing, 1880), p. 95. See also Crooke, *Popular Religion,* vol. 1, p. 73.

77. Frazer, *The Magic Art,* vol. 1, p. 284; Alvin Cohen, "Coercing the Rain Deities in Ancient China," *HR* 18 (1978): 247.

78. Middleton, *History of Theories of Rain,* pp. 5–7.

79. Ibid., pp. 9–10.

80. John Clarke, *Physical Science in the Time of Nero, being a Translation of the Quaestiones naturales of Seneca,* with notes by Sir Archibald Geikie (London: Macmillan, 1910), vol. 5, chaps. 1 and 4.

81. Middleton, *History of Theories of Rain,* p. 11.

Chapter 19

1. A. A. MacDonell, *Vedic Mythology* (Delhi: Motilal Banarsidass, 1974), p. 2.

2. William Crooke, "Dravidians (North India)," in *ERE,* vol. 5, p. 4.

3. See J. A. MacCulloch, "Earth-Gods," in *ERE,* vol. 5, pp. 127–131.

4. References, for example, that show inanimate objects worthy of worship according to the *Rig-Veda* are: Earth (1,89.4 and 5,84); Rivers (10,75 and 3,33); Stones (10,76; 10,94; and 10,175), and Mountains (7,34.23; 6,49.14; 3,54.20; 1,122.3; 1,132.6, and 3,53.1). The earth is also deified in *Atharva-Veda* (12,1 and 6,136.1).

5. While realizing that categorizing all Hindu philosophies under one roof is impossible (see John Bowker, *Problems of Suffering in Religions of the World* [London: Cambridge Univ. Press, 1970], p. 193; John B. Noss, *Man's Religions* [New York: Macmillan, 1969], p. 88), it is nevertheless true that the majority of these sacred writings tend toward the classical definition of pantheism, which equates everything with one divine spirit. See Ainslie T. Embree, *The Hindu Tradition* (New York: Vintage, 1972), p. 50; J.N.D. Anderson, *Christianity and Comparative Religion* (Downers Grove, Ill.: Inter-Varsity, 1970), pp. 76–78; and Raymond Hammer, "Men and Movements," in *Eerdman's Handbook to the World Religions,* R. Pierce Beaver et al., eds. (Grand Rapids: Eerdmans, 1982), p. 177.

6. *Rig-Veda* 10,89.4.

7. R. F. Gombrich, "Ancient Indian Cosmology," in Carmen Blacker and Michael Loewe, *Ancient Cosmologies* (London: George Allen & Unwin, 1973), p. 123.

8. *Rig-Veda* 10,90; 1,139.11; 10,129.6. *Atharva-Veda* 10,17.

9. *Rig-Veda* 7,95.1-2; 5,43.11; 6,61.11–12.

10. Ibid., 7,95.4–5; 2,30.8; 6,49.7.

11. See MacDonell, *Vedic Mythology,* p. 60.

12. *Rig-Veda* 2,20.8.

13. Ibid., 4,30,20.

14. Ibid., 1,52.8; 7,104.19.

15. Ibid., 8,89.9. Mountains were also held in reverence in sacred Sanskrit literature. The Himalayan chain was paid special homage. In return, the rugged peaks were said to dole out benefits to their adherents.

16. Ibid., 10,76; 10,94; 10,175.

17. Ibid.

18. A. A. MacDonell, "Magic (Vedic)," in *ERE,* vol. 8, p. 312; George B. Walker, *Hindu World II* (London: George Allen & Unwin, 1968), pp. 67–68.

19. Ibid.

20. Ibid., p. 313.

21. Ibid.; also Embree, *Hindu Tradition,* pp. 36–39.

22. *Rig-Veda* 3,33.1-12; 5,5; 10,98.

23. MacDonell, "Magic," p. 313.

24. Ibid., p. 317. See also M. Bloomfield, "On the 'Frog Hymn,' " *JAOS* 17 (1896): 173–179.

25. Crooke, *Popular Religion,* vol. 1, p. 73. Also M. N. Venketswami, "Superstitions Among Hindus in the Central Provinces," *IA* 28 (1899): 111.

26. T. C. Hobson, "The Nature Tribes of Manipur," *JAI* 31 (1901): 302; Walker, *Hindu World II,* p. 68.

27. M. Bloomfield, *Hymns of the Atharva-Veda, SBE,* vol. 42 (Oxford: Oxford Univ. Press, 1897) 249.

28. *Atharva-Veda* 1,8.2.

29. Ibid., 10,3.11.

30. Ibid., 19,26.1

31. *Mahabharata,* III.clxiii.14; I.xvii.5; I.xviii.1. Note also Lawrence A. Waddell, *Buddhism in Tibet* (London: W. Heffer and Sons, 1895), p. 78 and pp. 397ff; Hans Penner, "Cosmology as Myth in the Vishnu Purana," *HR* 5 (1966): 283–299; F. B. J. Kuiper, "Cosmogony and Conception: A Query," *HR* 10 (1970): 91–138; I. W. Mabbett, "The Symbolism of Mount Meru," *HR* 23 (1983): 65–83; S. Muzafer Ali, *The Geography of the Puranas* (New Delhi: People's, 1966); and Mircea Eliade, *The Myth of the Eternal Return, or Cosmos and History,* tr. by W. Trask (Princeton: Princeton Univ. Press, 1974), p. 16. *Anguttara Nikaya,* i,227, places the earth on water and water on air.

32. James G. Frazer, *The Golden Bough: Adonis, Attis, Osiris,* Part 4, vol. 1 (1890; rprt. New York: St. Martins, 1980), pp. 196–198.

33. J. Dyer Ball, "Light and Darkness (Chinese)," in *ERE,* vol. 8, p. 51.

34. Waddell, *Buddhism,* pp. 370f.

35. William Crooke, "Water, Water-Gods (Indian)," in *ERE,* vol. 12, p. 717.

36. Joseph Needham, *Science and Civilization in China* (Cambridge: Cambridge Univ. Press, 1956), vol. 3, p. 473.

37. R. F. Johnston, *Buddhist China* (London: John Murray, 1913), p. 245.

38. MacCulloch, "Mountains, Mountain-Gods," in *ERE,* vol. 8, p. 863. See, further, Anthony Christie, *Chinese Mythology* (London: Paul Hamlyn, 1968), pp. 68–69; Milton M. Chiu, *The Tao of Chinese Religion* (New York: Univ. Press of America, 1984), pp. 71–77; John C. Ferguson, "Chinese," in *MAR,* vol. 8, p. 61.

39. J. J. M. deGroot, *The Religious System of China* (1901; rprt. Taipei: Lit-

erature House, 1964), vol. 4, p. 109. Note also R. K. Douglas, *Confucianism and Taoism* (London: Society for Promoting Christian Knowledge, 1877), p. 244.

40. deGroot, *Religious System of China,* vol. 3, p. 947f. Also deGroot, *Religion in China* (New York: G. P. Putnam's Sons, 1912), pp. 285–314. See Confucius, *Shih Ching,* tr. by Ezra Pound (Cambridge: Harvard Univ. Press, 1954), vol. 3, p. 5.

41. Ball, "Light and Darkness," p. 51. For a more complete discussion of rainmaking magic in ancient China, see Alvin Cohen, "Coercing the Rain Deities in Ancient China," *HR* 18 (1978): pp. 243–248.

42. Pointing a finger at the rainbow was prohibited. See Douglas, *Confucianism and Taoism,* pp. 260–271.

43. See MacCulloch, "Mountains," p. 866. See also *Li Ki* III.ii.14–16; iii,6; VIII.ii.7; ii.12; *Shu Ching* II.i; III.i.9; V.iii.1; and *Shih Ching* i.8.

44. *Shih Ching* iii.5.

45. Needham, *Science and Civilization,* p. 464.

46. Ibid., p. 468.

47. *Shih Ching* II.viii.8.

48. James Hope Moulton, "Iranians," in *ERE,* vol. 7, p. 420.

49. MacCulloch, "Mountains," p. 866.

50. Moulton, "Iranians," p. 419.

51. Ibid., p. 420. See also James Hope Moulton, *Early Zoroastrianism* (London: Williams and Norgate, 1913), pp. 163f.

52. W. G. Aston, *Shinto: The Way of the Gods* (London: Longman's Green and Co., 1905), p. 330.

53. Ibid., p. 297.

54. W. D. Wallis, "Prodigies and Portents," in *ERE,* vol. 10, p. 369. *Ko-ji-ki,* tr. by B. H. Chamberlain (New York: C. E. Tuttle, 1982), p. 64.

55. Michael Revon, "Nature (Japanese)," in *ERE,* vol. 9, p. 234. See also Michael Revon, "Ancestor Worship and Cult of the Dead (Japanese)," in *ERE,* vol. 1, p. 456; Juliet Piggott, *Japanese Mythology* (London: Paul Hamlyn, 1969), pp. 12, 42; and Anderson, *Christianity and Comparative Religion,* p. 45.

56. *Ko-ji-ki,* p. 70; *Nihongi,* tr. by W. G. Aston (New York: C. E. Tuttle, 1971), i.22. See "Magic (Japanese)," in *ERE,* vol. 8, p. 298.

57. Revon, "Nature," p. 237.

58. W. G. Aston, "Shinto," in *ERE,* vol. 11, p. 466.

59. *Nihongi* ii.124.

60. Heber C. Kimball, in *Journal of Discourses,* Brigham Young, ed. (1859; rprt. Los Angeles: General, 1961), vol. 6, pp. 35–36. In vol. 5, p. 172, readers and listeners are told that the earth has a "spirit as much as a body has a spirit."

61. Bruce R. McConkie, *Mormon Doctrine* (Salt Lake City: Bookcraft, 1966), pp. 210–211, 251–252. See also Joseph Fielding Smith, *Doctrines of Salvation* (Salt Lake City: Bookcraft, 1954), vol. 1, pp. 73–74.

Chapter 20

1. Bernard Ramm, *The Christian View of Science and Scripture* (Grand Rapids: Eerdmans, 1954), p. 80.

2. J. W. Dawson, *Nature and the Bible* (New York: Robert Carter, 1875), pp. 23–25. See also, C. F. Whitley, *The Genius of Ancient Israel*, (Amsterdam: Philo Press, 1969), p. 61.

3. Charles Woodruff Shields, *The Scientific Evidences of Revealed Religion* (New York: Charles Scribner's Sons, 1900), p. 27. See also, Ramm, *Science and Scripture*, p. 71.

4. Robert E. D. Clark, *The Christian Stake in Science* (Chicago: Moody, 1967), p. 33.

5. Clarence J. Glacken, *Traces on the Rhodian Shore* (Berkeley: Univ. of California Press, 1967), p. 13.

6. For a more in-depth study of the rationality of nature, see Mario Bunge, *Causality and Modern Science* (New York: Dover, 1979).

7. Colin Chapman, *Christianity on Trial* (Wheaton, Ill.: Tyndale, 1975), p. 340.

8. R. Hooykaas, *Religion and the Rise of Modern Science* (Edinburgh: Scottish Academic Press, 1972), pp. 161–162. See also Eugene M. Klaaren, *Religious Origins of Modern Science* (Grand Rapids: Eerdmans, 1977).

9. C. F. Von Weizacker, *The Relevance of Science* (London: Collins, 1964), p. 163. See also Donald Mackay, *Science and Christian Faith Today* (London: CPAS, 1970), pp. 18–20.

10. H. and H. A. Frankfort, "The Emancipation of Thought from Myth," in *The Intellectual Advancement of Ancient Man*, H. Frankfort, ed. (Chicago: Univ. of Chicago Press, 1946), p. 363.

11. Hooykaas, *Rise of Modern Science*, pp. 7–9, 12–13.

12. Peter C. Craigie, *Psalms 1–50* (Waco, Tex.: Word, 1983), p. 181.

13. Derek Kidner, *Psalms 1–72* (Downers Grove, Ill.: Inter-Varsity, 1973), p. 99.

Chapter 21

1. C. F. Keil and F. Delitzsch, *Commentary on the Old Testament*, vol. 1, *The Pentateuch*, tr. by James Martin (n.d.; rprt. Grand Rapids: Eerdmans, 1978), p. 64.

2. *The Sacred Books of China*, tr. by James Legge, *SBE* (London: Clarendon, 1910), vol. 16, p. 355.

3. Ibid., pp. 425–427; vol. 27, p. 36; and vol. 28, pp. 203, 209, 218. See also *The Saddharma-Pundarika*, tr. by H. Kern, in *SBE*, vol. 21, p. 371; *The Zend-Avesta*, tr. by James Darmesteter and L. H. Mills, in *SBE*, vol. 31, p. 291; and *The Vendanta-Sutras*, tr. by G. Thibaut, in *SBE*, vol. 48, pp. 140, 365.

4. *The Upanishads*, tr. by F. Max Muller, in *SBE*, vol. 15, p. 260.

5. Robert E. D. Clark, *The Christian Stake in Science* (Chicago: Moody, 1967), p. 115.

6. Compare with the attempt by some to blame the Judeo-Christian religion for our current ecological problems: Lynn White, Jr., "The Historical Roots of Our Ecological Crisis," *Science* 155 (March 10, 1967): 1203–1207; Richard L. Means, "Why Worry about Nature?" *Saturday Review* (December 2, 1967), pp. 13–15; and Ian L. McHarg, *Design with Nature* (Garden City, N.Y.:

Natural History Press, 1969). Such accusations have been ably dealt with in Francis A. Schaeffer's *Pollution and the Death of Man* (Wheaton, Ill.: Tyndale, 1970). See also James Limburg, "What Does It Mean to 'Have Dominion Over the Earth'?" *Dialog* 10 (1971): 221–223; and Bruce Wrightman, "Man: Manager or Manipulator of the Earth?" *Dialog* 9 (1970): 200–210.

7. Some authors attempt to push these writings ahead to the Babylonian exile. Even if they are right, the thesis would remain unaffected. Evidence suggests, however, that the laws were in effect prior to the exile, though they were not closely observed. See R. Westbook, "Jubilee Laws," *ILR* 6 (1971): 209–226; R. North, *Sociology of the Biblical Jubilee* (Rome: Pontifical Biblical Institute, 1954), pp. 204f.

8. "Sabbatical Year," *MS*, vol. IX, p. 202.

9. A. Rendle Short, *Modern Discoveries and the Bible* (London: Intervarsity, 1942), p. 92.

10. John Peter Lange, *Leviticus: A Commentary on the Holy Scriptures*, tr. by Philip Schaff (Grand Rapids: Zondervan, 1876). p. 188.

11. Julian Morgenstern, "Year of Jubilee," *IDB*, vol. 2, p. 1001.

12. J. Barton Payne, *The Theology of the Older Testament* (Grand Rapids: Zondervan, 1962), p. 326.

13. D. Freeman, "Sabbatical Year," in *The New Bible Dictionary*, J. D. Douglas, ed. (Grand Rapids: Eerdmans, 1962), p. 1112.

14. See the excellent article by Christopher J. H. Wright, "What Happened Every Seven Years in Israel?" *EQ* 56 (1984): 129–138; 193–202. Other authors who deal with the humanitarian/religious aspect include Martin Noth (*Leviticus* [London: SCM, 1965], pp. 183f.) and Gordon J. Wenham (*The Book of Leviticus*, [Grand Rapids: Eerdmans, 1979], pp. 316–324).

15. Lange, *Leviticus*, p. 189; C. F. Whitley, *The Genius of Ancient Israel* (Amsterdam: Philo Press, 1969) p. 100.

16. Ibid., p. 188; Bernard Ramm, *The Christian View of Science and Scripture* (Grand Rapids: Eerdmans, 1954), p. 141.

17. See Michaelis, *Commentaries on the Laws of Moses* (London: Rivington, 1814), vol. 1, p. 376.

18. *MS*, vol. 4, p. 1042.

Chapter 22

1. Alfred Wegener, *Origin of Continents and Oceans*, tr. by John Biram, 1912 (Mineola, N.Y.: Dover, 1966).

2. Tom Alexander, "A Revolution Called Plate Tectonics Has Given Us a Whole New Earth," *The Smithsonian* 5 (January, 1975): p. 30.

3. Several sources deal at length with difficulties posed by the various methods used to date the earth. Two recent summaries written in easily understood terms by those who hold to the "young earth" position are provided by Paul D. Ackerman (*It's A Young World After All* [Grand Rapids: Baker, 1986]) and A. J. Monty White (*How Old Is the Earth?* [Welwyn, England: Evangelical Press, 1985]).

4. Trevor J. Major, "Plate Tectonics and Genesis," *RR* 6 (1986): 23–26.

Chapter 23

1. Roger Revelle, (Introduction) in Robert Cowen, *Frontiers of the Sea* (Garden City, N.Y.: Doubleday, 1969), p. 7.

2. A. O. Schnabel, *Has God Spoken?* (San Diego: Creation-Life, 1974), p. 31.

3. Warren E. Yasso, *Oceanography: A Study of Inner Space* (New York: Holt, Rinehart, and Winston, 1965), p. 11.

4. Francis P. Shepard, *Submarine Geology,* 3d ed. (New York: Harper and Row, 1973), p. 1.

5. The word *channels* used in 2 Samuel 22:16 literally means "stream bed" or "ravine." See *BDB,* p. 67.

6. Some writers claim more for these statements than seems credible. Schnabel (*Has God Spoken?*), p. 31, sees a link to the trench near the continental shelves and argues that Bible writers are describing where the ocean floor slides under the continents. There are several difficulties with such an interpretation, including the fact that many underwater canyons do not fit Schnabel's model.

7. Cuchlaine A. M. King, *An Introduction to Oceanography* (New York: McGraw-Hill, 1963), pp. 64–65. See also J. Tuzo Wilson, "Oceanic Ridges," *EB-MAC,* vol. 13, pp. 472–476.

8. Yasso, *Oceanography,* p. 85.

9. Ibid., p. 86.

10. Shepard, *Submarine Geology,* p. 2.

11. King, *Introduction to Oceanography,* p. 70.

12. Strabo was the first to write of these springs, sometime after 63 B.C.

13. Lawrence J. Kulp, in William J. Cromie, *Exploring the Secrets of the Sea* (New York: Prentice-Hall, 1962), p. 15.

14. For a general discussion of the history of oceanic knowledge, see Henry Chapin and F. G. Walton Smith, *The Ocean River* (New York: Charles Scribner's Sons, 1952), pp. 74–95.

15. F. G. Walton Smith, *The Seas in Motion* (New York: Thomas Y. Crowell, 1973), p. 182f.

16. Chapin and Smith, *Ocean River,* p. 95.

17. Matthew Fontaine Maury, *Physical Geology of the Sea,* John Leighly, ed. (1855; rprt. Cambridge: Belknap, 1963).

18. Cowen, *Frontiers of the Sea,* pp. 151–176.

19. Yasso, *Oceanography,* pp. 46–47.

20. Ibid., p. 48.

21. Chapin and Smith, *Ocean River,* p. 189.

22. Ibid., p. 174. See also S. Van Der Spoel and R. P. Heyman, *A Comparative Atlas of Zooplankton: Biological Patterns in the Oceans* (New York: Springer-Verlag, 1983); Ernest F. Thompson, "Plankton," *EA,* vol. 22, pp. 177–178; Per H. H. Halldal, "Plankton," *EB-MAC,* vol. 14, pp. 494–496; and J.E.G. Raymont, *Plankton and Productivity in the Oceans* (New York: Pergamon, 1963).

23. Chapin and Smith, *Ocean River,* p. 175.

Chapter 24

1. W. E. Middleton, *A History of the Theories of Rain and Other Forms of Precipitation* (Chicago: Univ. of Chicago Press, 1969), p. 2.

2. Ibid., p. 3.

3. Martin A. Uman, *Lightning* (New York: McGraw-Hill, 1969), p. 1.

4. In certain rare instances when lightning occurs in the clear sky, the streamers are suspended through the atmosphere.

5. Richard E. Orville, "Lightning," in *EB-MAC,* vol. 10, pp. 966–970.

6. B. J. Mason, *The Physics of Clouds* (Oxford: Clarendon, 1971).

7. D. J. Malan, *Physics of Lightning* (London: English Universities Press, 1963), pp. 165–166.

8. Ibid.

9. Clark C. Spence, *The Rainmakers* (Lincoln: Univ. of Nebraska Press, 1980).

10. Malan, *Physics of Lightning,* p. 165.

Abbreviations

AIM	*Annals of Internal Medicine*
AJDC	*American Journal of Diseases of Children*
AJM	*American Journal of Medicine*
AJPH	*American Journal of Public Health*
AJSLL	*American Journal of Semitic Language Literature*
AS	*American Scientist*
AUSS	*Andrews University Seminary Studies*
BA	*Biblical Archaeologist*
BASOR	*Bulletin of the American Society of Oriental Research*
BBC	*Beacon Bible Commentary*
BDB	Brown, Driver, and Briggs' *A Hebrew and English Lexicon of the Old Testament*
BHM	*Bulletin of the History of Medicine*
BSN	*Bible-Science Newsletter*
CA	*CA: A Cancer Journal for Clinicians*
CBC	*Cambridge Bible Commentary*
CG	*Clinical Gastroenterology*
CMAJ	*Canadian Medical Association Journal*
CPP	*Current Problems in Pediatrics*
CT	*Christianity Today*
CTM	*Concordia Theological Monthly*
Dae	*Daedalus*
EA	*Americana Encyclopedia*
EB	*Encyclopedia Britannica,* 9th edition
EBE	*Encyclopedia of Bioethics*
EB-MAC	*Encyclopedia Britannica-Macropaedia*

EDB	Vine's *An Expository Dictionary of Biblical Words*
EMH	*Encyclopedia of Medical History*
EQ	*Evangelical Quarterly*
ERE	*Encyclopedia of Religious Ethics*
FPP	*Family Planning Perspectives*
HR	*History of Religions*
HS	*History of Science*
IA	*Indian Antiquary*
IB	*Interpreter's Bible*
IBC	*International Bible Commentary*
IDB	*Interpreter's Dictionary of the Bible*
IDB-S	*Interpreter's Dictionary of the Bible: Supplement*
IJHS	*Indian Journal of the History of Science*
ILR	*Israel Law Review*
IS	*International Surgery*
ISBE	*International Standard Bible Encyclopedia*
ISBE-REV	*International Standard Bible Encyclopedia,* rev.ed.
JAI	*Journal of the Anthropological Institute*
JAMA	*Journal of the American Medical Association*
JAOS	*Journal of the American Oriental Society*
JBL	*Journal of Biblical Literature*
JCS	*Journal of Cuneiform Studies*
JD	*Journal of Discourses*
JEA	*Journal of Egyptian Archaeology*
JETS	*Journal of the Evangelical Theological Society*
JGR	*Journal of Geophysical Research*
JMP	*Journal of Medical Philosophy*
JTS	*Journal of Theological Studies*
JTVI	*Journal of the Transactions of the Victoria Institute*
JU	*Journal of Urology*
KB	Koehler and Baumgartner's *Lexicon in Veteris Testamenti Libros*
MAR	*The Mythology of All Races*
MCMT	*Main Currents in Modern Thought*
MMM	*Man, Myth, and Magic*
MS	McClintock and Strong's *Cyclopedia of Biblical, Theological, and Ecclesiastical Literature*
NEJM	*New England Journal of Medicine*
NH	*Natural History*
NYSJM	*New York State Journal of Medicine*
Or	*Orientalia*
Os	*Osiris*
PC	*Pulpit Commentary*

PCNA	*Pediatric Clinics of North America*
Ped	*Pediatrics*
PM	*Psychosomatic Medicine*
PRSM	*Proceedings of the Royal Society of Medicine*
PT	*Physics Today*
RA	*Revue d'Assyriologie*
RR	*Reason and Revelation*
SA	*Scientific American*
SBE	*Sacred Books of the East*
SGAB	*Societe de Geographis d'Alger Bulletin*
SHERK	*Schaff-Herzog Encyclopedia of Religious Knowledge*
SIJ	*Smithsonian Institute Journal*
ST	*Studia Theologica*
TB	*Tyndale Bulletin*
TL	*The Lancet*
TWOT	Harris, Archer, and Waltke's *Theological Wordbook of the Old Testament*
UJE	*Universal Jewish Encyclopedia*
WBC	*Wesleyan Bible Commentary*

Bibliography

Part One: The Body Inside

Ackerknecht, E. H. *A Short History of Medicine.* New York: Ronald Press, 1955.

Albright, W. F. *The Archaeology of Palestine.* Baltimore: Penguin, 1960.

———. *Yahweh and the Gods of Canaan.* Garden City, N.Y.: Doubleday, 1968.

Almy, T. P. "Therapeutic Strategy in Stress-Related Digestive Disorders." *CG* 6 (1977): 709–722.

American Scientific Affiliation. *Modern Science and the Christian Faith.* Wheaton, Ill.: Van Kampen, 1948.

Anesaki, Masahar. "Ethics and Morality (Buddhist)." *ERE.* Vol. 5, pp. 447–455.

Armstrong, Gail, and Friis, Robert. *Stress-Heart Disease Connection.* Irving, Calif.: Human Behavior Research Group, 1981.

Aston, W. G. "Shinto." *ERE.* Vol. 11, pp. 462–471.

Atkinson, D. T. *Magic, Myth and Medicine.* New York: World, 1956.

Bachman, L. H. "The Statistics of Circumcision and Penile Cancer." *CA* 34 (July/August, 1984): 238.

Badaway, Alexander. "Egypt, Ancient: Science and Technology." *EA.* vol. 10, pp. 60–62.

Bahlmann, J., and Liebau, H., eds. *Stress and Hypertension.* New York: S. Karger, 1982.

Bammer, Kurt, and Newberry, B. H., eds. *Stress and Cancer.* Lewiston, N.Y.: C. J. Hogrefe, 1981.

Bannan, E. A., and Judge, L. F. "Bacteriological Studies Relating to Handwashing." *AJPH* 55 (1965): 915–922.

Berenson, Abram S., ed. *Control of Communicable Diseases in Man.* New York: American Public Health Association, 1970.

Bettmann, Otto L. *A Pictorial History of Medicine.* Springfield, Ill.: Charles C. Thomas, 1956.

Bieber, I., ed. *Homosexuality—A Psychoanalytic Study.* New York: Basic Books, 1962.

Bieliauskas, L. A. *Stress and Its Relationship to Health and Illness.* Boulder, Colo.: Westview Press, 1982.

Biggs, R. D. "Medicine in Ancient Mesopotamia." *HS* 8 (1969): 94–105.

Binkin, Nancy J.; Koplan, Jeffrey P.; and Cates, Willard, Jr. "Preventing Neonatal Herpes." *JAMA* 251 (June 1, 1984): 2816–2821.

Bolling, G. M. "Disease and Medicine (Vedic)." *ERE.* Vol. 2, pp. 762–772.

________. "Vedic Literature." *EA.* Vol. 27, pp. 925–928.

Bouche-Le Clerq, Auguste. *Histoire de la Divinatione dans l'Antiquite.* 4 vols. Paris: E. Leroux, 1879–1882.

Bowen, James. *A History of Western Education.* Vol. 1. New York: St. Martin's, 1972.

Braunwald, E., ed. *Heart Disease.* Philadelphia: W. B. Saunders, 1984.

Bryan, C. P. *The Papyrus Ebers.* London: Geoffrey Bles, 1930.

Burnet, Sir McFarlane. *Natural History of Infectious Disease.* 4th ed. Cambridge: Cambridge Univ. Press, 1972.

Castiglione, Arturo. *A History of Medicine.* 2d ed. New York: Alfred A. Knopf, 1958.

Christie, A. B. "Infectious Diseases." *EB-MAC.* Vol. 9, pp. 532–559.

Cicero. *De divinatione.* A. S. Pease, ed. Urbana: Univ. of Illinois Press, 1920.

Civil, M. "Prescriptions medicales sumeriennes." *RA* 54 (1960): 57–72.

Clements, R. E. "Leviticus." *Broadman Bible Commentary.* Nashville: Broadman, 1980.

Clifford, Allen. *A Textbook of Psychosexual Disorders.* New York: Oxford Univ. Press, 1969.

Committee on Fetus and Newborn. "Report of the Ad Hoc Committee on Circumcision." *Ped* 56 (1975): 610.

Connor, Sonja L., et al. The Cholesterol/Saturated Fat Index: An Indication of the Hypercholesterolaemic and Atherogenic Potential of Food." *TL* 8492 (May 31, 1986): 1229–1232.

"Conquering the Quiet Killer." *Time*, January 13, 1975: 60–62.

Craigie, Peter C. *The Book of Deuteronomy.* Grand Rapids: Eerdmans, 1976.

Dagher, R; Selzer, M. L.; and Lapides, J. "Carcinoma of the Penis and the Anticircumcision Crusade." *JU* 110 (1973): 79–80.

Deanfield, John E., et al. "Silent Myocardial Ischaemia Due to Mental Stress." *TL* 8410 (November 3, 1984): 1001–1004.

de Boer, T. J. "Ethics and Morality (Muslim)." *ERE.* Vol. 5, pp. 501–512.

deGroot, J. J. M. *The Religious System of China.* 1901; rprt. Taipei: Literature House, 1964.

de Vaux, B. C. "Family (Muslim)." *ERE.* Vol. 5, pp. 742–744.

DeWelt, Don. *Leviticus.* Joplin, Mo.: College Press, 1975.

Dobson, C. B. *Stress: The Hidden Adversary.* Hingham, Md.: Kluwer Academic Publications, 1983.

Douglas, Mary. "Deciphering a Meal." *Dae* 101 (1972): 61–81.

Driberg, Tom. "Food and Drink." *MMM,* Vol. 4, pp. 1016f.

du Mas, Frank M. *Gay Is Not Good.* Nashville: Nelson, 1979.

Eby, Frederick, and Arrowood, Charles F. *The History and Philosophy of Education: Ancient and Medieval.* New York: Prentice-Hall, 1942.

Elliott, G. R., and Eisdorfer, C., eds. *Stress and Human Health.* New York: Springer, 1982.

Esler, M. D., and Goulston, K. T. "Levels of Anxiety in Colonic Disorders." *NEJM* 288 (1973): 16–20.

———. "An Irritable Mind or an Irritable Bowel?" *TL* 8415 (December 1, 1984): 1249–1250.

Evans, A. S., and Feldman, H. A. *Bacterial Infections of Humans: Epidemiology and Control.* New York: Plenum, 1982.

Fenner, E. T. "Rasayana Siddhi: Medicine and Alchemy in the Buddhist Tantras." Ph.D. diss., Univ. of Wisconsin, Madison, 1978.

Fetus and Newborn Committee, Canadian Pediatric Society. "Benefits and Risks of Circumcision: Another View." *CMAJ* 126 (1982): 1399.

Finegan, Jack. *Light from the Ancient Past.* 2d ed. London: Oxford Univ. Press, 1959.

Fisher, J. T., and Hawley, L. S. *A Few Buttons Missing.* New York: Lippincott, 1951.

Frazer, James G. *The Golden Bough: A Study in Magic and Religion.* 3d ed. London: Macmillan, 1955. Vol. 1: *The Magic Art and the Evolution of Kings.*

Friedman, Meyer, and Rosenman, R. H. *Type A: Behavior and Your Heart.* New York: Alfred A. Knopf, 1974.

Friis, Robert. *Stress and Physical Health: A Bibliography.* Vol. 4. Irving, Calif.: Human Behavior Research Group, 1984.

Gardiner, A. H. "Ethics and Morality (Egyptian)." *ERE.* Vol. 5, pp. 475–485.

Garfinkel, Lawrence. "Letter." *CA* 33 (September/October, 1983): 320.

Garrison, Fielding. *History of Medicine.* 4th ed. Philadelphia: W. B. Saunders, 1961.

Geers, F. W. "A Babylonian Omen Text." *AJSLL* 43 (1926–1927): 29–33.

Goetze, A. "An Incantation against Diseases." *JCS* 9 (1955): 8–18.

Gordon, B. L. *Medicine Through Antiquity.* Philadelphia: F. A. Davis, 1949.

Graboys, Thomas B. "Stress and the Aching Heart." *NEJM* 311 (August 30, 1984): 594–595.

Grissom, D. K. *Communicable Diseases.* Dubuque, Iowa: William C. Brown, 1971.

Groen, J. J., et al. *Psychosomatic Research: A Collection of Papers.* New York: Macmillan, 1964.

Guthrie, Douglas. *A History of Medicine.* Philadelphia: J. B. Lippincott, 1946.

Hackett, T. P., and Rosenbaum, J. F. "Emotion, Psychiatric Disorders and the Heart." In E. Braunwald, ed. *Heart Disease.* Philadelphia: W. B. Saunders, 1984.

Harrison, R. K. *Introduction to the Old Testament.* Grand Rapids: Eerdmans, 1970.

———. *Leviticus.* Downers Grove, Ill.: Inter-Varsity, 1980.

———. "Heal." *ISBE-REV.* Vol. 2, p. 642.

———. "Health, Healing." *IDB.* vol. 2, pp. 541–548.

Hasel, Gerhard F. "Health and Healing in the Old Testament." *AUSS* 21 (1983): 191–202.

Heinze, John E. "Bar Soap and Liquid Soap." *JAMA* 251 (June 22/29, 1984): 3222–3223.

Hierholzer, Walter J., Jr. "Nosocomial Bacterial Infections." In *Bacterial Infections of Humans: Epidemiology and Control.* A. S. Evans and H. A. Feldman, eds. New York: Plenum, 1982.

Hoernle, A. F. R. *The Bower Manuscript.* Calcutta: Superintendent of Government Printing, 1893.

Holt, L. Emmett, Jr., and McIntosh, Rustin. *Holt Pediatrics.* 12th ed. New York: Appleton-Century-Crofts, 1953.

Huard, Pierre, and Wong, Ming. *Chinese Medicine.* New York: McGraw-Hill, 1968.

Hudson, Robert P. *Disease and Its Control: The Shaping of Modern Thought.* Westport, Conn.: Greenwood, 1983.

Hume, E. E. *The Military Sanitation of Moses in the Light of Modern Knowledge.* Carlisle Barracks, Penn.: Medical Field Service School, 1940.

Inglis, Brian. *A History of Medicine.* New York: World, 1965.

Jeremias, Alfred. "Ethics and Morality (Babylonian)." *ERE.* Vol. 5 pp. 444–447.

Jerome, Lawrence. *Astrology Disproved.* Buffalo: Prometheus, 1977.

Johnson, David L. *A Reasoned Look at Asian Religions.* Minneapolis: Bethany House, 1985.

Jolly, Julius. "Disease and Medicine (Hindu)." *ERE.* Vol. 4, pp. 753–755.

———. "Food (Hindu)." *ERE.* Vol. 6, pp. 63–65.

Josephus, Flavius. *Against Apion.* Tr. by William Whiston. Grand Rapids: Associated Publishers, 1860.

Jung, C. G. *Modern Man in Search of a Soul.* New York: Harcourt, Brace and World, 1933.

Kaplan, G. W. "Circumcision—An Overview." *CPP* 7 (1977): 10.

Katz, Joseph. "The Question of Circumcision." *IS* 62 (1977): 490–492.

Keith, A. B. "Marriage (Hindu)." *ERE.* Vol. 8, pp. 449–454.

Kochen, M., and McCurdy, S. "Circumcision and the Risk of Cancer of the Penis." *AJDC* 134 (1980): 484–486.

Konig, Edward. "Defilement and Purification." *SHERK.* Vol. 3, p. 388.

LaWall, C. H. *Four Thousand Years of Pharmacy.* Philadelphia: Lippincott, 1927.

Leake, Chauncey D. *The Old Egyptian Medical Papyri.* Lawrence: Univ. of Kansas Press, 1952.

Leff, Samuel, and Leff, Vera. *From Witchcraft to World Health.* New York: Macmillan, 1957.

Leftik, M. I.; Miller, J. W.; and Brown, J. D. "Penicillin-resistant Gonococcal Polyarthritis." *JAMA* 239 (1978): 134.

Leiter, E., and Lefkovits, A. M. "Circumcision and Penile Cancer." *NYSJM* 75 (1975): 1520–1522.

Lenski, R. C. H. *The Interpretation of the Acts of the Apostles.* Minneapolis: Augsburg, 1961.

Lindsey, Jack. *The Origins of Astrology.* New York: Barnes and Noble, 1971.

Macht, D. I. "An Experimental Pharmacological Appreciation of Leviticus 11 and Deuteronomy 14." *BHM* 27 (1953): 444–450.

Madow, Leo. *Anger.* New York: Charles Scribner's Sons, 1972.

Majno, Guido. *The Healing Hand: Man and Wound in the Ancient World.* Cambridge: Harvard Univ. Press, 1975.

Major, R. H. *A History of Medicine.* Springfield, Ill.: Charles C. Thomas, 1954.

Marx, Jean L. "The Immune System 'Belongs in the Body.' " *Science* 227 (March 8, 1985): 1190–1192.

McGrew, Roderick E. *EMH.* New York: McGraw-Hill, 1985.

McMillan, C. W.; Weis, A. E.; and Johnson, A. M. "Acquired Coagulation Disorders in Children." *PCNA* 19 (1972): 1034.

McMillen, S. I. *None of These Diseases.* Old Tappan, N.J.: Revell, 1963.

———. *None of These Diseases,* rev. ed. Old Tappan, N.J.: Revell, 1984.

McQuade, Walter, and Aikman, Ann. *Stress.* New York: Bantam Books, 1975.

Medalie, J. H., et al. "Angina Pectoris Among 10,000 Men: 5 Year Incidence and Univariate Analysis." *AJM* 55 (1973): 583.

Mulhern, James. *A History of Education.* 2d ed. New York: Ronald Press, 1959.

Needham, Joseph. *Science and Civilization in China.* 3 vols. Cambridge: Cambridge Univ. Press, 1956.

Neuberger, Max. *History of Medicine.* London: Oxford Univ. Press, 1910.

Noth, Martin. *The Laws in the Pentateuch and Other Studies.* Edinburgh: Oliver and Boyd, 1966.

Oppenheim, A. Leo. *Ancient Mesopotamia.* Rev. ed. Chicago: Univ. of Chicago Press, 1977.

Peck, George Kerlin. "Divination." *EB-MAC.* vol. 5, pp. 916–920.

Perkins, David V. "The Assessment of Stress Using Life Events Scales." In Leo Goldberger and Schlomo Breznitz, eds. *Handbook of Stress: Theoretical and Clinical Aspects.* New York: Raven Press, 1982, pp. 319–331.

Philo, Judaeus. *The Works of Philo.* Tr. by F. H. Colson. Cambridge: Harvard Univ. Press, 1935.

Pingree, D. "Astronomy and Astrology in India and Iran," *Isis* 54 (1963): 229–246.

Rencontre Assyriologique Internationale. *La Divination en Mesopotamie Ancienne et dans les Regions Voisines.* Paris: Presses Universitaires de France, 1966.

Rinaldi, R. Z.; Harrison, W. O.; and Peng, Thim Fan. "Penicillin-resistant, Gonococcal Arthritis." *AIM* 97 (1982): 43–45.

Risse, Guenter B. "Medicine: History." *EA.* Vol. 18, pp. 624–636.

Rosen, George. *History of Public Health.* New York: M D Publications, 1958.

Ruutu, P., et al. "Septicemia Caused by Penicillinase-producing Gonorrhea." *JAMA* 251 (April 13, 1984): 1836.

Ryan, Miriam. "Venereal Diseases Increase in the Third World." *NS* 106 (May 16, 1985): 18.

Sachs, A. J. "Babylonian Horoscopes." *JCS* 6 (1952): 49–75.

Sadler, William. *Practice of Psychiatry.* St. Louis: C. V. Mosby, 1953.

Saggs, H. W. F. *The Greatness That Was Babylon.* New York: New American Library, 1962.

Sarton, George. *A History of Medicine.* Cambridge: Harvard Univ. Press, 1959.

"Science vs. Astrology: New Battle, Old War." *Science News* 108 (1975): 166.

Seabrook, Charles. "Stress." *The Atlanta Journal and Constitution Magazine,* July 8, 1979, p. 15.

Seidel, A. K. "Taoism." *EB-MAC.* Vol. 17, pp. 1034–1044.

Selye, Hans. *The Physiology and Pathology of Exposure to Stress.* Montreal: Acta Press, 1950.

———. *The Stress of Life.* New York: McGraw-Hill, 1956.

Short, A. Rendle. *Modern Discoveries and the Bible.* London: Inter-Varsity, 1942.

———. *The Bible and Modern Medicine.* Chicago: Moody, 1953.

Sigerist, H. E. *A History of Medicine.* Oxford: Oxford Univ. Press, 1951.

Sikdar, J. C. "Jaina Alchemy." *IJHS* 15 (1980): 6–17.

Siwolop, Sana. "New Drugs for Herpes." *Discover* 5 (July, 1984): 31–33.

Solomon, R. F., and Moos, R. H. "The Relationship of Personality to the Presence of Rheumatoid Arthritis in Asymptomatic Relatives of Patients with Rheumatoid Arthritis." *PM* 27 (1965): 350.

Sorenson, Herbert, and Malm, Margurite. *Psychology for Living.* New York: McGraw-Hill, 1957.

Spence, Lewis. "Circumcision (Introductory)." *ERE.* Vol. 3, pp. 659–670.

Sprunt, K.; Redman, W.; and Leidy, G. "Antibacterial Effectiveness of Routine Handwashing." *Ped* 52 (1973): 264–271.

Steere, A. C., and Mallison, G. F. "Handwashing Practices for the Prevention of Nosocomial Infections." *AIM* 83 (1975): 683–690.

Steindorff, George, and Seele, Keith C. *When Egypt Ruled the East.* Chicago: Univ. of Chicago Press, 1957.

Taff, G. A., and Friis, Robert. *Stress and Cancer: An Annotated Bibliography.* Irving, Calif.: Human Behavior Research Group, 1983.

Thompson, R. Campbell. "Medical History." *PRSM* 17 (1924): 2–22.

———. "Assyrian Prescriptions for Stone in the Kidneys, for the 'Middle', and for Pneumonia." *Arch. Orientforschung* 11 (1936–37): 336–340.

Thompson, W. G. *The Irritable Gut: Functional Disorders of the Alimentary Canal.* Baltimore: University Park Press, 1979.

Thomsen, R. J. *The Bible: Book of Medical Wisdom.* Old Tappan, N.J.: Revell, 1974.

Thorwald, Jurgen. *Science and Secrets of Early Medicine.* Tr. by Richard and Clara Winston. New York: Harcourt, Brace and World, 1963.

Unschuld, P. U. "Concepts of Illness in Ancient China: The Case of Demonological Medicine." *JMP* 5 (1980): 117–132.

Ursin, H., and Murison, R., eds. *Biological and Psychological Basis of Psychosomatic Disease.* Oxford: Pergamon, 1980.

Vernant, J. P., et al. *Divination et Rationalite.* Paris: Editions du Seuil, 1974.

"VD: The Epidemic." *Newsweek* (January 24, 1972): 46.

Vidal, E. "Les idees des Assyriens et des Egyptiens sur la vie et la mort, le sant et la maladie, 3000 ans avant Jesus Christ." *SGAB* 7 (1912): 569–596.

Vis, W. R. in American Scientific Affiliation *Modern Science and the Christian Faith.* Wheaton, Ill.: Van Kampen, 1948.

Wain, Harry. *A History of Preventive Medicine.* Springfield, Ill.: Charles C. Thomas, 1970.

Walker, George B. *Hindu World.* 2 vols. London: George Allen & Unwin, 1968.

Wallerstein, Edward. *Circumcision: An American Health Fantasy.* New York: Springer, 1980.

Warner, E., and Strashin, E. "Benefits and Risks of Circumcision." *CMAJ* 125 (1981): 967–976.

Washington, A. Eugene; Cates, Willard, Jr.; and Zaidi, Akbar A. "Hospitalizations for Pelvic Inflammatory Disease." *JAMA* 251 (May 18, 1984): 2529–2533.

Wenham, Gordon J. *The Book of Leviticus.* Grand Rapids: Eerdmans, 1979.

Wheatley, David, ed. *Stress and the Heart.* 2d ed. New York: Raven, 1981.

Xenophon. *Memorabilia.* tr. by E. C. Marchant. Loeb Classical Library. Cambridge: Harvard Univ. Press, 1923.

Zales, M. R., ed. *Stress in Health and Disease.* New York: Brunner-Mazel, 1984.

Zamula, Evelyn. "Syphilis and Gonorrhea: Old-Fashioned VD Still Flourishing." *FDA Consumer* 20 (April, 1986): 5–9.

Zelnik, Melvin, and John F. Kantor, "Sexual Activity, Contraceptive Use and Pregnancy among Metropolitan Teenagers." *FPP* 12 (1980): 230–237.

———. "Sexual and Contraceptive Experience of Young Unmarried Women in the United States." *FPP* 9 (1977): 55–71.

Zimmer, Robert Heinrich. *Hindu Medicine.* Baltimore: Johns Hopkins Univ. Press, 1948.

Zoltan, Imre. "Ignaz Philipp Semmelweis." *EB-MAC.* Vol. 16, pp. 529–530.

Part Two: The Sky Above

Abell, George. *Exploration of the Universe.* 2d ed. New York: Holt, Rinehart and Winston, 1969.

Allen, Ronald Barclay. *Praise! A Matter of Life and Breath.* Grand Rapids: Zondervan, 1980.

Allis, Oswald T. *The Five Books of Moses.* Nutley, N.J.: Presbyterian and Reformed, 1977.

Angrist, S. W. "Perpetual Motion Machines." *SA* 218 (1968): 120–121.

Arp, Halton C. "The Evolution of Galaxies." In Owen Gingerich, ed. *Frontiers of Astronomy.* San Francisco: W. H. Freeman, 1970, pp. 212–223.

Asimov, Isaac. *The Universe: From Flat Earth to Quasar.* New York: Avon, 1966.

________. "In the Game of Energy and Thermodynamics You Can't Even Break Even." *SIJ* 4 (June, 1970): 6.

Barnett, Lincoln. *The Universe and Dr. Einstein.* New York: New American Library, 1957.

Blumenthal, W. H. "Astronomy." *UJE.* Vol. 1, p. 572.

Boettner, Lorraine. *Roman Catholicism.* Philadelphia: Presbyterian and Reformed, 1962.

Bolt, Bruce A. *Earthquakes: A Primer.* San Francisco: W. H. Freeman, 1978.

Bowie, W. R. "The Book of Genesis." *IB.* Vol. 1, p. 472.

Branley, Franklyn. "Conceptions of the Universe." *NH* 79 (December, 1970): 30–35.

Bridgman, P. W. "Reflections on Thermodynamics." *AS* 41 (October, 1953): 549.

Broderick, James. *Galileo: The Man, His Work, His Misfortunes.* New York: Harper and Row, 1964.

Brown, Francis, Driver, S. R. and Briggs, Charles A. *A Hebrew and English Lexicon of the Old Testament.* 1907; rprt. with corrections. Oxford: Clarendon, 1958.

Browne, E. H. *Genesis.* New York: Scribners and Armstrong, 1873.

Bruce, F. F. *The Books and the Parchments.* 3d ed. Old Tappan, N.J.: Revell, 1963.

________. *International Bible Commentary.* Grand Rapids: Zondervan, 1986.

Budge, E. A. Wallis. *Gods of the Egyptians.* London: Peter Smith, 1904.

Cassuto, U. *A Commentary on the Book of Genesis.* Tr. by Israel Abrahams. Jerusalem: Magnes, 1961.

Christianson, Gale E. *This Wild Abyss.* New York: Free Press, 1978.

Clark, Robert E. D. *The Christian Stake in Science.* Chicago: Moody, 1967.

Clayton, John. *The Source.* Mentone, Ind.: Superior, 1976.

Cornford, Francis. *Plato's Cosmology.* London: Kegan Paul, 1937.

Corswant, W. *A Dictionary of Life in Bible Times.* Tr. by A. Heathcote. Bungay, Suffolk: Hodder and Stoughton, 1960.

Costelloe, M. J. "Astral Religion." *EDR.* Vol. 1, p. 296.

———. "Astronomy." *EDR.* Vol. 1, pp. 296–297.

Crawford, C. C. *Genesis.* Joplin, Mo.: College Press, 1985.

Cremer, A. H. "Heaven." *SHERK.* Vol. 5, pp. 180–181.

Cumont, Franz. *Astrology and Religion Among the Greeks and Romans.* Mineola, N.Y.: Dover, 1912.

Dampier, Sir W. C. *A History of Science.* 4th ed. London: Cambridge Univ. Press, 1948.

d'Arezzo, Ristoro. *La Composizione del Mondo.* Rome: Bibliotacarara, 1859.

Das, Sukumar Ranjan. "Scope and Development of Indian Astronomy." In *Os.* George Sarton, ed. Bruges, Belgium: St. Catherine Press, 1936. Vol. 2, pp. 197–219.

Davidson, R. *Genesis 1–11. CBC.* Vol. 1. Cambridge: Cambridge Univ. Press, 1971.

Davis, John J. *Paradise to Prison: Studies in Genesis.* Grand Rapids: Baker, 1975.

Dreyer, John L. E. *A History of Astronomy.* 2d ed. Rev. by W. H. Stahl. Mineola, N.Y.: Dover, 1952.

Dunham, David W.; Sofia, Sabatino; Fiala, Alan D.; Herald, David W.; and Muller, Paul M. "Observations of a Possible Change in the Solar Radius between 1715 and 1979." *Science* 210 (1980): 1243–1245.

Eddy, John A., and Boornazian, Aram A. "Analyses of Historical Data Suggest Sun Is Shrinking." *PT* 32 (September, 1979): 17–19.

Edwards, D. M. "Seal." *ISBE.* Vol. 4, p. 2708.

Epiphanius. *Adversus Haereses.* In J. P Migne *Patrologia Graeca.* Oxford: Basil B. Blackwell, 1858.

Fallaize, E. M. "Sun, Moon, and Stars (Primitive)." *ERE.* Vol. 12, pp. 62–65.

Fenn, John B. *Engines, Energy, and Entropy.* San Francisco: W. H. Freeman, 1982.

Ferguson, John C. "Chinese." *MAR.* Vol. 8, pp. 61–63.

Fosdick, H. E. *The Modern Use of the Bible.* New York: Macmillan, 1924.

Francisco, Clyde T. *Genesis.* Rev. ed. Nashville: Broadman, 1969.

Fu, T. "Sun, Moon, and Stars (Chinese)." *ERE.* Vol. 12, pp. 74–80.

Funk, Wilfred. *Word Origins and Their Romantic Stories.* New York: Bell, 1950.

Gaenssle, C. "A Look at Current Biblical Cosmologies." *CTM* 23 (1952): 738–749.

Gaussen, L. *The Divine Inspiration of the Bible.* 1841: rprt. Grand Rapids: Kregel, 1971.

Geden, A. S. "Sun, Moon, and Stars (Hindu)." *ERE.* Vol. 12, pp. 83–85.

Giles, H. A. *Confucianism and Its Rituals.* London: Williams and Northgate, 1915.

Gilmore, G. W. "Stars." *SHERK.* Vol. 11, pp. 68–69.

———. "Sun and Sun Worship." *SHERK.* Vol. 9, p. 137.

———. "Hebrew Conceptions of the Moon." *SHERK.* Vol. 7, pp. 492–494.

Girdlestone, Robert Baker. *Girdlestone's Synonyms of the Old Testament.* 3d ed. Donald White, ed. Grand Rapids: Baker, 1983.

Golden, Frederic. *The Trembling Earth.* New York: Charles Scribner's Sons, 1983.

Grant, Edward. *In Defense of Earth's Centrality and Immutability: Scholastic Reaction to Copernicanism in the Seventeenth Century.* Philadelphia: American Philosophical Society, 1984.

Graubard, Mark A. *Astrology and Alchemy: Two Fossil Sciences.* New York: AMS, 1953.

Graves, Robert, and Patai, Raphael. *Hebrew Myths: The Book of Genesis.* Garden City, N.Y.: Doubleday, 1965.

Green, Jay P., Sr., ed. *The Interlinear Bible: Hebrew-English.* Grand Rapids: Baker, 1976.

Green, W. H. *The Higher Criticism of the Pentateuch.* 1895. rprt. Grand Rapids: Baker, 1978.

Grote, George. *Plato.* London: John Murray, 1885.

Guier, W. H., and Newton, R. R. "The Earth's Gravity Field—Doppler Tracking of Five Satellites." *JGR* 70 (September 15, 1965): 4613-4626.

Haines, Lee. "Genesis and Exodus." *WBC,* Vol. 1. Grand Rapids: Eerdmans, 1967.

Halacy, D. S., Jr. *Earthquakes.* Indianapolis: Bobbs-Merrill, 1974.

Harris, R. Laird; Archer, Gleason L., Jr.; and Waltke, Bruce K.; eds. *TWOT.* Chicago: Moody, 1980.

Hasel, Gerhard F. "The Polemic Nature of the Genesis Cosmology." *EQ* 46 (1974): 81–102.

Heide, Fritz. *Meteorites.* Chicago: Univ. of Chicago Press, 1964.

Heidel, Alexander. *The Babylonian Genesis.* 2d ed. Chicago: Univ. of Chicago Press, 1951.

Hippolytus. *Philosophumena.* Tr. by F. Legge. Vol. 1. London: Society for Promoting Christian Knowledge, 1921.

Hornung, Erik. *Concepts of God in Ancient Egypt.* Tr. by John Baines. Ithaca: Cornell Univ. Press, 1982.

Hoyle, Fred. *Astronomy.* New York: Doubleday, 1962.

Jerome, Lawrence. *Astrology Disproved.* Buffalo: Prometheus, 1977.

Jobes, Gertrude, and Jobes, James. *Outer Space: From the Emergence of History to the Present Day.* New York: Scarecrow, 1964.

Kaufman, Reuben. "Astrology." *UJE.* Vol. 1, pp. 570–571.

Keith, A. Berriedale. "Indian." *MAR.* Vol. 6, pp. 15–40.

Kidner, David. *Psalms 73–150.* Downers Grove, Ill.: Inter-Varsity, 1975.

Kilmister, Clive. *The Nature of the Universe.* New York: E. P. Dutton, 1971.

King, L. W. *The Seven Tablets of Creation.* London: Luzac, 1902.

Kitchen, K. A. *Ancient Orient and the Old Testament.* Downers Grove, Ill.: Inter-Varsity, 1966.

Klein, Martin J. "Thermodynamics in Einstein's Universe." *Science* 157 (1967): 509–516.

Kloetzli, W. Randolph. "Maps of Time—Mythologies of Descent: Scientific Instruments and the Puranic Cosmograph." *HR* 25 (1985): 116–147.

Koch, Robert H. Review of *Mass Loss from the Stars. Science* 167 (February 13, 1970): 971.

Koehler, Ludwig and Baumgartner, Walter. *Lexicon in Veteris Testamenti Libros.* Leiden: E. J. Brill, 1953.

Kohlenberger, John R., III, ed. *The NIV Interlinear Hebrew-English Old Testament.* Grand Rapids: Zondervan, 1979.

Kramer, S. N. *Mythologies of the Ancient World.* Garden City, N.Y.: Doubleday, 1961.

Kurfees, M. C. *Instrumental Music in the Worship.* 1911. rprt. Nashville: Gospel Advocate, 1969.

Lambert, W. G. "A New Look at the Babylonian Genesis." *JTS* 16 (1965): 288f.

Lang, Walter. "Science Verifies Scripture." *BSN* 9 (June, 1971): 8.

Lapaz, Lincoln, and Lapaz, Jean. *Space Nomads.* New York: Holiday House, 1961.

Lawton, April. "From Here to Infinity." *Science Digest* 89 (January/February, 1981): 98–105.

Lerner, Lawrence S., and Gosselin, Edward A. "Galileo and the Specter of Bruno." *SA* 255 (November, 1986):126–133.

Littman, Mark, and Yeomans, Donald K. *Comet Halley: Once in a Lifetime.* Washington: American Chemical Society, 1985.

Livingston, George Herbert. "Genesis." *BBC.* Vol. 1. Kansas City: Bacon Hill, 1969.

Lyon, T. C. *Witness in the Sky.* Chicago: Moody, 1961.

Maunder, E. W. "Astronomy." *ISBE.* Vol. 1, pp. 300–316.

McCall, Gerald Joseph. *Meteorites and Their Origin.* New York: John Wiley, 1973.

Millard, A. R. "A New Babylonian Genesis Story." *TB* 18 (1968): 3–18.

Morowitz, Harold. "Biology as a Cosmological Science." *Main Currents in Modern Thought,* 28 (1972): 151.

Morris, Henry M. "The Day-Age Theory Revisited." In *The Decade of Creation.* Henry M. Morris and Donald H. Rohrer, eds. San Diego: Creation-Life, 1981.

Mulfinger, George. "Our Degenerating Universe." In *A Challenge to Education.* Walter Lang, ed. Caldwell, Idaho: Bible-Science, 1972.

Newman, R. C., and Eckelmann, H. J., Jr. *Genesis One and the Origin of the Earth.* Downers Grove, Ill.: Inter-Varsity, 1977.

Orr, James. "World: Cosmological." *ISBE.* Vol. 5, p. 3106.

Pannekoek, Antonie. *A History of Astronomy.* New York: Interscience Publishers, 1961.

Parker, E. N. "The Solar Wind." In *Frontiers in Astronomy.* Owen Gingerich, ed. San Francisco: W. H. Freeman, 1970.

Parker, R. A. "Ancient Egyptian Astronomy." In *The Place of Astronomy in the Ancient World.* F. R. Hodson, ed. London: Oxford Univ. Press, 1974, pp. 51–66.

Payne-Gaposchkin, Cecilia. *Stars and Clusters.* Cambridge: Harvard Univ. Press, 1979.

Pippard, A. B. *Elements of Chemical Thermodynamics for Advanced Students.* Cambridge: Cambridge Univ. Press, 1966.

Plutarch. *Isis et Osiris.* Mario Meunier, ed. Paris: L'Artisan du livre, 1924.

Plumley, J. M. "The Cosmology of Ancient Egypt." in *Ancient Cosmologies.* Carmen Blacker and Michael Loewe, eds. London: George Allen & Unwin, 1975, pp. 17–41.

Proctor, R. A. "Astronomy." *EB.* 9th ed. Vol. 2, pp. 744–763.

Redondi, Pietro. *Galileo Eretico.* Turin: Guilio Einaudi Editore, 1983.

Reichen, Charles-Albert. *A History of Astronomy.* New York: Hawthorn, 1963.

Renou, Louis. *The Nature of Hinduism.* Tr. by Patrick Evans. New York: Walker, 1962.

Ricks, D. R. *Early Greek Astronomy to Aristotle.* Ithaca: Cornell Univ. Press, 1970.

Sagan, Carl, and Druyan, Ann. *Comet.* New York: Random House, 1985.

Saggs, H. W. F. *The Greatness That Was Babylon.* New York: New American Library, 1962.

Sale, George. tr. *The Koran.* By Muhammed. London: Frederick Warne, 1909.

Sarna, Nahum M. *Understanding Genesis.* New York: Schocken Institute, 1970.

Sarton, George. *A History of Science.* 2 vols. Cambridge: Harvard Univ. Press, 1959.

Saville, B. W. "On Heathen Cosmogonies Compared with the Hebrew." *JTVI* 10 (1877): 274–275.

Sayce, A. H. "Babylonia." *EB.* 9th ed. Vol. 3. pp. 182–194.

Schnabel, A. O. *Has God Spoken?* San Diego: Creation-Life, 1974.

Schroeder, H. J. *Canons and Decrees of the Council of Trent.* St. Louis: Herder, 1950.

Simpson, C. A. "Genesis." *IB.* Vol. 1, p. 467.

Smick, Elmer B. "Mythology and the Book of Job." *JETS* 20 (1970): 101–108.

Stadelmann, L.I.J. *The Hebrew Conception of the World.* Rome: Pontifical Bible Institute, 1970.

Taton, Rene. *History of Science: Ancient and Medieval Science.* New York: Basic Books, 1963.

Taylor, John. "Pleiades." In *A Dictionary of the Bible.* James Hastings, ed. New York: Scribner's, 1900.

Thierens, A. E. *Astrology in Mesopotamian Culture.* New York: Gordon, 1977.

Thomas, D. W., ed. *Documents from Old Testament Times.* New York: Harper and Row, 1958.

Thomas, E. J. "Sun, Moon, and Stars (Buddhist)." *ERE.* Vol. 12, pp. 71–73.

Tiel, Rudolf. *And There Was Light.* New York: Alfred A. Knopf, 1957.

Torczyner, H. "The Firmament and the Clouds." *ST* 1 (1948): 188–196.

Tozer, H. F. *History of Ancient Geography.* 2d ed. Cambridge: Cambridge Univ. Press, 1935.

Van Der Kamp, Walter. "I Make Its Pillars Firm." *BSN* 14 (January, 1976):3.

Vine, W. E. *An Expository Dictionary of Biblical Words.* rev. by Merrill F. Unger and William White. Nashville: Nelson, 1985.

———. *An Expository Dictionary of Old Testament Words.* F. F. Bruce, ed. Old Tappan, N.J.: Revell, 1978.

von Oefele, F. "Sun, Moon, and Stars (Introduction)." *ERE.* Vol. 12, pp. 48–62.

Vos, Howard F. *Genesis.* Chicago: Moody, 1983.

Wallace, William A. "Galileo." *Isis* 76 (1985): 379–380.

Wallis, W. D. "Prodigies and Portents." *ERE.* Vol. 10, pp. 362–376.

Walker, George Benjamin. *Hindu World.* 2 vols. London: George Allen & Unwin, 1968.

Warren, W. F. *The Earliest Cosmologies.* New York: Eaton and Mains, 1909.

Watterson, Barbara. *The Gods of Ancient Egypt.* New York: Facts on File, 1984.

Westermann, Claus. *Genesis 1–11.* Minneapolis: Augsburg, 1984.

Whitelaw, Thomas. "Genesis." In *The Pulpit Commentary.* H. D. M. Spence and Joseph S. Excell, eds. Vol. 1. 1881. rprt. Grand Rapids: Eerdmans, 1952.

Whitley, C. F. *The Genius of Ancient Israel.* Amsterdam: Philo Press, 1969.

Williams, Arthur F. "The Genesis Account of Creation." In *Why Not Creation?* Walter E. Lammerts, ed. Grand Rapids: Baker, 1970.

Wolff, Hans Walter. *Joel and Amos.* tr. by Waldemar Janzen, S. Dean McBride, Jr., and Charles A. Muenchow. Philadelphia: Fortress, 1977.

Wyatt, Stanley. *Principles of Astronomy.* 2d ed. Boston: Allyn and Bacon, 1971.

Xenophon. *Memorabilia.* tr. by E. C. Marchant. (Loeb Classical Library) Cambridge: Harvard Univ. Press, 1923.

Young, Edward. *Thy Word Is Truth.* Grand Rapids: Eerdmans, 1957.

Young, Louis, ed. *Exploring the Universe.* New York: McGraw-Hill, 1963.

Zodhiates, Spiros. "Lexical Aids to the Old Testament." *The Hebrew-Greek Key Study Bible.* Grand Rapids: Baker, 1984.

Part Three: The Earth Beneath

Ackerman, Paul. *It's A Young World After All.* Grand Rapids: Baker, 1986.

Adams, Frank Dawson. *The Birth and the Development of the Geological Sciences.* New York: Dover, 1954.

Alexander, Tom. "A Revolution Called Plate Tectonics Has Given Us a Whole New Earth." *The Smithsonian* 5 (January, 1975): 30–40.

________. "Plate Tectonics Has a Lot to Tell Us About the Present and Future Earth." *The Smithsonian* 5 (February, 1975): 38–47.

Ali, S. Muzafer. *The Geography of the Puranas.* New Delhi: People's, 1966.

Anderson, J. N. D. *Christianity and Comparative Religion.* Downers Grove, Ill.: Inter-Varsity, 1970.

Aristotle. *Meteorologica.* Loeb Classical Library, No. 397. Cambridge: Harvard Univ. Press, 1952.

Ball, J. Dyer. "Light and Darkness (Chinese)." *ERE.* Vol. 8, pp. 51–52.

Barrow, John D., and Tipler, Frank J. *The Anthropic Cosmological Principle.* Oxford: Oxford Univ. Press, 1986.

Biddulph, J. *Tribes of the Hindoo Koosh.* Calcutta: Office of the Superintendent of Government Printing, 1880.

Bloomfield, M. *Hymns of the Atharva-Veda.* SBE. Vol. 42. Oxford: Oxford Univ. Press. 1897.

———. "On the 'Frog Hymn.' " *JAOS* 17 (1896): 173–179.

Bowker, John. *Problems of Suffering in Religions of the World.* London: Cambridge Univ. Press, 1970.

Budge, E. A. Wallis. *Egyptian Religion.* 1900. rprt. New York: Bell, 1959.

Bunge, Mario. *Causality and Modern Science.* New York: Dover, 1979.

Burns, I. F. "Cosmogony and Cosmology (Greek)." *ERE.* Vol. 4, pp. 148–151.

Campbell, Joseph. *The Masks of God: Oriental Mythology.* New York: Viking, 1962.

Cassidy, Vincent H. *The Sea Around Them.* Baton Rouge: Louisiana State Univ. Press, 1968.

Chapin, Henry, and Smith, F. G. Walton. *The Ocean River.* New York: Charles Scribner's Sons, 1952.

Chapman, Colin. *Christianity on Trial.* Wheaton, Ill.: Tyndale, 1975.

Christie, Anthony. *Chinese Mythology.* London: Paul Hamlyn, 1968.

Chui, Milton M. *The Tao of Chinese Religion.* New York: University Press of America, 1984.

Clarke, John. *Physical Science in the Time of Nero, being a Translation of the Quaestiones naturales of Seneca.* London: Macmillan, 1910.

Clayton, John. *The Source.* Mentone, Ind.: Superior Printing, 1976.

Clogett, Marshall. *Greek Science in Antiquity.* New York: Abelard-Schuman, 1955.

Cohen, Alvin. "Coercing the Rain Deities in Ancient China." *HR* 18 (1978): 243–248.

Confucius. *Shih Ching.* tr. by Ezra Pound. Cambridge: Harvard Univ. Press, 1954.

Corliss, William R. *Mysteries Beneath the Sea.* New York: Thomas Y. Crowell, 1970.

Cowen, Robert. *Frontiers of the Sea.* Garden City, N.Y.: Doubleday, 1969.

Craigie, Peter C. *Psalms 1–50.* Waco, Tex.: Word, 1983.

Cromie, William J. *Exploring the Secrets of the Sea.* New York: Prentice-Hall, 1962.

Cronin, Vincent. *The View from Planet Earth.* New York: William Morrow, 1981.

Crooke, William. *Popular Religion and Folklore of Northern India.* 2 vols. Westminster: Archibald Constable, 1896.

_______. "Dravidians (North India)." *ERE.* Vol. 5, pp. 1–21.

_______. "Water, Water-Gods (Indian)." *ERE.* Vol. 12, pp. 716–719.

Custance, Arthur. *Evolution or Creation?* Grand Rapids: Zondervan, 1976.

Dawson, J. W. *Nature and the Bible.* New York: Robert Carter, 1875.

Douglas, R. K. *Confucianism and Taoism.* London: Society for Promoting Christian Knowledge, 1877.

Eliade, Mircea. *Patterns in Comparative Religion.* New York: New American Library, 1958.

deGroot, J. J. M. *Religion in China.* New York: G. P. Putnam's Sons, 1912.

_______. *The Myth of the Eternal Return, or Cosmos and History.* tr. by W. Trask. Princeton: Princeton Univ. Press, 1974.

Embree, Ainslie. *The Hindu Tradition.* New York: Vintage, 1972.

Evans, Joan. *Magical Jewels of the Middle Ages and the Renaissance.* Oxford: Oxford Univ. Press, 1923.

Frankfort, H., and Frankfort, H. A. "The Emancipation of Thought from Myth." In *The Intellectual Advancement of Ancient Man.* H. Frankfort, ed. Chicago: Univ. of Chicago Press, 1946.

Frazer, James G. *The Golden Bough: The Magic Art and the Evolution of Kings.* Part 1, 2 vols. 1890. rprt. New York: St. Martin's, 1980.

Freeman, D. "Sabbatical Year." In *The New Bible Dictionary.* J. D. Douglas, ed. Grand Rapids: Eerdmans, 1962.

Gardner, E. A. "Water-Gods." *ERE.* Vol. 12, pp. 713–716.

Glacken, Clarence J. *Traces on the Rhodian Shore.* Berkeley: Univ. of California Press, 1967.

Godwin, George Stanley. *Vancouver, A Life, 1757–1798.* London: P. Allan, 1930.

Gombrich, R. F. "Ancient Indian Cosmologies." In *Ancient Cosmologies*. Carmen Blacker and Michael Loewe, eds. London: George Allen & Unwin, 1973, pp. 110–139.

Gray, William R., et al. *The Powers of Nature.* Washington: National Geographic, 1978.

Halacy, D. S., Jr. *Earthquakes: A Natural History.* Indianapolis: Bobbs-Merrill, 1974.

Halldal, Per H. H. "Plankton." *EB-MAC.* Vol. 14, pp. 494–496.

Hammer, Raymond. "Men and Movements." In *Eerdmans' Handbook to the World Religions.* R. Pierce Beaver et al, eds. Grand Rapids: Eerdmans, 1982.

Hobson, T. C. "The Nature Tribes of Manipur." *JAI* 31 (1901): 302.

Hooykaas, R. *Religion and the Rise of Modern Science.* Edinburgh: Scottish Academic Press, 1972.

Johnston, R. F. *Buddhist China.* London: John Murray, 1913.

Keil, C. F., and Delitzsch, F. Commentary on the Old Testament. Vol. 1. *The Pentateuch.* tr. by James Martin. n.d. rprt. Grand Rapids: Eerdmans, 1978.

Kidner, Derek. *Psalms 1–72.* Downers Grove, Ill.: Inter-Varsity, 1973.

King, Cuchlaine A. M. *An Introduction to Oceanography.* New York: McGraw-Hill, 1963.

Klaaren, Eugene M. *Religious Origins of Modern Science.* Grand Rapids: Eerdmans, 1977.

Kofahl, Robert, and Seagraves, Kelly. *The Creation Explanation.* Wheaton, Ill.: Shaw, 1975.

Ko-ji-ki. tr. by B. H. Chamberlain. New York: C. E. Tuttle, 1982.

Kuiper, F. B. J. "Cosmogony and Conception: A Query." *HR* 10 (1970): 91–138.

Lange, John Peter. *Leviticus: A Commentary on the Holy Scriptures.* tr. by Philip Schaff. Grand Rapids: Zondervan, 1876.

Lehmann, Johann Gottlob. *Traite de la Physique.* Vol. 1. Paris: J. T. Herissant, 1759.

Lewis, Naphtali. *Life in Egypt Under Roman Rule.* Oxford: Clarendon, 1983.

Limburg, James. "What Does It Mean to 'Have Dominion over the Earth'?" *Dialog* 10 (1971): 221–223.

Livy. *Roman History.* Loeb Classical Library, Vol. 7, no. 301. tr. F. G. Moore. Cambridge: Harvard Univ. Press. 1943.

Mabbett, I. W. "The Symbolism of Mount Meru." *HR* 23 (1983): 65–83.

MacCulloch, J. A. "Earth, Earth-Gods." *ERE.* Vol. 5, pp. 127–131.

———. "Mountains, Mountain-Gods." *ERE.* Vol. 8, pp. 963–868.

MacDonell, A. A. *Vedic Mythology.* Delhi: Motilal Banarsidass, 1974.

———. "Magic (Vedic)." *ERE.* Vol. 8, pp. 311–321.

Mackay, Donald. *Science and Christian Faith Today.* London: CPAS, 1970.

Mackenzie, Donald. *Egyptian Myth and Legend.* 1907. rprt. New York: Bell, 1978.

Major, Trevor J. "Plate Tectonics and Genesis." *RR* 6 (1986): 23–26.

Malan, D. J. *Physics of Lightning.* London: English Universities Press, 1963.

Mason, B. J. *The Physics of Clouds.* Oxford: Clarendon, 1971.

Maury, Matthew Fontaine. *Physical Geology of the Sea.* John Leighly, ed. 1855. rprt. Cambridge: Belknap, 1963.

McConkie, Bruce R. *Mormon Doctrine.* Salt Lake City: Bookcraft, 1966.

McDowell, Josh. *Understanding Non-Christian Religions.* San Bernardino: Here's Life, 1982.

McHarg, Ian L. *Design with Nature.* Garden City, N.Y.: Natural History Press, 1969.

Means, Richard. "Why Worry about Nature?" *Saturday Review,* December 2, 1967, pp. 13–15.

Mercer, S.A.B. "Water, Water-Gods (Babylonian)." *ERE.* Vol. 12, pp. 708–710.

———. "Water, Water-Gods (Egyptian)." *ERE.* Vol. 12, pp. 710–712.

Michaelis. *Commentaries on the Laws of Moses.* London: Rivington, 1814.

Middleton, W. E. *A History of the Theories of Rain and Other Forms of Precipitation.* Chicago: Univ. of Chicago Press, 1969.

Morgenstern, Julian. "Year of Jubilee." *IDB.* Vol. 2, p. 1001.

Moulton, James Hope. "Iranians." *ERE.* Vol. 7, pp. 418–420.

———. *Early Zoroastrianism.* London: Williams and Norgate, 1913.

Morrison, A. Creasy. *Seven Reasons Why a Scientist Believes in God.* Westwood, N.J.: Revell, 1963.

Nevins, Stuart. "Planet Earth: Design or Accident?" In *The Battle for Creation.* Henry M. Morris and Duane Gish, eds. San Diego: Creation-Life, 1976.

Nihongi. Tr. by W. G. Aston. New York: C. E. Tuttle, 1971.

North, R. *Sociology of the Biblical Jubilee.* Rome: Pontifical Biblical Institute, 1954.

Noss, John B. *Man's Religions.* New York: Macmillan, 1969.

Noth, Martin. *Leviticus.* London: SCM, 1965.

Orville, Richard E. "Lightning." *EB-MAC:* Vol. 10, pp. 966–970.

Pausanias. *Description of Greece.* Loeb Classical Library, No. 298. Cambridge: Harvard Univ. Press, 1935.

Payne, J. Barton. *The Theology of the Older Testament.* Grand Rapids: Zondervan, 1962.

Penner, Hans. "Cosmology as Myth in the Vishnu Purana." *HR* 5 (1966): 283–299.

Piggott, Juliet. *Japanese Mythology.* London: Paul Hamlyn, 1969.

Plato. *Timaeus.* tr. by Francis Cornford. New York: Liberal Arts Press, 1959.

———. *Laws.* E. B. England, ed. 1921. rprt. Salem, N.H.: Ayer, 1976.

Plattes, Gabriel. *A Discovery of Subterranean Treasure.* London: I. Okes for Jasper Emery, 1639.

Plumley, J. M. "The Cosmology of Ancient Egypt." In *Ancient Cosmologies.* Carmen Blacker and Michael Loewe, eds. London: George Allen & Unwin, 1975.

Pollard, W. G. "Science and the Bible." *IDB-S.* Nashville: Abingdon, 1976, pp. 789–791.

Ramm, Bernard. *The Christian View of Science and Scripture.* Grand Rapids: Eerdmans, 1954.

Raymont, J. E. G. *Plankton and Productivity in the Oceans.* New York: Pergamon, 1963.

Rehwinkel, A. M. *Wonders of Creation.* Grand Rapids: Baker, 1974.

Revon, Michael. "Ancestor Worship and Cult of the Dead (Japanese)." *ERE.* Vol. 1, pp. 455–457.

———. "Nature (Japanese)." *ERE.* Vol. 9, pp. 233–240.

Sacred Books of China. tr. by James Legge. London: Clarendon, 1910.

Schaeffer, Francis A. *Pollution and the Death of Man.* Wheaton, Ill.: Tyndale, 1970.

Schonland, B. F. J. *The Flight of the Thunder Bolts.* Oxford: Clarendon, 1950.

Seneca. *Naturales Quaestiones.* Loeb Classical Library, No. 457. Cambridge: Harvard Univ. Press, 1972.

Shephard, Francis P. *Submarine Geology.* 3d ed. New York: Harper and Row, 1973.

Shields, Charles Woodruff. *The Scientific Evidences of Revealed Religion.* New York: Charles Scribner's Sons, 1900.

Smith, F. G. Walton. *The Seas in Motion.* New York: Thomas Y. Crowell, 1973.

Smith, Joseph Fielding. *Doctrines of Salvation.* Salt Lake City: Bookcraft, 1954.

Spence, Clark C. *The Rainmakers.* Lincoln: Univ. of Nebraska Press, 1980.

"Taming of Earthquakes." *Time,* September 7, 1970, p. 46.

Taylor, Edward B. *Researches into the Early History of Mankind.* 1878. rprt. London: Luzac, 1929.

Thomas, N. W. "Animals." *ERE.* Vol. 1, pp. 483–535.

Thompson, Ernest F. "Plankton." *EA.* Vol. 22, pp. 177–178.

Uman, Martin A. *Lightning.* New York: McGraw-Hill, 1969.

Van Der Spoel, S., and Heyman, R. A., *A Comparative Atlas of Zooplankton: Biological Patterns in the Oceans.* New York: Springer-Verlag, 1983.

Venketswami, M. N. "Superstitions among Hindus in the Central Provinces." *IA* 28 (1899): 111.

Von Weizacker, C. F. *The Relevance of Science.* London: Collins, 1964.

Waddell, Lawrence A. *Buddhism in Tibet.* London: W. Heffer and Sons, 1895.

Walker, Bruce, et al. *Earthquake.* Alexandria: Time-Life, 1982.

Wegener, Alfred. *Origin of Continents and Oceans.* tr. by John Biram. 1912. rprt. Mineola, N.Y.: Dover, 1966.

Wenham, Gordon J. *The Book of Leviticus.* Grand Rapids: Eerdmans, 1979.

Westbrook, R. "Jubilee Laws." *ILR* 6 (1971): 209–226.

White, Andrew Dickson. *A History of the Warfare of Science with Theology.* New York: Free Press, 1965.

White, A. J. Monty. *How Old Is the Earth?* Welwyn, England: Evangelical press, 1985.

White, Lynn, Jr. "Historical Roots of Our Ecological Crisis." *Science* 155 (March 10, 1967): 1203–1207.

Wilson, J. Tuzo. "Oceanic Ridges." *EB-MAC.* Vol. 13, pp. 472–476.

Wright, Christopher J. H. "What Happened Every Seven Years in Israel?" *EQ* 56 (1984): 129–138; 193–202.

Wright, Ruth V., and Chadbourne, Robert. *Gems and Minerals of the Bible.* New York: Harper and Row, 1970.

Wrightman, Bruce. "Man: Manager or Manipulator of the Earth?" *Dialog* 9 (1970): 200–210.

Yasso, Warren E. *Oceanography: A Study of Inner Space.* New York: Holt, Rinehart, and Winston, 1965.

Young, Brigham. *Journal of Discourses.* 1859. rprt. Los Angeles: General, 1961.